CW00767433

SEMIOLOGIES OF TRAVEL: FROM GAUTIER TO BAUDRILLARD

Semiologies of Travel is the first book to explore comprehensively the role of semiology and signs in the encounter with foreign cultures as it is expressed in travel writing. David Scott focuses on major French writers of the last 200 years, including Théophile Gautier, André Gide, Henri Michaux, Michel Leiris, Claude Lévi-Strauss, Roland Barthes and Jean Baudrillard, to show how ethnology, politics, sociology and semiotics, as well as literature, are deeply bound up in travel experience and the writing that emerges from it. Scott also shows how the concerns of Romantic writers and theorists are still relevant to reflections on travel in today's post-modern world. The book follows an itinerary through jungle, desert and Utopia, as well as through Disneyland and Chinese restaurants, and will be of interest to specialists in French studies and cultural studies as well as to readers of travel writing.

DAVID SCOTT holds a personal chair in French (Textual and Visual Studies) at Trinity College Dublin. He is the author of *Pictorialist Poetics* (Cambridge, 1988), *Paul Delvaux: Surrealising The Nude* (1992) and *European Stamp Design: A Semiotic Approach* (1995).

SEMIOLOGIES OF TRAVEL

From Gautier to Baudrillard

DAVID SCOTT

CAMBRIDGE
UNIVERSITY PRESS

PUBLISHED BY THE PRESS SYNDICATE OF THE UNIVERSITY OF CAMBRIDGE
The Pitt Building, Trumpington Street, Cambridge, United Kingdom

CAMBRIDGE UNIVERSITY PRESS
The Edinburgh Building, Cambridge CB2 2RU, UK
40 West 20th Street, New York, NY 10011–4211, USA
477 Williamstown Road, Port Melbourne, VIC 3207, Australia
Ruiz de Alarcón 13, 28014 Madrid, Spain
Dock House, The Waterfront, Cape Town 8001, South Africa

http://www.cambridge.org

© David Scott 2004

This book is in copyright. Subject to statutory exception
and to the provisions of relevant collective licensing agreements,
no reproduction of any part may take place without
the written permission of Cambridge University Press.

First published 2004

Printed in the United Kingdom at the University Press, Cambridge

Typeface Adobe Garamond 11/12.5 pt.   *System* LATEX 2$_\varepsilon$ [TB]

A catalogue record for this book is available from the British Library

Library of Congress Cataloguing in Publication data
Scott, David H. T.
Semiologies of travel: from Gautier to Baudrillard / David Scott.
p.   cm.
Includes bibliographical references and index.
ISBN 0 521 83853 3
1. French literature – 19th century – History and criticism.   2. French literature –
20th century – History and criticism.   3. Semiotics.   1. Title.
PQ283.S388   2004
840.9′32′014 – dc22   2003065453

ISBN 0 521 83853 3 hardback

Em memória do meu querido amigo,
o poeta e erudito
Philadelpho Menezes (1960–2000),
o meu guia aos recantos culturais e desportivos
de São Paulo e do Brasil,
entre 1996 e 2000

Contents

Illustrations

Acknowledgements

My first thanks go to Malcolm Bowie and Clive Scott to whom I trace the source of this project in my reading, while a postgraduate at the University of East Anglia in the 1970s, of the books recommended for their undergraduate course on literature of travel and escape. I am also grateful for the feedback and stimulus of students of Trinity College Dublin since the early 1980s on whom I have tried out various travel-related courses and approaches. More specifically, I would like to thank Linda Bree and her colleagues at Cambridge University Press, for their valuable support and guidance through the publication phase. Finally, I am grateful to Trinity College Dublin for research funding support through both the Arts and Social Sciences Benefaction Fund and the Research Committee's Maintenance and Research Incentive scheme.

All translations from French to English are by David Scott.

Introduction: nostalgies du symbole

Avec l'Amérique indienne je chéris le reflet, fugitif même là-bas, d'une
ère où l'espèce était à la mesure de son univers et où persistait un
rapport adéquat entre l'exercice de la liberté et ses signes.

(Claude Lévi-Strauss, 1955: 171)

Encore aujourd'hui la nostalgie d'une référence naturelle du signe est
vivace.

(Jean Baudrillard, 1976: 79)

L'imaginaire d'un retour à l'origine du signe prend naissance [chez
Michaux] dans cet idéogramme [chinois] indéchiffrable, qui a suscité
la nostalgie d'une *lisibilité primitive*.

(Jean-Pierre Martin, 1994: 391)

Tout rite est analogique.

(Marc Augé, 1994b: 110)

SYMBOL AND ANALOGY

The relationship between sign systems and travel, the symbolic and the real,
seems to have been of fundamental concern to European writers from the
beginning of the age of exploration – on both a hermeneutic and semiotic
level. This is because from the Renaissance period onward, fresh encounters with the real in newly discovered and far-off lands tended to initiate
reflection on the phenomena encountered as much in terms of their status as signs as the problems they posed to interpretation. As early as 1516,
Thomas More in his *Utopia*, recounting an imaginary voyage across the
Atlantic to a newly discovered country, is as deeply concerned with its
modes of symbolic representation – as we shall see in Chapter 4, he goes so
far as to invent for it an alphabet and language, rooted in Greek – as with the
physical aspects of its culture and environment. This preoccupation continued well into the seventeenth century when, as Paul Cornelius has shown

I

(1965), the interest in both imaginary voyages and imaginary languages was founded on a realistic basis: linguists were searching for traces of the originary or universal language that it was believed was shared by humankind throughout the world before Babel, while theorists and practitioners of the newly developing sciences were interested in the possibility – often worked out in experimental terms in the literature of imaginary voyages – of languages or other symbolic systems in which the relationship between sign and object was philosophically motivated: '[In seventeenth-century Europe], there was much discussion about the possibility of making language a perfect representation of material reality, and there were a number of attempts to make an artificial language which imitated the European notion of the language of China – a scientific, universal language, with ideograms that represented the things and concepts for which they stood' (Cornelius, 1965: 2).

So while European thought was negotiating the complicated transition between a pre-Renaissance, analogical mode of thinking and a post-sixteenth-century rational approach to knowledge – what Foucault (1966), as we shall see below, refers to as the Enlightenment *épistèmè* – it was at the same time exploring the possibility of superimposing an iconic (or visually motivated) system of representation on a symbolic (or conventionally logical) one. The link between this epistemological project and travel to unexplored countries, real or imagined, is symptomatic of a deeper impulsion in the early modern European sensibility – that of a desire to relate the new – whether scientific or utopian – to the past – whether historical or mythological. In this way, the quest for the new and the different is paradoxically accompanied by a nostalgia for an integrated semiotic system. This nostalgia becomes, after the nineteenth century, an integral part of the appeal of the exotic, part of whose underlying project, as Chris Bongie suggests, is 'to recover the possibility of this total "experience", this concrete apprehension of others that is [. . .] typical of traditional communities but has been [. . .] eliminated from our own' (1991: 9).

This curiosity/nostalgia relation becomes integral to travel writing, in particular from the end of the Enlightenment period. So, although the voyage theme goes back in Europe at least as far as Homer's *Odyssey*, travel writing, increasingly important in Europe from the sixteenth century's voyages of discovery (Affergan, 1987a; Cornelius, 1965), became a major literary genre in the modern period (nineteenth and twentieth centuries). Its early expansion coincided with the development of a more scientific approach to history, anthropology and semiotics, and evolved against a background in which the scientific/rationalist model of thinking of the Enlightenment was beginning to come to terms with the relativisation of knowledge and of cultural prestige that a study of history, and, later, semiotics and anthropology, brought to European understanding. It also reflected a heightening of that nostalgia in the early modern period for a holistic, analogical pre-Renaissance approach to knowledge, the equivalent of which anthropologists were rediscovering in so-called primitive societies. For ethnographers were uncovering in native cultures epistemological structures in which the sign still seemed to have a motivated or sacred connection with its object, a link that each ethnic group's social organisation and ritual activity were structured to strengthen and maintain.

For travel writers, in the wake of Enlightenment rationalism and scepticism, and the decline in religious belief, such epistemic models were irresistibly attractive, offering in terms of the real what the Romantic imagination was committed to salvaging – but, in effect, only in terms of literature. This attractiveness was still powerful well into the twentieth century, the anthropological project of Lévi-Strauss, for example, being, as we shall see, in part motivated by a profound nostalgia for a primitive state in which human society was bound to both itself and the natural world by a unified and integral symbolic order.[1] From the nineteenth century, then, an important motivation governing travel writing (though in some earlier cases it was not formulated systematically or consciously) was the quest for an ideal model of human interaction with the social and natural worlds. While the Utopian strain implicit in this ambition will be investigated more specifically in a later section (Chapter 4), this book's aim in general is to investigate the ways in which confrontation of difference – through anthropology and history – and the clarification of the operations of the sign – through semiotics – became fundamental strategies in modern French travel writing in the pursuit of this quest.

For a model describing the fundamental categories different cultures use to shape their representation of the world, this study will in particular adapt that outlined by Michel Foucault in *Les Mots et les choses* (1966). In framing the concept of the *épistémè*, Foucault clarifies the way the basic epistemological structures of a culture organise themselves, establishing codes governing knowledge and custom (1966: 11–13). Each *épistémè* is relative both historically and in its claim to knowledge of the world, myths of one kind or another forming an integral part of every one. But each *épistémè* has an internal coherence and is in theory comprehensive within the given culture or ethnic group it governs. It is only in the modern period that western cultures have become aware of the *épistémès* governing their own outlook, as a result both of the work of anthropologists from the nineteenth century onwards in uncovering that of other ethnic groups, and of the work of modern historians. It is against this background indeed that Foucault, as historiographer and philosopher of history, produced in *Les Mots et les choses* his theory of the *épistémè*. In effect each ethnographer attempts to describe the *épistémè* of a culture, in particular the myths and prohibitions governing its rituals, social organisation and knowledge, which Foucault refers to as the 'codes fondamentaux d'une culture' (1966: 11). These codes are often 'deep' or hidden – Foucault refers to the necessity of an archeology to unearth them – and the 'structuralist' anthropology of a one-time geologist, Claude Lévi-Strauss, was developed precisely in an attempt to reconstruct their complex ramifications. In a sense, every serious travel writer is an ethnographer, and in confronting a new *épistémè*, is faced by a surprise or a bewilderment comparable to that felt by a reader of Borgès's Chinese encyclopedia, cited by Foucault in the preface of *Les Mots et les choses* (1966: 7). For Borgès's encyclopedia proposes categories and classifications inconceivable to, incompatible with the Enlightenment *épistémè* that, Foucault argues, still governs much western thinking.

Foucault cites Borgès's Chinese dictionary as a model of knowledge comparable to that governing pre-Enlightenment European epistemology. Before the Renaissance, western thinking had much in common with the pre-scientific, analogical models operative not only in an imaginary China but in many still existing so-called primitive societies. Such *épistémès* were capable of integrating monsters and myths into a scheme which also accommodated what we might still today describe as 'scientific fact': divisions between the imagined and the scientifically proven were still fluid. The analogical model, Foucault argues, was largely superseded in the Enlightenment by an *épistémè* that established universal, scientific principles, capable in theory of accounting for all experience, able to acclimatise all difference. Foucault's distinction is of special interest to any study of travel writing in that the latter invariably expresses, in one form or another, a clash of the analogical and rational *épistémès*. With the nineteenth-century shift into what Foucault describes as the modern period, such epistemic clashes become relativised, as historical and anthropological perspectives added to and nuanced all branches of knowledge. A corresponding increase in complexity is evidenced in travel writing, in which a nostalgia for holistic, mythical models of truth has to be correlated with the realities of a modern, scientific age. In this respect, there is a travel literature for each age: Homer and Marco Polo, with their real itineraries leading to mythical beasts – golden fleece or dragons, both explore a pre-Renaissance *épistémè*; in the eighteenth century, James Cook and Bougainville investigate an Enlightenment globe, while a panoply of modern writers, particularly English and French, seek out the fast-disappearing traces of once magical worlds.

The nostalgia for an *analogical* as opposed to a rational approach to experience or knowledge (to use Foucault's distinction, 1966: 44–5) is in part a function of the *épistémè* or paradigm shift marked by Romantic and early modern European literature. As Foucault states it, in the Renaissance period the *hermeneutic*, the science of making signs speak – 'l'ensemble des connaissances et des techniques qui permettent de faire parler les signes et de découvrir leur sens' (1966: 44) – was ideally in correlation with the *semiological*, the science of sign recognition – 'l'ensemble des connaissances et des techniques qui permettent de distinguer où sont les signes' (1966: 44); however, there was always a gap or *décalage* between these two grids which was sufficient to problematise knowledge. The Romantics sought, after the Enlightenment separation of the scientific disciplines, to superimpose again, this time in *imaginative* terms, hermeneutics on semiology as in Renaissance thinking and theories of resemblance. However, since the scientific/rationalist revolution of the seventeenth and eighteenth centuries, such a superimposition was viewed as increasingly problematic and relegated to more imaginative realms of cultural expression such as literature. As a model, it could only be found playing a central role in other cultures, considered more 'primitive'. Correspondingly travel writing, as a (pseudo-)ethnography, will seek to re-enchant the world, expressing in the process a nostalgia for and desire to experience other, seemingly more integral, signifying systems (Foucault, 1966: 48).

The Romantic concern with *metaphor* forms part of an awareness, expressed in travel writing as well as in lyric poetry, of the mythical nature of analogical thinking. As Foucault argues: 'Connaître une bête, ou une plante, ou une chose quelconque de la terre, c'est recueillir toute l'épaisse couche des signes qui ont pu être déposés en elles ou sur elles' (1966: 55) [To know an animal, a plant or any earthly phenomenon is to apprehend fully the thick layer of signs that have been deposited in or on them]. This 'thick layer of signs' provides the basis of both the so-called 'primitive logic' as studied by ethnography and the poetic logic which through metaphor links the real to the imaginary and *vice versa*. So, just as primitive societies or exotic cultures offer the possibility of experiencing an earlier, pre-rationalist *épistémè*, so Romantic writing once again strives to propose a textual model that both is linked to the real and yet, through a complex layering of signs, liberates the imagination. Travel writing is a paradox in that it is a rite of passage both to the *real* – that is, to an epistemic system different from that of the writer and which thus provokes a profound re-assessment of experience and values – and to the *ideal* – that is, to a world of renewed and heightened meaning. Likewise, travel writing's search for the exotic shares another paradox with the Romantic project, being built in part upon the nostalgia that came with the discovery of the historical dimension to all experience (and thus the desire to rehabilitate the *previously known*) and in part on anticipation of the new and strange (the desire to discover the *differently known*). The theory of the exotic is given ultimate expression by late Romantic writers such as Segalen, after whom later twentieth-century travel writers either mourn the exotic's passing or begin to explore, in a post-colonial context, new configurations of intercultural communication.[2]

The complex form Romantic cultural nostalgia takes may in part be a function of the fact that Europeans were never really able to sustain for long an originating myth of their own: their culture and beliefs are a function of a long history and pre-history of successive invasions – military, cultural, ideological – depriving them of the millennial stability enjoyed by other civilisations – Indian, Chinese – and the numberless so-called primitive societies of the Americas and Australasia. The word 'civilisation' is indeed problematic when applied to European culture which – unlike Egyptian, Greek, Chinese, Indian – has never – except perhaps during the Christian Middle Ages – been stable for long enough to establish a unifying system. Europa was only ever a raging farmyard animal, an iconoclastic bull, tossing about and eventually shattering the icons and belief systems of previous or other cultures – a power-house of energy but one never able to live at peace with itself. This relative cultural rootlessness may be one of the reasons why travel writing has been more elaborated in European than in other cultures.

Of course the comparative stability of other, non-European cultures and civilizations is partly illusory, a function of the nostalgic, idealising European gaze seeking a millennial permanence in societies outside itself which appear less prone (until the modern period at any rate) to historical change. In a sense, of course, it is Europe's exceptionally tumultuous recent history (in particular the last millennium) that has in part provoked its nostalgia for permanence and stable meaning. Once again, as Foucault correctly observed, the Renaissance was a watershed: apart from historical factors (the wars of religion and those waged in nationalist power struggles), the Enlightenment compartmentalisation of knowledge led to the outstripping of some disciplines in relation to others (e.g. science over theology) and to a clash of ideologies within the system. This in turn led, in conjunction with economic and industrial expansion, to an acceleration of history unparalleled in any other culture or recorded civilisation. Of course, in seeking to escape this acceleration by reference to other, non-European ethnic groups, Europeans simply brought about, through colonialism and other forms of cultural interchange, a corresponding acceleration of history in other cultures. This acceleration has in turn resulted in an upsurge of travel-related writing from formerly colonised countries, especially in Africa with its growing literature of exile in Europe.[3]

The problematic status of history in so-called primitive societies has become a major topic of discussion in contemporary ethnology, whether it be the difficulty of identifying historical change in societies without writing (as analysed for example by Lévi-Strauss in the introduction to *Anthropologie structurale*, 1958) or the problem of what happens when European history, through colonialism, impinges on other cultures (as discussed by Marc Augé in the context of contemporary Africa, *Le Sens des autres*, 1994a). Discussion of such problems has also filtered into some recent travel writing. It is paralleled by the modern (that is post-mid-nineteenth-century) concern with *tourism*, a phenomenon that has in the twentieth century increasingly exercised sociology and ethnography as well as travel writing.[4] Like all foreign influences, tourism ultimately destroys the object – the exotic, the Other – that it seeks to possess, converting it into matter for consumption comparable to the manufactured or industrialised objects it offers to primitive or colonial or post-colonial societies in exchange. Popular travel is now estimated by the various branches of the human sciences to be not just a product but also a defining characteristic of postmodern society.

In addition to history[5] and instead, as it were, of civilisation, Europe offers the rest of the world an 'intellectual tradition' whose main vocation, based in particular on its classical Greek ancestry, has been to question and problematise both its own and other cultures' belief systems. Drawing its knowledge from a heterogeneous and successive series of sources, post-Renaissance Europe has leant increasingly away from holistic and religious models towards a science based on questioning and experiment, away – as has been shown in the context of Foucault – from the analogical principle towards the rational. The multiplicity of sciences – physical and human – in Europe is in part a function of the lack of a unifying belief system: after the Renaissance, theology branches into philosophy (reason), science (empiricism) and literature (imagination). Emerging from the relatively stable period of the Middle Ages, when the Christian Church and Latin language provided a spiritual and conceptual frame within which major issues of faith, truth and knowledge could be contained, the Renaissance, with its revival of the vernacular and of alternative systems of representation (in particular Greek) initiated a process of desacralisation which today shows no sign of abating.

The loosening of the sacred bond between sign and object that brought about this desacralisation is a central issue of semiotics. As has been shown, Foucault in *Les Mots et les choses* sees the separation of hermeneutics from semiology as being part of the birthright of the Enlightenment, whose project it was, while attempting to systematise the relation between *words* and *things*, precisely to separate irrevocably the sign from its object. So, while metaphysics was re-invented by Descartes and his followers in part as a counter to scepticism and the decline in religious belief – belief in the Word as the word of God, the divine and all-knowing principle – proposing instead a truth based on reason and logical deduction, it also inaugurated the liberation of the true from the sacred, the word from the Book. The thesis of Descartes's *Discours de la méthode* (1637) was thus that if the meaning of signs (words) could be clearly and distinctly defined and the relation between them plotted logically, then Truth could be accessed. There was no longer any need for an *iconic* relation (similitude) between sign and object if reason were able clearly and distinctly to grasp the link between the separate but analogous systems constituted by signs and objects. Indeed iconic relations between sign and object were to be distrusted given the potentially deceptive nature of the *sensual* apprehension on which they were often based. In this respect, the arbitrariness of the European alphabetic language systems proved a definite advantage: lacking the iconic similitude of pictographic (Egyptian) or ideogrammatic (Chinese) languages, the truth of the relation between sign and object was lodged not in its signifying surface or signifier, but in its internal logic, i.e. what it signified. So, while on the one hand non-iconic sign systems make the relation between sign and object more difficult to grasp, on the other they constitute an unrivalled system for analysis and for the accommodation of countless words and concepts from the outside (Foucault, 1966: 100).

In re-inventing metaphysics, however, Descartes also re-invented metaphysical doubt and was only able to circumvent it, as Pascal clearly saw, through metaphysical sophistry. Doubt is always the result of the emergence of an alternative sign system which undermines or problematises that which precedes it.[6] The rapid and catastrophic collapse of so-called primitive systems of belief has mostly been the function of contamination by contact in the post-Renaissance period with European sign systems, just as Christianity slowly collapsed beneath the onslaught of alternative models and sources of knowledge. In so-called primitive societies it is not access to but maintenance of the Truth that is of the essence: primitive societies are self-contained – their myths are both integral and inviolable, but, like all human phenomena, susceptible to forgetting and decay. Hence the vital role of ritual in constantly rehearsing the myths binding the community. The semiological project of primitive societies as analysed by Lévi-Strauss and theorized by Baudrillard is essentially one of repeatedly re-assigning the sign to its object in a sacred bond and thus maintaining a stable environment for meaning. In this respect, European colonisation of American and African worlds is a revisiting of cultural aggression as catastrophic as that visited on Europe in pre-historic and early historic times. As has already been noted, the other side to this restless intellectual inquiry is the nostalgia for a fixed or stable belief system, one capable of surviving the aggressions or encroachments of other knowledge systems. This nostalgia is accompanied, however, by a paradox we have already mentioned in the context of history and tourism: to seek and to find an alternative and authentic tradition is almost certainly to destroy it through the contamination of contact.

This fear of contamination through contact may be a major factor in the historic mistrust between Moslem (Near and Middle Eastern) and Christian (European) civilisations. As the Iranian philosopher Javad Tabatabai convincingly demonstrates in his essay 'L'Incompréhension des civilisations: le cas de la Perse' (2002), for the last millennium the opposition of Islam and Europe is a concomitant of the respective states of fixity and crisis the two civilisations represent:

L'identité telle qu'elle est entendue dans le monde de l'islam – contrairement à la conception européenne – est l'identité en tant qu'uniformité, monotonie et monolithisme; l'identité de l'Europe n'est ce qu'elle est que parce qu'elle est plurielle et en devenir; elle vit de la crise et dans celle-ci, et le mode de l'islam ne peut guère comprendre cette situation de la crise permanente, puisque l'identité dans le monde de l'islam est notre 'authenticité', qui n'est d'ailleurs authentique que parce qu'elle demeure intouchable, inchangée et inchangeable. (Javad Tabatabai, 2002: 72–3)

[Identity as it is understood in the world of Islam – contrary to the European conception – is identity as uniformity, monotonous and monolithic; European identity is what it is only because it is plural and evolving; it lives off and in a state of crisis; Islamic thinking has difficulty understanding this state of permanent crisis, since identity in the world of Islam is our 'authenticity', which is moreover authentic only because it remains untouchable, unchanged and unchangeable.]

For Tabatabai, almost from its Greek beginnings, European thought has been a reflection on change, on successive crises and moments of decline, one that from the Renaissance has progressively accelerated. Within the more homogeneous conceptual frameworks of Islamic thinking, on the other hand, such a reflection was impossible. The result of this, Tabatabai argues, was that Islamic thinking was unable, first, to grasp and, second, to evaluate what was at stake in European self-analysis, taking it literally as a sign of cultural decadence rather than of intellectual creativity. In semiotic terms, the effect of this was that Islam, through its relative stasis, has preserved the violence of signs – a unified religious, legal and social code observing a fixed, sacred and non-negotiable link between sign and object – whereas, in the Greek period and since the Renaissance in particular, Europe has tended progressively to separate sign from object, liberating thought from any attachment to the real and so from immovable violent hierarchies.[7]

SEMIOTICS AND TRAVEL

The separation during the European Enlightenment of semiology and hermeneutics and the subsequent early modern nostalgia for their super-imposition no doubt had some bearing on the subsequent development, in both philosophy and the new science of linguistics, of theories of signs. For although sign theories originated in ancient Greek philosophy, it was only after the paradigm shift from the Enlightenment to the early modern period that semiotic theories developed sufficiently to provide a foundation for the modern human sciences. This basis was provided in particular by two thinkers, one a philosopher, the other a linguistician, Charles Sanders Peirce (1839–1914) and Ferdinand de Saussure (1857–1913). Although both elaborated semiotic theories comprehensive enough to embrace both the *hermeneutic* and *semiological* aspects of sign articulation and recognition as analysed by Foucault (1966: 44–5), the emphasis in each tends towards one or other of these two. In Peirce, it is the mechanisms of interpretation (or hermeneutics) that are given more extensive elaboration than in Saussure, while the latter focuses more particularly on the internal structure of the sign (or semiology). Peirce is father of Semiotics in the broadest sense of the term. Saussure, on the other hand, though he coined the word 'semiology', was primarily concerned with one branch of this new general science – that of Linguistics, a study area that his *Cours de linguistique générale* (1916) was the first to establish on a truly scientific footing – and it was correspondingly to the linguistic sign that he devoted his closest attention.

The difference of emphasis between these two seminal semioticians is worth pursuing here to the extent that it clarifies the nature of the theo-retical models developed in modern ethnography and sociology, and the responses to difference and the other as explored in modern French travel writing. To summarise, one might say that Saussurian semiology is concerned with *difference*, whether within a given system or as between different *systems*, while Peircian hermeneutics is concerned with the other, in particular in so far as it approaches the *real*. This difference is reflected in the varying structural emphasis of the Peircian and Saussurian systems: Saussure works within a format of binary opposition – same/different – while Peirce's thinking is essentially triadic. Where Saussure, bracketing the sign's referent, concentrates his attention on the internal structure of the sign – the relation of the signifier as visual or acoustic sign to the signified as concept or idea – Peirce is concerned with the triangular relation between sign, interpretant and object; that is, not only with the relation between signifier (sign) and interpretant (signified) but also with the sign's relation to the object (whether the latter be a thing, an idea or another sign). The *hermeneutic* process – 'l'ensemble des connaissances et des techniques qui permettent de faire parler les signes et de découvrir leur sens' (Foucault, 1966: 44) – is clarified in particular in Peirce's theory of the sign by his analysis of the interpretative process: the interpretant's grasp of the sign as a function of different but complementary *logics* – deductive (or immediate), abductive (imaginative) or inductive (epistemological). At the same time, the *hermeneutics/semiology* distinction as made by Foucault is maintained in Saussure's distinction between *parole* – a hermeneutic activation of signs – and *langue* – the theoretical disposition enabling the signifying process to operate: semiology.[8]

Within the French tradition of the human sciences in the twentieth century, it is clearly Saussure's theory which, as a semiology, has had the greatest impact, the influence of Peirce only beginning to make itself felt in the last quarter of the century. In particular Saussure's analysis of the sign into signifier and signified (*signifiant/signifié*) together with his distinction between language as a system (*langue*) and as a praxis (*parole*) played a crucial role in providing a theoretical basis for structuralist analysis. For ethnologists (such as Claude Lévi-Strauss) and sociologists and political/economic theorists (such as Jean Baudrillard), such distinctions provided a basis for a more scientific approach to the infinitely complex semiotic structure constituting human societies. So, for example, the real but often obscure relation between a surface feature and a deeper, underlying structure, on the level both of individual signs (the signifier/signified relationship) and of sign systems (the *langue/parole* distinction), made it possible to produce a model of the *épistémè* structuring the myths, rituals and other cultural practices of a given society or ethnic community. In their turn, such theoretical tools have increasingly provided conceptual devices within recent French travel writing (Barthes, Baudrillard) as well as providing a basis for critical analysis of other travel texts in which such distinctions are not consciously applied.

It is as a metatextual, critical tool in particular that Peirce's sign theory will be brought to bear in this study since none of the writers consciously frame the problematics explored in their travel texts in Peircian terms. In particular Peirce provides critical distinctions enabling an analysis of certain travel writers' attempts to express the Other and the real (Segalen, Gide, Bouvier), notably, the distinction between the immediate and dynamic object and the corresponding mechanism of immediate and dynamic interpretant. For the immediate object as indicated by the sign is not the same as the dynamic or *real* object which is ultimately not completely knowable and certainly not expressible in linguistic or indeed in any sign-related terms. This will not prevent travel writers, such as those just mentioned, trying to get as near as possible – in terms both of experience and of expression – to the real and the Other. Thus even a semiotician as sceptical as Baudrillard, who argues that signs in the post-modern era have become increasingly simulacral, mere symbols whose referential scope has been seriously reduced, disconnecting rather than linking interpretant and object, nonetheless recognises a persistent nostalgia for a natural referent to the sign – 'Encore aujourd'hui la nostalgie d'une référence naturelle du signe est vivace' (Baudrillard, 1976: 79) [Even today the nostalgia for a natural reference to the sign is still very much alive].

The exploration in this study of this nostalgia for authentic symbols or for a world in which signs appeared naturally to correspond with their objects implies a fundamentally western or European perspective on travel experience and the confrontation of other cultures. Europe's repeated and ongoing crises of identity and semiotic modelling means that recent western writers bring a particular urgency and intensity to their reflection on alternative semiotic and cultural systems, one in which the theoretical or methodological issues raised by the approaches adopted are often integral to the travel-writing project. Since the field opened up here is already large, the temptation to explore beyond the Eurocentric, anthropomorphic perspective outlined so far will be resisted. In part this is possible because much valuable study has been devoted recently to post-colonial writing, in particular in so far as it devotes itself to exploring the identity and semiotic crises of those cultures on the receiving end of European political and ideological imperialism,[9] and to investigating the increasing dialogue initiated between European and non-European writers.

The European nostalgia for sign systems that appear to offer a more authentic link with their object is also, of course, partly based on a certain cultural imperialism. Since the Renaissance, if not since the Greeks, most European travelogue and ethnographic writing has been to some degree predicated on a sense of the superiority of western knowledge and cultural praxis. As Edward W. Said has convincingly argued, this has led to a series of often deeply violent and counterproductive antitheses or binary oppositions being established between the 'West' and other important cultural systems in the world, in particular Islam (as analysed in *Orientalism*, 1978) and those of the formerly colonised countries of Africa and Latin America (as explored in *Culture and Imperialism*, 1993). While the question of Orientalism will be returned to in my concluding chapter, it would perhaps be helpful here briefly to situate the quest for alternative meaning systems pursued by the European writers studied in what follows within the framework of cultural imperialism as analysed by Said. In the first place, the very ability or power of writers (whether travellers, ethnographers or novelists) consciously to make different cultural choices already attests to the privilege of the position from which they are operating. At the same time, what differentiates the former two categories from the novelists who form the principal basis of Said's analysis in *Culture and Imperialism* is the explicit search for different or alternative meaning systems. This implies both a critical perspective on the home culture and a recognition that other cultures might offer authentic, if not superior, alternatives to it. For the writers studied here, as I have argued above, are not just seeking difference or the exotic, but the Other as a real and viable alternative or complement to the known, western, system. It is in part for this reason that anxiety and ambivalence, as well as enthusiasm and delight, characterise many of the texts explored in this book.

THE FRENCH CONNECTION

A fundamental aim of this book is to show more specifically how French writers over the last two centuries have made a special contribution to an understanding of the signifying processes at stake within the larger European problematic of travel in the post-Renaissance period. This contribution is a function not only of a rich corpus of travel literature – this can be found also in the English and to a lesser extent the German and Italian traditions – but also of a marked French tendency to elaborate a conceptual basis for their experience. In this process, they seem especially committed not only to theorising what they feel most keenly, but also to investigating how cultural confrontation and change impact not only on human experience itself but also on the human sciences to whose study human experience is submitted. In this respect, this book will identify a particular

French lineage within the wider European travel-writing tradition, one in which the relation between writing and the human sciences (and to a lesser extent the fine arts) is an exceptionally fertile one. The selection of texts in the field of French travel writing over the last two centuries to be studied here is thus governed by the strong presence of critical and theoretical as well as narrative and descriptive intelligence in them. The extraordinary richness of the critical debate in France in the recent structuralist and post-structuralist periods, as I shall argue in the next section, inevitably means that such seminal writers of the human sciences as Barthes, Lévi-Strauss, Derrida and Baudrillard figure prominently. At the same time, the nineteenth- and early twentieth-century period in France is also very rich in writers sensitive to fundamental aesthetic and cognitive issues relating to travel, even if they do not conceptualise their experience as systematically as their post-war successors. So, for example, a nineteenth-century writer such as Théophile Gautier's remarkable awareness of semiotic and identity, as well as aesthetic and cultural issues, makes of his *Voyage en Espagne* an exemplary foil in the discussion of later writers' confrontation of related questions. (The potential richness of such historical dialogue will be discussed further below.) This does not of course imply that the French travel writing is sealed off from its various counterparts in the European tradition: as we shall see, writers such as Conrad will reappear frequently as fertile points of reference in modern French writers. But the intertextual awareness in the French of writers in their own tradition (as exemplified for instance by Derrida in *Retour de l'URSS*) constitutes a particularly rich vein for study.

This book thus sets out to explore, across a representative selection of French travel writers between the early nineteenth and late twentieth centuries, the nostalgia for epistemic systems in which the symbol maintains an authentic connection with the real or sacred. The focus will be in particular on a corpus of authors who, within a travelogue format, confront issues relating to ethnography, semiotics or ideal societies or political systems. Not surprisingly this corpus includes texts by ethnologists (Lévi-Strauss, Augé, Leiris), semioticians (Barthes, Baudrillard) and sociologists / political theorists (Tocqueville, Custine, Baudrillard), as well as by literary writers who display a real though less systematically elaborated concern with such issues in their travel writing – Gautier (semiotics), Michaux, Segalen (ethnography), Gide (politics). Indeed, one of this book's important themes is precisely the relationship between ethnology and travel writing.[10] In addition texts by other literary writers (Chateaubriand, Nerval, Fromentin, Loti,

Butor, Bouvier, Boman) are studied insofar as they cast further light on the themes just outlined. The overall disciplinary frame of the study is semiotics, not only because travel experience and writing are nothing if not a matter of reading sign systems, but also because the related disciplines (anthropology, politics, sociology) have, in the twentieth century at least, been profoundly marked by structuralist semiology.[11]

SELECTING A CORPUS

In the light of the position just outlined, the corpus of texts selected in this study will privilege travel journal rather than fiction; real not imaginary journeys; *utopies réalisées* not fictive utopias.[12] For this book's particular focus on travel journals is a function of their more explicit and conscious concern with topics central to its argument: the sign, identity, the self/other relation, politics and ethnology. Less complicated by narrative, fictive or character-related concerns, the travel journal is able to explore a range of issues across a spectrum of scientific disciplines, bringing together perceptions, concepts and arguments in a richly suggestive fabric. The focus on a particular genre, especially one as richly developed as the travel journal, also of course facilitates the relatively uncomplicated cross-reference that will become a particular strategy of this study's argument as it unfolds over the following pages (a point that will be returned to in the penultimate section of this chapter). The link between travel writing and fundamental human science preoccupations (politics, sociology, ethnology, semiology) is indeed, as I have said, central to this project and to the books that constitute its corpus. Moreover, a number of the texts central to it (such as those by Augé, Barthes, Baudrillard, Leiris, Lévi-Strauss) straddle the literature / *sciences humaines* divide and bring unique insights to bear on the problematics at issue. Thus in the travel writings of Augé, Leiris, Lévi-Strauss and Segalen, the different but related themes of autobiography, travel diary and ethnography are intertwined in varying dosages, in some cases (as in some texts of Augé and Segalen) being staged or semi-fictionalised into the form of *ethnoromans*. In Barthes, Baudrillard and, to a lesser extent, Butor (whose *Mobile* is a kind of sociological novel), fundamental issues relating to semiotics that underlie their writings in general take a particular turn in their travel texts, in which they are made more explicit or defined in a more memorable and graphic way. Thus, for example, *L'Empire des signes* brings to a memorably graphic head a number of issues Barthes had explored in earlier works such as *Mythologies* (1957), while Baudrillard's *Amérique* (1986) is a vivid exemplification of the theories relating to the semiotics of the consumer society that he had worked out more systematically in *La Société de consommation* (1970) and *Pour une critique de l'économie politique du signe* (1972). To this extent, the works of French semioticians such as Barthes and Baudrillard are crucial in clarifying the deeper issues at stake in modern travel since they show how it both reflects and magnifies the processes of signification characterising modern capitalist consumer society. In this respect, the travel journal, in its mixture of analysis and description, discourse and scientific observation, seems uniquely suited to bringing together theory and sign.

In addition, the corpus selected in this study includes the work of a few writers who are also artists (Fromentin, Gauguin, Michaux), though in all cases these figures are viewed primarily as writers: this is not a book about the art history of travel or of travel illustration. The aim here is rather to explore the extent to which meditation on the status of the sign and a certain graphic register of signification find expression in both textual and visual terms, and the degree to which the visual image may enhance or complete the textual, or vice versa. In this way the dozen images incorporated in the text function as illustrations of the striking recurrence of certain visual motifs in some artists' and writers' reflection on travel experience. So the white horse as viewed by Delacroix, Gautier, Fromentin and Gauguin, that will tell us so much about these artists' and writers' view of the relativity of colour, exemplifies one of those chains of images that can provide telling insight into a cultural tradition. A second example is provided by the graphic mark, whether primitive scribble or ideogrammatic sign as encountered by Lévi-Strauss, Michaux and Barthes, one which in its few cursive strokes can tell us as much about a symbolic system as many pages of text. A third example is the photographic sign of the smile as successively recorded in textual and/or visual terms by Butor, Barthes and Baudrillard, one which opens up unsuspected perspectives onto the Other and the exotic cultural context from which it is drawn.

THEMATIC FOCUS AND HISTORICAL DIALOGUE

The corpus of French travel writing, even if restricted to the last 200 years, is vast and would need more than one volume to be explored adequately. It is not however the aim of this book to produce a historical survey or even highlight landmarks in the travelogue genre. Rather it aims, within the general field of French travel writing, to identify certain fundamental problematics — identity, the sign, the Other, political utopias, etc. – and to analyse them closely across a compact but representative cluster of texts. The advantage of this approach is that it enables clear and coherent perspectives to be maintained across what might otherwise be a bewildering range of texts. Most importantly, such an approach enables the texts studied from different periods within the two centuries to be brought into dialogue with each other. This is especially important in the light of the complementary relation between much nineteenth- and twentieth-century writing, in which the essential themes raised and developed more or less consciously by Romantic and early modern writers are subsequently submitted by postmodern writers to systematic theorisation and critical analysis. In this way the persistence of certain major underlying problematics over the two centuries can be effectively identified and the evolution of different positions in relation to them thoroughly investigated.

Such a dialogue can be particularly illuminating to the extent that it clarifies genealogies of preoccupation or thinking evidenced in travel writing from the Romantic through the modern to the post-modern periods. To this effect, the pairing or grouping in the chapters of this book of certain key writers from these three distinct periods is a conscious strategy. So the first great travel journal of the French tradition after 1800, Chateaubriand's *Itinéraire de Paris à Jérusalem* (1811) can be illuminatingly re-read in the light of one of the most recent and controversial French travel texts, that of Baudrillard's *Amérique*. French travel writers' profound preoccupation with the sign can be traced fruitfully from the Romantic Gautier, through the modern Segalen, to the post-modern Barthes. The recurrent meditation over the last two centuries on utopian political systems opens up a particularly rich field of investigation and comparison in French travel writing: in the 1830s, two major figures, Custine and Tocqueville, set out diametrically opposed but complementary positions in relation to both political systems and the manner of analysing them, positions that will be engaged with in varying ways subsequently in both modern (Gide) and post-modern (Derrida, Baudrillard) utopian writing. The recent post-modern discussion of utopia in terms of Disneyland in turn invites a comparison of three takes on the issue made by three major contemporary writers – Augé, Baudrillard, Marin, each bringing to bear on the issues at stake a related but contrasting disciplinary frame (ethnology, sociology, semiotics respectively). Finally, this strategy seems justified in that, in the event, it elicits substantial reference to most of the great travel writers in the French tradition over the last 200 years.

The recurrent presence of certain writers across the different thematic headings (Gautier in the nineteenth century; Barthes, Leiris, Michaux and Gide in the early twentieth or modern period; and Lévi-Strauss and Baudrillard in the structuralist and post-structuralist period of the later twentieth) is a mark of the particular richness of their sensitivity to fundamental travel issues (it is for this reason that Gautier rather than Chateaubriand figures as a key name in this book's title). The occasional references to pre-nineteenth-century French travel writers, such as Jean de Léry, cited from time to time *en filigrane* in the notes, functions not merely as a discreet reminder of the vast body of pre-Romantic travel writing that lies beyond the scope of this study, but also as beacons marking certain exceptionally fertile precursors. Lévi-Strauss himself (Léry, [1578] 1994: 5–14) identifies Léry's anticipation of the major issues of ethnology, cultural relativity and sign status that re-emerge in the foreground of twentieth-century writing. Thomas More's *Utopia* is, exceptionally, foregrounded as an essential point of reference for the Romantic, modern and post-modern texts discussed in Chapter 4.

DOMINANT THEMES

As the above remarks suggest, and subsequent chapter headings confirm, this book is structured around a series of central themes explored through clusters of key writers. Focussing on fundamental problematics rather than literary historical survey, the book nevertheless strives to present a comprehensive view of a rich topic over a significant period. Since the theoretical framework proposed is that of semiotics, issues relating to the nature and status of the sign are pursued in different ways throughout the seven chapters. In addition, each chapter will to a greater or lesser extent aim to apply as cogently as possible certain semiotic methodologies in an attempt to show how they offer valuable tools of analysis and criticism across a range of different travel issues.

So, in Chapter 1, 'Reading signs', a basically Saussurian approach to sign analysis is employed, focussing in particular on the way the signifier aspect of the sign is apprehended by successive writers as a means of coming to terms more effectively with the novelty and difference that the travel experience inevitably presents. The question of how signs operate within a *system* as much as as an index of or prelude to meaning is pursued in a Saussurian spirit, in relation both to individual writers' responses to the problem and to the way structuralist and post-structuralist writers theorise the semiotic process itself. The trajectory via Gautier and Segalen to Barthes, Butor and Baudrillard is an interesting one to the extent that it reflects the increasingly conscious tendency towards the separation of signifier from signified in the travel encounters with signs.

By way of contrast, Chapter 2, 'The other as interpretant', brings a Peircian approach to the problem of the nature and structure of human identity. Peirce's close attention to that part of the interpretative process that is the *interpretant* led him to elaborate a set of logical categories or strategies that provide a valuable framework for the analysis of human experience, especially as it negotiates those moments of disorientation consistently provoked by travel. So the complex mental processes undergone by Segalen or Michaux in attempting to come to terms with the Other can be pinpointed and compared with greater precision using Peircian terminology. In particular, Peirce's categories of 'immediacy' and 'dynamism' in relation to both the object and the interpretant will, as I hope to show, clarify the two-way dynamic between subject and object, self and other, and the difficulty experienced in matching signs immediately to the dynamic complexity of the other or exotic object.

In Chapter 3, 'Identity crises', elements of Peircian and Saussurian semiotics are supplemented by insights from Foucault's analysis of folly in *Les Mots et les choses* and applied across a series of travel texts from Gautier and Nerval in the nineteenth century to Gauguin and Bouvier in the twentieth. The aim here is in particular to show how the diverse and often disconcerting experiences of travel bring out the problematic nature of the subject – notably the degree to which the 'I' is perceived as other, and the disturbing mental consequences that accompany this realisation. The problem of madness as theorised by Foucault thus retrospectively illuminates aspects of the Van Gogh / Gauguin relationship as well as the personal crises of writers such as Nerval and Bouvier. So, as an anticipatory counter to the semiotic scepticism of Baudrillard and other post-modern theorists, writers such as Paul Gauguin and Victor Segalen were at the beginning of the twentieth century still hoping to experience the unthinkable or *impensable* as defined by Foucault in the context of Borgès's Chinese encyclopedia, and/or the real as equivalent to the exotic Other.

Chapter 4, 'Utopias and dystopias', brings into dialogue a range of contemporary semiotic approaches, emanating from sociological, ethnological and philosophical disciplines, with political writers of the Romantic and the early modern period. Thus early nineteenth-century reflections on democracy and absolutism as articulated by such major figures as Tocqueville and Custine are subsequently re-contextualised in the experience of Gide in his *Retour de l'URSS* of 1936, and, more particularly, in the more theoretically informed experience of post-modern writers such as Augé, Baudrillard, Derrida and Marin. Derrida's *Moscou: aller-retour* of 1992 offers a particularly valuable paradigm in its awareness of the intertextual nature of travel writing and experience, evoking as it does the writings of Tocqueville and Gide in its attempt to come to terms with the changing political regime in Russia. Similarly, Baudrillard's exploration of the paradox of the *Utopie réalisée* that he sees America as currently exemplifying enters into an illuminating intertextual dialogue with Tocqueville.

Chapter 5, 'Signs in the desert', returns to Foucault's important distinction between the *semiological* and the *hermeneutic* and applies it – using in addition Peircian categories of sign definition – to a close analysis of western experience of desert travel. Peirce's elaboration of sign categories into the three orders of qualisigns, sinsigns and legisigns; of icons, indexes and symbols; of rhemes, dicisigns and arguments, provides a panoply of instruments permitting a fine calibration of European travellers' apprehension of the desert scene. So from a seemingly abstract void, signs surge forth in Chateaubriand's experience of the deserts of Greece or Judea into the observing consciousness and activate a spectrum of semiotic mechanisms. The control of such mechanisms is a major concern of second- and third-generation French Romantic writers such as Fromentin and Loti, while in the twentieth-century American desert, Baudrillard gets as near as he ever will to experiencing the pre-semiotic, that is a hallucinatory vision of a pre-human, pre-biological, even pre-organic world in which time is obliterated and only the physical real exists in all its religious majesty.

Chapter 6, 'Jungle books', observes an opposite semiotic trajectory to the extent that it traces the development of semiological and hermeneutic strategies in the face of an overwhelming plethora of phenomena. So the Jungle, in its obliteration of recognisable signs of civilisation and orientation, and the exposure it offers to natural elements, tends to elicit from the French travellers exploring it (Michaux, Gide, Leiris) a desire to rediscover and re-impose signs, if only in the hope of imposing some sense of order on the chaos which confronts them. In the case of Leiris, this problem is complicated by the ethnographic project in which he is engaged (the Dakar–Djibouti expedition of 1931–3), in which the confrontation of other semiological systems demands intense hermeneutic investigation. An upshot of this is that Leiris in his African journal works out for himself semiotic models that bear an uncanny relation to the structures Peirce had elaborated on a theoretical level, in particular the sign/object/interpretant triad.

Finally, Chapter 7, 'Grammars of gastronomy', pinpoints another group of travel writers whose semiotic project starts closer to the familiar and everyday, beginning indeed where many people first experience the exotic: in the local Chinese or Indian restaurant. The question such writers raise is: to what extent is food and the way it is consumed a route to the centre of a culture? In the light of Foucault's stress on the role of language and classification systems in providing or indicating the deep structures of a cultural or ethnic group, the work of writers in this group can be read in terms of the gastronomic grammars encountered. Lévi-Strauss's monumental study *Le Cru et le cuit* (1964), the first of his *Mythologiques*, provides a point of departure, in showing not only how primitive cosmologies and myths of origin (in particular of fire and thus the ability to cook properly) are deeply bound up with basic human needs, but also how in human societies it is at bottom the symbolic – that which differentiates humans from the rest of creation – that is prior and superior to the real. The 'syntaxe de la mythologie sud-américaine' (Lévi-Strauss, 1964: 16) explored in *Le Cru et le cuit* provides a model that is taken up by Barthes in his evocation of Japanese cooking in *L'Empire des signes* (1970) to the extent that the structures of Japanese preparation and consumption of food exemplify a grammar – radically different from that of the West – of the way the far eastern world constructs itself. Similarly in Boman's *Le Palais des Saveurs-Accumulées* (1989), the western reader is regaled with accounts of Chinese meals that share some of the outlandish structure and heterogeneous content evident in the taxonomies of Borgès's Chinese encyclopedia cited by Foucault in *Les Mots et les choses* (1966: 7–16). Finally, in *L'Afrique fantôme* (1934), Michel Leiris's study of and participation in the possession rituals of the native inhabitants of Abyssinia lead him to compare and reflect on not only the difference between western and native 'grammars' of gastronomy, but also the extent to which they are symptomatic of symbolic activity in general.

A short concluding chapter, 'Writing difference – coming home to write', investigates the extent to which the reading of travel texts brings home the essentially problematic nature of the real/symbolic relation and the infinite mobility of the signifying process. A particular complication of this is the way the travel writer's desire to re-establish contact with the real, and to enjoy the heightening of experience it in theory offers, is ineluctably accompanied by a desire to commit such experience to the symbolic – through writing or art – a mediation that inevitably distances the real from the reader. The writing-up process thus becomes as central a part of the

travel project as the encounter with the other and activates a correspondingly double interpretative process in the reader. So, in most cases perhaps,
what travel writing, like travel experience, ultimately offers the reader is as
much a heightened awareness of the semiotic as of the exotic – a situation
that both reflects and illuminates the increasingly semiotic orientation of
today's mediatised world.

CHAPTER I

Reading signs: foregrounding the signifier – from Gautier to Baudrillard

[Les] étrangers, grands lecteurs d'enseignes, s'il en fut.
(Théophile Gautier, [1840] 1981: 156)

Toutes ces promesses autour des signes.
(Victor Segalen, [1907] 1982: 199)

La lune au-dessus de l'enseigne Coca-Cola.
(Michel Butor, 1962: 442)

[Des] signes coupés de l'alibi référentiel par excellence: celui de la chose vivante.
(Roland Barthes, [1970] 1980: 13)

[I]l n'est de vrai dépaysement que celui incarné par les signes.
(François Cheng, 1979: 133)

La seule lecture des signes indispensables à la survie crée une sensation extraordinaire de lucidité réflexe.
(Jean Baudrillard, 1986: 55)

Travel writers are sign-readers in many senses of the word.[1] For when they encounter not just difference but the *other*, they are faced with an *épistémè* in which is at stake not only the strangeness to the outsider of the sign itself but also the nature of its relations to its object. It is here that the various possible conceptions of the sign, that is of the way signs work, come into question. For the post-Enlightenment, rationalist European, signs are primarily perceived as arbitrary symbols; but they can also, in certain circumstances – such as in art or religion – be perceived as being motivated, having, as Peirce would say, a *real* connection with their object (Peirce, 1966: vol. VIII). Furthermore, in so-called primitive societies, as indeed in some areas of Pre-Renaissance European culture, signs can also be understood in certain circumstances or through exceptional processes such as exorcism and magic, to *act on* or *modify* their object (see Malinowski, [1922] 1966: 392–463; Foucault, 1966; and Goody, 1979: 250). It is the business of ethnography to study in a given culture both the *how* and the *what* of semiosis, not only the way signs interact but also the way they may be understood from a native perspective to act on and transform the real.[2] Ethnography sets out to do this as scientifically as possible while running the risk of a certain inevitable degree of subjectivity, a tendency to impose western logical categories (see Johannes Fabian, 1983), with the very presence of the outside observer having a certain impact on the object of study.[3] Travel writing, on the other hand, while often still operating within a project broadly analogous to that of ethnography, seeks to focus more on how the other or a different *épistémè* is experienced by the individual consciousness. As in ethnology, this continues to involve a questioning of the way meaning is produced (cf. Malinowski, [1922] 1966: 509–18), a widening of the understanding of the various ways signs may be understood to work. The focus, however, is above all on the impact – alienating or stimulating – such readjustments produce in the experience of the individual. Such alienation and/or stimulation characterises the encounter with what is often perceived by the traveller to be a more integral, analogical world, that is, one in which there seem to be more and different ways in which signs can be understood to work and one which correspondingly opens to wider interpretation.

This chapter adopts a double approach to these two perspectives on other sign systems. In the first part, the sign as it may be supposed to be perceived by the native will be investigated, in particular the degree to which consciousness of the sign is born when a competing semiotic system irrupts into the primitive *épistémè*. This will imply a primarily ethnographic perspective in which the confrontation of radically different sign systems is observed as a general phenomenon. Such an angle is provided by Lévi-Strauss – notably in *Tristes Tropiques* in which ethnography, ethnology (for the difference between these two see Lévi-Strauss, 1958: 10–11) and autobiographical reflection and experience are closely bound up with each other. It is also to be found in the ethno-fiction of Victor Segalen, notably *Les Immémoriaux* in which Segalen creates a fictive reconstruction of the clash of European and Polynesian sign systems. The second part of the chapter will investigate some of the ways in which sign systems are perceived from the outside by western travellers and the strategies they employ to enrich the semiotic process, with the aim of maintaining as far as possible the promise of the sign and thus the illusion of a more integral cultural system. In the case of Gautier's *Voyage en Espagne*, of Barthes's *L'Empire des signes* and of Baudrillard's *Amérique*, the writers' exploration of ways of applying semiotic grids becomes an integral part of their investigation of different cultures. For all three writers aim to experience the other in terms of an already partly elaborated ideal or utopian vision – one in which signs are highly motivated in their link to their object. In all cases this high level of motivation is linked to a certain aestheticism. Gautier will seek in Spain images and experiences that confirm the visions that art, and especially painting, have already imaginatively created for him. In Japan, Barthes explores sign systems that, far from inviting specific interpretation, on the contrary indefinitely defer and problematise meaning. Here, it is the very surface of the signifier itself, in all its strangeness and beauty, that suggests multiple signifying procedures, of equal though differing potential, thus satisfying a nostalgia for a world in which the very tangibility of the sign constitutes part of its significance. Meanwhile Baudrillard, exploring further Marshall McLuhan's theory that 'the medium is the message' (1962), will seek and find in the United States an only slightly more vivid replay of the cinematographic and televisual images that have already long shaped his vision of American culture. All three writers thus confirm, in their different ways, an important link, visible in travel writing from the nineteenth century in France, between aestheticism and exoticism. For the aesthetic becomes the motivating dynamic that relates the sign to its object or to its signifying function with an intensity otherwise lost to the rational post-Enlightenment European experience.

Of course there is an element of naivety in the post-Enlightenment western nostalgia for an integral, analogical world, in which signs still appear to have a tangible link with their objects and in which the recognition of meaning is still bound up with the sacred. For the symbolic contract dictates that, for those native to the system, signs must be observed (in both senses of the word): there is little scope for individual initiative or fantasy, no choice in how signs are to be interpreted. An essential part of the power of religious systems lies in their control of signs and how they are interpreted: to break the sacred pact of sign and object is to practice *heresy* and is thus taboo. The elaborate ritual of so-called primitive societies is motivated thus by a desire to maintain the integrity of the signifier/signified link and, in the process, social cohesion. In reality such worlds, as Baudrillard reminds us, are cruel and despotic:

Si nous nous prenons encore à rêver – aujourd'hui surtout – d'un monde de signes sûrs, d'un 'ordre symbolique' fort, soyons sans illusions: cet ordre a existé, et ce fut celui d'une hiérarchie féroce, car la transparence et la cruauté des signes vont de pair. Dans la société des castes, féodales ou archaïques, sociétés *cruelles*, les signes sont en nombre limité, de diffusion restreinte, chacun a sa pleine valeur d'interdit, chacun est une obligation réciproque entre castes, clans ou personnes: ils ne sont donc pas arbitraires. L'arbitraire du signe commence lorsque, au lieu de lier deux personnes par une réciprocité infranchissable, il se met, signifiant, à renvoyer à un univers désenchanté du signifié, dénominateur commun du monde réel, envers qui personne n'a plus d'obligation. (Baudrillard, 1976: 78).

[If we continue still to fantasise – today especially – about a world of fixed signs, of a strong 'symbolic order', let us have no illusions about it: this order did once exist and it was that of a ferocious hierarchy, for the transparency and the cruelty of signs go together. In feudal, archaic or caste-based societies – cruel societies – signs are limited in number and of limited circulation, each having its value as a prohibition, each signifying a reciprocal obligation between castes, clans or persons; these signs are thus far from being arbitrary. The sign becomes arbitrary only when, instead of linking two persons in an unbreakable relation of reciprocity, it sets out, as *signifier*, to refer to the disenchanted universe of the *signified*, common denominator of the real world, towards which nobody has any obligation any more.]

What Baudrillard describes in the latter part of this passage is the double movement of disenchantment and liberation that comes about once the hegemony of a single sign system is broken. For when the sign becomes detached from its object (and therefore conceptualised), which happens when an alternative sign system is apprehended, the spell of the integral primitive world is broken. As soon as an alternative or a choice is introduced into a signifying system, the arbitrary nature of the sign/object, signifier/signified link becomes apparent. To the native of a so-called primitive society, this introduction of semiotic choice is both liberating and disenchanting:[4] he/she discovers the possibility of individual interpretation and therefore personal destiny as opposed to the primarily communal understanding of meaning and collective fate established hitherto by the primitive society. At the same time, however, the magical unity and integrity of sign system and environment is irrevocably broken as competing systems strive to assert their control over the meaning process. Sign systems imply knowledge that in turn implies power. Conflicting sign systems engage in a power struggle in which the newly individual consciousness is caught up in a relation of often irresolvable tension.

The most powerful sign systems are those that involve writing (see Lévi-Strauss, 1955: 352–5; Goody, 1979). This is not only because writing enables knowledge to be stored, remembered, elaborated and disseminated widely but also because it can be used as an instrument of exploitation and control.[5] The following passage, much commented on, from *Tristes Tropiques* illustrates this well:

On se doute que les Nambikwara ne savent pas écrire [. . .]. Comme chez les Caduveo, je distribuai pourtant des feuilles de papier et des crayons dont ils ne firent rien au début puis un jour je les vis tous occupés à tracer sur le papier des lignes horizontales ondulées. Que voulaient-ils donc faire? Je dus me rendre à l'évidence: ils écrivaient [. . .]. Pour la plupart, l'effort s'arrêtait là; mais le chef de bande voyait plus loin. Seul, sans doute, il avait compris la fonction de l'écriture. Aussi m'a-t-il réclamé un bloc-notes et nous sommes pareillement équipés quand nous travaillons ensemble. Il ne me communique pas verbalement les informations que je lui demande, mais trace sur son papier des lignes sinueuses et me les présente, comme si je devais faire lire sa réponse. Lui-même est à moitié dupe de sa comédie; chaque fois que sa main achève une ligne, il l'examine anxieusement comme si la signification devait en jaillir, et la même désillusion se peint sur son visage. Mais il n'en convient pas; et il est tacitement entendu entre nous que son grimoire possède un sens que je feins de déchiffrer; le commentaire verbal suit presque aussitôt et me dispense de réclamer les éclaircissements nécessaires.

Or, à peine avait-il rassemblé tout son monde qu'il tira d'une hotte un papier couvert de lignes tortillées qu'il fit semblant de lire et où il cherchait, avec une hésitation affectée, la liste des objets que je devais donner en retour des cadeaux offerts: à celui-ci, contre un arc et des flèches, un sabre d'abatis! à tel autre, des perles! Pour ses colliers . . . Cette comédie se prolongea pendant deux heures. Qu'espérait-il? Se tromper lui-même, peut-être; mais plutôt étonner ses compagnons, les persuader que les marchandises passaient par son intermédiaire, qu'il avait obtenu l'alliance du blanc et qu'il participait à ses secrets. (1955: 349–50)

[As one might suspect, the Nambikwara don't know how to write (. . .). As with the Caduveo, I nevertheless handed out sheets of paper and pencils with which they did nothing at first, then one day I saw them all occupied in tracing wavy horizontal lines across the paper. What were they doing? I had to accept the evidence: they were writing (. . .). For the most part, their efforts stopped there; but their chief realised there was more to it than that. He alone seems to have realised the function of writing. So he asked me for a note-pad, with which we were both equipped when working together. He did not communicate to me verbally the information that I asked of him but traced on the paper wavy lines that he then passed to me as if I should in this way read his reply. He himself was in part a dupe to his own play-acting: each time that his hand completed a line, he examined it anxiously as if its meaning were about to spring forth, and his face expressed the same disillusion every time. But this wouldn't do: it was tacitly agreed between us that his mumbo jumbo contained a meaning that I pretended to decipher; his verbal commentary followed almost immediately, obviating any necessity on my part to ask for further clarification.

Now, scarcely had he reassembled his people than he drew from a basket a piece of paper covered in wavy lines that he pretended to read and in which he sought, with affected hesitation, to identify the list of objects I should give in exchange for the presents offered: to so-and-so, an abatis sword in exchange for a bow and arrows; to someone else, beads. For these necklaces . . . This charade continued for two hours. What did he hope to achieve? To deceive himself, perhaps; or rather to astonish his fellow tribesmen, to persuade them that the merchandise was traded through him, that he had formed an alliance with the white man and that he shared his secrets.]

Before the Nambikwara chief's action here, as observed by Lévi-Strauss, it may be assumed that for members of the Nambikwara and other so-called primitive tribes, signs were believed to have a real connection with their object: to possess the sign *is* to possess the thing to which it refers. So in (mis-)appropriating the sign system of the white ethnographer, the Nambikwara chief might be imagined by his fellows also to be appropriating the objects attached to the borrowed signs, or at least that his (pretended) grasp of the new instrument empowered him to assure the transfer of objects from the other to the native community, or between native communities, and vice versa, in an exchange that was both symbolic and real. In fact though, the Nambikwara chief's action may have been – this is what Lévi-Strauss seems to imply – also a function of an obscure realisation of the power of the written sign *as a sign*, in particular in that, by its very agency, regardless of its content (of which he has only a hazy understanding), it offers possibilities of action different from or alternative to those already operative in his native system. However, the dawning realisation that the link between word and object may not be necessary or real, may be one of the causes of the subsequent unease felt by the Nambikwara tribesmen and, indeed, may have been a factor in the subsequent demotion of the chief who had in this way (mis-)appropriated western writing. Henri Michaux's graphic work such as that shown in figure 1, taken from *Par la voie des rythmes* (1974), seems to reveal, on one level, an intuitive grasp of what was at stake in the kind of motivated scribble that the Nambikwara chief was attempting to reproduce: a form of sign *that acted on* the object(s) to which it was presumed to refer in a new and mysterious way, the potential functional efficacy of which was recognised even if the actual content of the sign was obscure.[6]

A similar if more elaborated fable of the relation of signs to their objects and of the fascination of signs – aural or written – in relation to their power potential is recounted by Victor Segalen in his 'ethnographic' novel *Les Immémoriaux*. Segalen, like Lévi-Strauss, explores both the semiotic and power issues at stake in the confrontation of sign systems.[7] So we find in *Les Immémoriaux* the connection between words and beings, 'mots' and 'êtres', subject to political manipulation, and observe the trauma experienced by a native consciousness when a new sign system imposed from the outside ousts the native system. The Polynesian chief, Vaïraatoa, for example, like the Nambikwara chief described by Lévi-Strauss, is aware of the importance of asserting his power in terms of *signs* as well as actions. He not only invades the Piraè Valley, he also obliterates the names formerly used by its native inhabitants to describe its various parts:

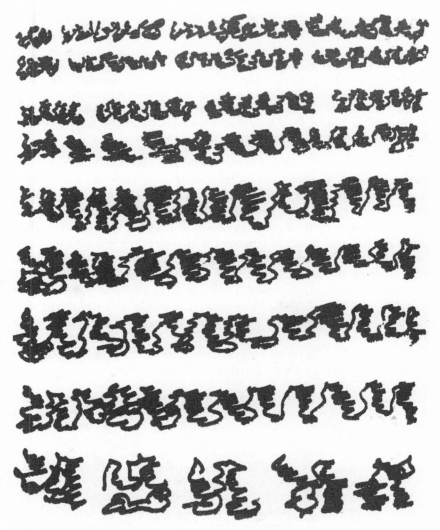

Figure 1 Drawing from Henri Michaux: *Par la voie des rythmes*

Pour affirmer sa conquête dans la vallée Piraè, il [Vaïraatoa, chef polynésien] en avait aboli tous les noms jadis en usage.

Car on sait qu'aux changements des êtres, afin que cela soit irrévocable, doit s'ajouter l'extermination des mots, et que les mots périssent en entraînant ceux qui les ont créés. Le vocable ancien de la baie, Vaï-été, frappé d'interdit, était donc mort à la foule. Les prêtres seuls le formulaient encore, dont le noble parler, obscur, imposant et nombreux, se nourrit de tous les verbes oubliés. (Segalen, [1907] 1982: 31)

[To affirm his conquest of the Piraè Valley, he (Vaïraatoa, the Polynesian chief) had abolished all the names previously in use.

For we know that to make changes to beings irrevocable, you must also exterminate words and that in perishing words should bring with them their creators. The old language of the bay, Vaï-été, irrevocably forbidden, was thereafter dead to the mass of the people. Only the priests still used it, their noble speech, obscure, imposing and extensive, still drawing on the old language.]

In this way, the magical bond between sign and object is broken, and the native is doubly dispossessed, losing ownership of both the native valley and the signs that formerly bound him to it.[8] It is notable here that the original, and therefore *sacred*, place names are still remembered by the native priests: religions originate in sites to which they become indissolubly attached by sacred bonds of language. A change in the words of the latter would ineluctably undermine the religion itself. Religion's attachment to place is later asserted by the hero of *Les Immémoriaux*, Paofaï when he responds to the question of his Christian interrogator Noté 'Quels sont tes dieux?' ['who are your gods?'] by saying: 'Dis-moi le nom de la terre où je mange' (Segalen [1907] 1982: 227–8) ['Tell me the name of the land where I eat'].

Solid though Paofaï's resistance is to western religion and language, he is nonetheless alert to the potential of the latter's *written* status:

Les étrangers blêmes, parfois si ridicules, ont beaucoup d'ingéniosité: ils tatouent leurs étoffes blanches de petits signes noirs qui marquent des noms, des rites, des nombres. Et ils peuvent, longtemps ensuite, les rechanter tout à loisir. [. . .]

Quand, au milieu de ces chants, – qui sont peut-être récits originels, – leur mémoire hésite, ils baissent les yeux, consultent les signes, et poursuivent sans erreur. Ainsi leurs étoffes peintes valent mieux que les mieux nouées des tresses aux milliers de nœuds. [. . .]

Or, Paofaï, – ayant incanté jadis contre les hommes au nouveau-parler; ayant dénoncé les fièvres et les maux dont ils empliraient ses terres; les ayant méprisés pour leur petitesse et leurs maigres appétits – Paofaï, néanmoins, se prend à envier leurs signes. ([1907] 1982: 125)

[The white-skinned foreigners, sometimes so ridiculous, are nevertheless very ingenious: they tattoo their white fabric with little black signs that mark names, rites, numbers. This enables them a long time after to call up again everything at their will. (. . .)

When, in the middle of their utterances – which are perhaps ancient stories – their memory falters, they lower their eyes, consult the signs, and continue without error. In this way their painted fabric is more valuable than the most knotted of our memory ropes with their thousands of tyings. (. . .)

Now Paofaï, having raged previously against the Men of New Speech, having denounced the diseases and ills with which they filled his land, having despised them for their small size and their puny appetites – Paofaï nevertheless begins to envy them their signs.]

Whereas in Polynesian culture, meaningful signs are tattooed to the object to which they refer ('Ils avaient des dieux fétii, des dieux maori, vêtus du maro, ou bien nus de poitrine, de ventre et de visage; et tatoués de nobles marques': [1907] 1982: 230), in western writing it is the neutral and exchangeable page that is 'tattooed', allowing the sign a movement and circulation that has had an incalculable effect on the development and ultimate domination of western alphabetic civilisation (see Goody, 1979). Confrontations between civilisations are thus in the end always battles of signs and the semiotic system that is the most flexible and transparent is ultimately always the victor, even though it may be the one that has the least indexical or iconic relation to the objects it represents or to which it refers.

A fascination with indexical or iconic signs undoubtedly constitutes a significant part of European travellers' nostalgia for an analogical world in which signs are attached to their objects. As a result, the question of the sign's decipherability becomes, from the nineteenth century, central to European travel texts. If the sign is to re-awaken a magical sense of the presence or at least immanence of the object, it must offer some of the latter's *resistance*. And, like the object it must be perceived as being part of the real, or at least contiguous with it, having a sensuous presence or even beauty in its own right. This is reflected in the travel writer's concern with the *signifier*, that part of the sign that confirms its semiotic status but which is at the same time perceptible without the corresponding signified necessarily being identified, and meaning thus adduced. The travel writer's aim is thus to keep open as long as possible the dynamic potential of the object before the interpretant ascribes immediacy and thus intelligibility to it. In some cases, such as the Michaux of the purely graphic texts (for example, in Michaux, 1974; figure 1), the sign will remain ultimately indecipherable, allowing the reader to experience both the primitive's first confrontation with graphic signs and the untutored westerner's first encounter with far-eastern ideographic systems. Similarly, the success of Barthes's project in *L'Empire des signes* depends on the language of his exotic empire being non-alphabetic. Finally, even a country as close to his own as Spain offers Gautier the advantage of a language offering a resistance – if only in its graphic style of transcription – that borrows something from the more radically different Arabic system.

An exemplary account of the issues at stake in the travel-writer's deciphering of foreign signs is provided by Gautier in the following passage from his *Voyage en Espagne* that deals with his arrival in the capital Madrid:

Une chose qui est vraiment surprenante, c'est la fréquence de l'inscription suivante: *Juego de villar*, qui se reproduit de vingt pas en vingt pas. De peur que vous ne vous imaginiez qu'il y a quelque chose de mystérieux dans ces trois mots sacramentels, je me hâte de les traduire: ils signifient seulement *jeu de billard*. [. . .] Après les *juegos de villar*, l'inscription la plus fréquente est celle de *despacho de bino* (débit de vin). [. . .] Les *confiterias* et *pastelerias* sont aussi très nombreuses [. . .]. Toutes ces enseignes sont écrites en caractères abréviés, avec des lettres entrelacées les unes dans les autres, qui en rendent d'abord l'intelligence difficile aux étrangers, grands lecteurs d'enseignes, s'il en fut. ([1840] 1981: 155–6)

[A really astonishing thing is the frequent recurrence of the following sign: *Juego de villar*, which you see every twenty yards. Lest you imagine that there be something mysterious in those three sacramental words, I hasten to translate them: all they mean is *Billiard Room*. (. . .) After *juegos de villar*, the next most common sign is *despacho de bino* (wine shop). (. . .) The *confiterias* and *pastelerias* are also numerous (. . .). All these shop-signs are written in abbreviated forms, with letters interlaced, which makes it difficult at first for travellers – great readers of signs if ever there were any – to decipher them.]

Here, the foreignness of the language provides the charm of signifiers, exotic both in their graphic presentation – 'Toutes ces enseignes sont écrites en caractères abréviés, avec des lettres entrelacées les unes dans les autres' – and in their relation to their signifieds: 'De peur que vous ne vous imaginiez qu'il y a quelque chose de mystérieux dans ces trois mots sacramentels, je me hâte de les traduire'. The abbreviation of words so that they may be accommodated within the restricted format of the shop-sign, along with the elaborate arabesques of their graphic presentation, makes them in themselves an object of fascination even before the moment for deciphering comes. Before they are interpreted, the words *Juego de villar* are described as being 'mysterious' and 'sacramental', in other words as signs of quasi-religious significance, signs that communicate with their object according to a sacred or mystical bond. As shop signs, the words are also contiguous with the object to which they refer and are thus doubly indexical, pointing both to a meaning (game of billiards) and to an object (place where the game can take place). Although Gautier in this passage hastens to translate Spanish into French so that his reader may understand the meaning of the sign – in both senses of the word (*signe/enseigne*) – the link of the signifier to its signified comes as an anticlimax: the exotic strangeness of the sign becomes attached to a banal immediate object and the magical potential of the signifier is lost in signification. This process is repeated with other exotic signs Gautier encounters on his entry into Madrid – *despacho de bino, confiterias, pastelerias* – the foreign traveller of course being dependent on signs to orientate himself in a strange city and to find the objects, services or places he needs. With gradual acquisition of knowledge of the city and its facilities, the reading of signs by the visitor becomes less important and the exotic strangeness of the place becomes banalised through familiarity.

In order to maintain the exotic even within a culture that is beginning to become familiar to him, the traveller sometimes devises other semiotic strategies. In the case of Gautier, the desire to re-authenticate the sign is worked out in terms of aesthetics. In the secular world of the post-Enlightenment, art becomes a substitute for religion: artists (in particular visual artists, painters) restore or re-motivate the link between signs and objects – or rather they arrange signs in such a way that their symbolic potential is maximised. They do this in particular by manipulating and co-ordinating the signifier or signifying aspect of the sign (colour, composition, the plastic qualities of paint), with the aim of recreating a magical world, one in which signs become as real (that is, powerful in meaning) as their objects. Indeed the painting becomes in itself an object, but one which, unlike a thing selected from the natural world, is already deeply imbued with significance. Beauty is perceived as difference on the level of the signifier that is subsequently translated into a signified which restores a full and sometimes unexpected meaning. The traveller seeks in the real world aesthetic impressions whose authenticity is confirmed if they become recognised as the signified of a work of art, something to which the work of art has already referred and therefore on which it has already conferred meaning. Gautier therefore looks everywhere in Spain for pictures or *tableaux* in the real world which either refer to existing works of art – especially by Decamps, Delacroix or others in the French Orientalist school, or by Goya and others in the Spanish school – or suggest imaginary paintings. Strange or other worlds are more susceptible to revitalisation of the sign/object, signifier/signified link than the familiar world since the gap between the two related elements is wider. It is in the gap between sign and object, signifier and signified that the potential for new or richer meaning lies.

This process is exemplified in this passage from Gautier's *Voyage en Espagne*:

Nous étions secoués comme des souris que l'on ballotte pour les étourdir et les tuer contre les parois de la souricière, et il fallait toute la sévère beauté du paysage pour ne pas nous laisser aller à la mélancolie et à la courbature; mais ces belles collines aux lignes austères, à la couleur sobre et calme, donnaient tant de caractère à l'horizon sans cesse renouvelé, que les cahots de la galère étaient compensés et au-delà. Un village, un ancien couvent bâti en forteresse, variaient ces sites d'une simplicité orientale, qui rappelaient les lointains du *Joseph vendu par ses frères*, de Decamps.

Dueñas, situé sur une colline, a l'air d'un cimetière turc; les caves, creusées dans le roc vif, reçoivent l'air par de petites tourelles évasées en turban, qui ont un faux air de minaret très singulier. Une église de tournure moresque complète l'illusion. A gauche, dans la plaine, le canal de Castille fait apparition de temps à autre; ce canal n'est pas encore terminé.

A Venta de Trigueros, l'on attela à notre galère un cheval *rose* d'une singulière beauté (l'on avait renoncé aux mules), qui justifiait pleinement le cheval tant critiqué du *Triomphe de Trajan*, d'Eugène Delacroix. Le génie a toujours raison: ce qu'il invente existe, et la nature l'imite jusque dans ses plus excentriques fantaisies. ([1840] 1981: 116)

[We were being jiggled like mice in traps that are shaken to stun and then kill them against the sides of the mouse-trap, and we needed all the severe beauty of the scenery to prevent us from giving ourselves up to melancholy and stiffness; but these beautiful hills with their austere lines and peaceful, sober colours gave so much interest to the incessantly moving horizon that the jolts of the carriage were a price more than worth paying. A village, an ancient convent built like a fortress, gave an oriental touch to the setting, which recalled the background of Decamps's painting *Joseph Sold by his Brothers*.

Dueñas, situated on a hilltop, looks like a Turkish cemetery; the caves hollowed out of solid rock, are ventilated by small towers shaped into turbans, which makes them seem like little minarets. A church in a seemingly Moorish style completes the illusion. On the left, the Castille Canal, not yet completed, can occasionally be glimpsed across the plain.

At Venta de Trigueros, a *pink* horse of singular beauty was harnessed to our carriage (the mules having been given up at this stage), an animal that fully justified the horse that received so much criticism in Eugène Delacroix's painting *The Justice of Trajan*. Genius is always right: what it invents exists, and nature will follow it even in its most eccentric fantasies.]

Here, despite – or perhaps ultimately as a function of – the boredom, melancholy and discomfort of foreign travel, a heightening of awareness is induced in the writer. For the landscape through which Gautier travels in this passage seems to have been touched by a magic that renders the banal exotic. The sensation of authenticity which satisfies a nostalgia for an integral, analogical world, is experienced here as a state in which reality seems to become once again fully or vividly re-attached to significance, or significance re-attached to reality. What is the semiotic process that has brought this situation about – one in which, as in an ideal or primeval world, the real fits the sign, or in which the object coincides fully with its own (aesthetic) significance? It seems to depend on the action of the interpretant which in a movement of abduction or imagination is able to render the object of the subject's gaze dynamic, and thus real, through the intermediary of an aesthetic sign. This latter is supplied by a work of art, in this case by images from French paintings (Decamps, Delacroix) that provide mental blueprints sufficiently compelling to induce their re-imposition on scenes in real life. Painting is thus able to reactivate or rejuvenate the semiotic process by creating imaginary objects that stimulate in the viewer a desire for their realisation in the objective world. So the pink horse that Delacroix included in his painting *The Justice of Trajan* (figure 2) having in the recent past embedded itself in Gautier's memory and imagination, returns as a dynamic interpretant capable of transforming the fragment of Spanish scenery into a *sign*. Although the passage employs in its description the vocabulary of deception – 'faux air', 'illusion', 'fantaisies' – this in no way undermines the validity of the semiotic process it embodies. Rather it underlines the necessary element of illusion or deception in all semiotic processes that venture beyond the immediate; for access to the dynamic object is always a privilege that is in some way motivated by desire for the fulfilment of some mythic intention. As the end of the passage just cited makes clear, Gautier rationalises this process in terms of genius and imagination which, like religion and myth, are the ultimate forces governing relations between signs and their objects.

In human culture, structuralist anthropology tells us (Lévi-Strauss, 1955), the symbolic precedes the real. It becomes increasingly the aim of later twentieth-century travel writers to rediscover this precedence in the difference or other they encounter on their travels. It is therefore in the symbolic that Roland Barthes in *L'Empire des signes* ([1970] 1980) sets out to experience difference without it being semiotised or rationalised into a meaning comprehensible in western terms. Barthes's aim becomes, as the following passage makes clear, to find and to experience the other in terms of signs and to understand how other sign systems (re-)construct the real:

Le rêve: connaître une langue étrangère (étrange) et cependant ne pas la comprendre: percevoir en elle la différence, sans que cette différence soit jamais récupérée par la socialité superficielle du langage, communication ou vulgarité; connaître, réfractées positivement dans une langue nouvelle, les impossibilités de la nôtre; apprendre la systématique de l'inconcevable; défaire notre 'réel' sous l'effet d'autres découpages, d'autres syntaxes; découvrir des positions inouïes du sujet dans l'énonciation, déplacer sa topologie; en un mot, descendre dans l'intraduisible, en éprouver la secousse sans jamais l'amortir, jusqu'à ce qu'en nous tout l'Occident

Figure 2 Eugène Delacroix, *The Justice of Trajan* (1840) oil on canvas, 490 × 390 cm

s'ébranle et que vacillent les droits de la langue paternelle, celle qui nous vient de nos pères et qui nous fait à notre tour, pères et propriétaires d'une culture que précisément l'histoire transforme en 'nature'. ([1970] 1980: 11)

[Who has not dreamed of a foreign (strange) language and yet of not understanding it; of perceiving difference in it without this difference ever being attenuated by the superficial sociability of language, communication or vulgarity; of becoming acquainted with the shortcomings of our own language positively refracted in that of another; of learning the system of what was hitherto inconceivable; of undoing our 'real' according to the effect of other ways of seeing, other syntaxes; of discovering unheard of positions of the enunciated subject, of re-situating our topographical bearings; in a word, of descending into the untranslatable and feeling its shock without ever fully absorbing it, until the whole system of western culture trembles and the rights of the paternal language shake to their foundations – that native language that our fathers handed down to us and which makes us in our turn fathers and proprietors of a culture which history has the effect of transforming into 'nature'.]

Writing a hundred years after Gautier and in the wake of half a century of linguistics and structural anthropology, Barthes is of course fully conscious of the ethnographic and linguistic/semiotic issues at stake in the exploration of a radically foreign culture. This awareness is evidenced in his concern with the structure of the sign, the necessity of grasping the underlying systems or *épistémè* supporting a given culture, and the importance of language as a major structuring element in cultural expression – he refers, for example, to Whorf's work on languages of North American Indians and to Granet's study of Chinese ([1970] 1980: 12). Also, though, like Gautier, Barthes is aware, from the point of view of the travel writer, of the value of personal experience of exotic sign systems, and the fascination they exert, before they are fully analysed and understood. As a result, even more than Gautier, Barthes focusses on the signifier, privileging the signs of Japan over the *real* Japan, making it clear from the start that for him Japan is a quasi-fictitious semiotic system ([1970] 1980: 7). Like Gautier, Barthes also has an ulterior motive – shared by many western travel writers: that of escaping – if only momentarily – the determinism and essentialism of western linguistic and cultural structures. So the 'masse bruissante d'une langue inconnue' ['the rustling mass of an unknown language'] is able to protect Barthes from all the 'aliénations de la langue maternelle' ['alienations of the mother tongue'], substituting in its stead a system far richer in sign possibilities ([1970] 1980: 17–18).

For Barthes then, Japan seems to offer a unique opportunity to experience cultural difference on a more abstract level, one on which it is the operations of signs as much as their content that is of primary concern. Japanese culture is able to lend itself to such an analysis because of the relative fragility of its physical reality and the disproportionate importance of its sign markings. A centreless archipelago of tortuous and mountainous islands, so densely populated that physical space is at a premium, Japan is a country so beset by the dangers of earthquakes, volcanic eruptions and tidal waves that fragility and adaptability become the aim of most of its physical constructions. Added to this, a racial type of apparent homogeneity, in which uniform skin, hair and eye colour, a small and light frame (the Sumo wrestler constitutes a striking exception to this rule), and a pattern of social practice as ritualistic as it is discreet, together create a backdrop of uniform insubstantiality against which the sign stands out in striking relief. In other words, for Barthes, in Japan, reality becomes a mere support for the sign, one in which 'le mur est détruit par l'inscription' ([1970] 1980: 145) ['the inscription obliterates the wall']. Meaning is experienced not as a profound revelation in three-dimensional space but as a series of flickers against a papery, semi-transparent and insubstantial surface. The Japanese fascination with – and skill in handling – paper is of course fundamental here, for paper is used in Japan as a primary material in building, decorating, clothing and cooking, as well as in painting and writing. Its primary role in the latter as a *support for signs*, through contagion, thus also seems to affect the other uses to which it is put, so that Japanese culture as a whole appears to Barthes as a fragile text to be *read*. For him then, Japanese culture becomes a diagram of the semiotic process, one whose heuristic value in semiotic terms is enhanced by the underlying void:

le lieu public est une suite d'événements instantanés qui accèdent au notable dans un éclat si vif, si ténu que le signe s'abolit avant que n'importe quel signifié ait eu le temps de 'prendre'. On dirait qu'une technique séculaire permet au paysage ou au spectacle de se produire dans une pure signifiance, abrupte, vide, comme une cassure. Empire de signes? Oui, si l'on entend que ces signes sont vides et que le rituel est sans dieu. ([1970] 1980: 145)

[public places are a series of instantaneous events that achieve noteworthiness in such a sudden flash that the sign is abolished before any signified has had time to 'take'. One would say that a centuries-old technique enables a landscape or spectacle to appear as a pure signifying surface, abrupt, empty, like a sudden break. Empire of Signs? Perhaps, to the extent that these signs are empty and that the ritual governing them presupposes no deity.]

   Correspondingly, in Barthes's adventures in the land of the Signifier, food (a subject that will be examined in Chapter 7), gifts, theatre, sport and other entertainments are explored and enjoyed not only for their difference from western equivalents but also for the way they each throw light on the semantic void underlying them. The fascination of the *haiku* is exemplary here. For Barthes, the haiku is an arrangement of words or signs in which signifiers are indeed attached to signifieds but in a relation that shares little of the motivating dynamic governing meaning construction in western sign systems.[9] For what is at stake in the haiku is the possibility of sense,

Figure 3 *Mu, le vide* (Japanese ideogramme) in Roland Barthes, *L'Empire des signes*

not depth of meaning. Such writing does not propose messages; rather is created the impression that any sense or meaning which is deduced comes as an accident, as a side effect, or, as Barthes puts it, is *exempted*. Meaning is merely one element in the overall aesthetic enjoyment offered by the text, a mere supplement to the attractiveness of the signifier as form (as in the Japanese calligraphic character itself, figure 3) in all its lightness and spatial airiness. Intellectual enjoyment of the haiku is a function not of any idea, argument or theory that the haiku text might itself propose but precisely of the way any such possibilities seem to be shut out. In this way, the art of the haiku is the art of manipulating the potential of signs without necessarily fully realising it, the art of using language without necessarily stimulating *thought* in the western understanding of the word. The following text by

Bashô, Japanese master of the haiku, as cited by Barthes, exemplifies the process:

> *Comme il est admirable*
> *Celui qui ne pense pas: 'La Vie est éphémère'*
> *En voyant un éclair!*   ([1970] 1980: 94).
>
> *[How admirable is he*
> *Who does not think 'How ephemeral life is'*
> *On seeing a lightning flash!]*

For Barthes, the haiku, as an exercise in exemption of sense, is a literary manifestation of the Zen Buddhism that he sees as providing a basic component of the *épistémè* underlying Japanese thinking. The philosophy of Zen, like Borgès's Chinese encyclopedia, deeply disturbs the logical categories operative in western thinking. The Buddhist recommendation to avoid assertion, negation, ambiguity and ambivalence, has the effect, as Barthes notes ([1970] 1980: 95), of destroying the linguistic paradigm as constructed by structural linguistics: *A – non-A – ni A, ni non-A (degré zéro) – A et non-A (degré complexe)*. If Buddhism is proposing such a radical blockage of sense-making structures, what possibilities of meaning remain? As an alternative, Buddhist teaching proposes a meditation on the sign, using a *koan* or some other fragment of text 'non de le résoudre, comme s'il avait un sens, non même de percevoir son absurdité (qui est encore un sens), mais de le remâcher "jusqu'à ce que la dent tombe"' ([1970] 1980: 97) ['not to resolve it, as if it had a meaning, nor even to notice its absurdity (which is still a meaning of sorts), but to chew it over it until there is nothing left to chew']. The aim of this is to reflect on the sign *as sign*, not as meaning but as an operation: 'En somme, c'est le symbole comme opération sémantique qui est attaqué' ([1970] 1980: 98).

In confirming that the value of East/West comparisons is not just knowledge of difference, but, more vitally, a confrontation of *épistémès* as revealed in different strategies of symbolisation, Barthes writes:

L'Orient et l'Occident ne peuvent donc être pris ici comme des 'réalités', que l'on essayerait d'approcher et d'opposer historiquement, philosophiquement, culturellement, politiquement. [. . .] Ce qui peut être visé, dans la considération de l'Orient, ce ne sont pas d'autres symboles, une autre métaphysique, une autre sagesse (encore que celle-ci apparaisse bien désirable); c'est la possibilité d'une différence, d'une mutation, d'une révolution dans la propriété des systèmes symboliques. [. . .] Aujourd'hui il y a sans doute mille choses à apprendre de l'Orient: un énorme travail de *connaissance* est, sera nécessaire [. . .]; mais il faut aussi que, acceptant de laisser de part et d'autre d'immenses zones d'ombre [. . .], un mince filet de lumière cherche, non d'autres symboles, mais la fissure même du symbolique. ([1970] 1980: 7–8)

[The East and the West cannot therefore be taken here as 'realities' that one might attempt to bring together or oppose in historical, philosophical, cultural or political terms. (. . .) What might be envisaged, in any consideration of the East, is not other symbols, another metaphysics, another wisdom (however desirable this latter might seem), but rather the possibility of a difference, mutation or revolution in the properties of symbolic systems. (. . .) There are no doubt today many things to learn from the East; a huge effort of understanding is or would be necessary for this (. . .); but what is also necessary is that, even if we accept that large zones remain in the shadows (. . .) a narrow beam of light should seek not other symbols but a split in the symbolic system itself.]

This passage also suggests a model for travel writing which, as a genre between semiotics and anthropology, temporarily suspends itself in 'la fissure même du symbolique', momentarily inhabiting the space between sign and object, signifier and signified, experiencing it as pure difference. Barthes achieves this aim in *L'Empire des signes* not only in the way, on the level of theory, he places it lucidly in its semiotic and anthropological context, but also in the way, on the level of writing as practice, he tries to recreate the confrontation of *symboliques*, to provoke comparison and contrast of different symbolising systems. Thus Barthes's text itself offers a profusion of different signifiers in which the heterogeneous mixture of French and Japanese text, fragments of Japanese calligraphy and characters, paintings, photographs, drawings, maps and other symbolic forms of representation, leads the reader in different ways to confront the gap between sign and object, between signifier and signified, and between sign systems. In this way Barthes's text in itself becomes the fictitious Japan its author announces his intention to explore at the beginning of the book, its pages a series of fissures which cut up and fragment in various ways the symbolic system that is their ultimate object. The final clue to the signifying process operative within it are the photographs which, like a chiasmus, open and close the volume (figure 4): both show a virtually identical image of a young Japanese actor: the *difference* between them is minimal, indeed they are identical, except for the smile, *au sourire près*. In other words they represent *the smile of the sign*, there being, as in Zen interpretation of the sign, nothing other to grasp. As Barthes says in the book's last words, which immediately precede the photograph's second appearance, and in which even typography as signifier changes from italics to hand-written script: 'il n'y a rien à *saisir . . .* **au sourire près**' ([1970] 1980:146).

Figure 4 Photographs reproduced as frontispiece and tailpiece in Roland Barthes,
L'Empire des signes

Figure 4 (*cont.*)

The smile that Jean Baudrillard encounters in the United States, like the one Barthes meets in Japan, can also be read as a symbol of the sign:

Sourire autoprophétique, comme tous les signes publicitaires: souriez, on vous sourira. Souriez pour montrer votre transparence, votre candeur. Souriez si vous n'avez rien à dire, ne cachez surtout pas que vous n'avez rien à dire, ou que les autres vous sont indifférents. Laissez transparaître spontanément ce vide, cette indifférence profonde dans votre sourire, *faites don* aux autres de ce vide et de cette indifférence, illuminez votre visage du degré zéro de la joie et du plaisir, souriez, souriez . . . A défaut d'identité, les Américains ont une dentition merveilleuse. (Baudrillard, 1986: 37)

[Autoprophetic smile, like all publicity signs: smile, you will be smiled at in return. Smile to show how transparent, how candid you are. Smile if you have nothing to say, certainly never hide that you have nothing to say or that you are indifferent to others. Let the void, the profound indifference in your smile appear spontaneously. *Make a gift* to others of this void, this indifference, light up your face to a zero degree of pleasure or joy, smile, smile. Even if they lack identity, Americans have perfect teeth.]

If, for post-structuralist sociologists/semioticians, it is in its manipulation of signs that a culture betrays its deeper epistemic structure, then for Baudrillard, it is the American smile, with its perfect dentition, that is synonymous with the publicity image that provides the model of semiosis in the capitalist democratic *épistémè*. For the publicity process, in promoting the image of a product (jeans, soft drinks, media star), attempts *to pass off the same as different* merely through marketing and packaging. The process it employs is paradoxical since it involves both blandness and difference: the blandness lies in the physical presentation of the object through the sign – regularity, smoothness, a certain transparency; the difference is added through the suggestion of some mythical association (the cowboy, Yankee vigour, the American Venus). In a society of democratic uniformity this process quickly becomes extended to the whole system of sign exchange and meaning creation, one which the cinematographic, televisual and, most recently, the computer/electronic media have massively facilitated. So, as Baudrillard notes, the US president can be a former B-movie cowboy star, his wife a former sex kitten, their photogenic smiles bearing no relation to their political or social functions.

As is the case with Barthes's take on the sign, though for different reasons, Baudrillard's analysis of the smile also leads to the conclusion that it is the signifier of a void. The void in Baudrillard's case however is not that arrived at through an exercise in Zen Buddhist spiritual asceticism, but is rather a function of the general emptying of significance of signs within the capitalist consumer world. In the West, the smile, the sign, is there to be consumed as a sign, but without an understanding of what is at stake in the signifying process entering into, and therefore potentially undermining, the consumer process. The sign operates therefore for what it suggests at the level of the signifier without entering into any real contract as to what it will in fact deliver on the level of the signified: it becomes, as Baudrillard says (his italics), '*la fiction matérielle de l'image*' (1986: 57). America is a culture in which a derisory object – a pair of jeans, a soft drink, a second-rate actress – is through the publicity process packaged and marketed (that is semiotised) in such a way as to become an object of quasi mythic significance.

In this respect, it is interesting to contrast Barthes's juxtaposition of photographs of a Japanese male successively serious and smiling with another object of desire, the smile of Marilyn Monroe as reproduced in a Warhol silkscreen print (figure 5) which appears on the cover of the French paperback edition of *Amérique* (1986). The first thing to say about the face of Marilyn Monroe is that, unlike that of Greta Garbo or Audrey Hepburn, as analysed by Barthes in *Mythologies* (1957: 70–1), it represents neither *Idée* (Idea) nor *Evénement* (Event), but Image.[10] For, as with the whole of American culture as analysed by Baudrillard, Monroe's face is manipulated to operate cinematographically, as a pure sign. Even before it appears before the camera, the face's basis in the biological real has been profoundly altered – by plastic surgery to the chin, dyeing and permanent waving of the hair, improved dentition, make-up. The aim of the face thus is not to express personality or individuality but to be *photogenic*. Warhol's silkscreen print, by multiplying further the process of the image's mediatisation before it is presented to the viewer/consumer, both clarifies and extends the layers of semi-transparent metamorphosis that the image undergoes in its transformation from index to simulacrum. First, the black and white photo is transferred to a silkscreen image; second, colour is added, the deliberate lack of synchronisation between it and the surfaces to which it is applied emphasizing the *écart* or fissure between make-up and face, photographic image and silkscreen technique – the crude technicolour hues employed (turquoise, peroxide yellow, geranium red) adding to the image's artificiality; third, the image is transferred to canvas where it receives the ideological gloss of the connotation 'work of art'; at the same time, the image is multiplied so that it appears like a series of temporarily arrested frames from a moving picture or film. What Warhol reproduces in visual terms is then exactly the process Baudrillard identifies in American sign culture: the signifier as a series of transparent layers which themselves simultaneously construct and occlude

Figure 5 Andy Warhol, *Marilyn* (1967) silkscreen print, 80 × 80 cm

the signified, leaving the latter virtually divorced from the object to which the sign (as combined signifier/signified) supposedly refers. In this way, the consumer grasps a sign that is practically *autosemiotic* or *hyperreal*, since it minimises the interpretative process while also mimicking and blocking access to the real.[11]

Baudrillard's project in *Amérique* is to apply this model to the whole of American culture and geography that he sees as being hyperreal in all its aspects. This is because there is no part of America or its culture that has not always already been experienced – televisually, cinematographically or in some other popular mediatised form – by the European traveller for whom it is impossible for the 'real' as encountered in America (except possibly for the desert, to which we will return in Chapter 5) to dislodge the hyperreal of its previous media representations or rather simulations:

Tout est repris par la simulation. Les paysages par la photographie, les femmes par le scénario sexuel, les pensées par l'écriture, le terrorisme par la mode et les médias, les événements par la télévision. Les choses semblent n'exister que par cette destination étrange. On peut se demander si le monde lui-même n'existe qu'en fonction de la publicité qui peut en être faite dans un autre monde. (1986: 35)

[Everything is taken up again by simulation. Landscapes by photography, women by sexual scenarios, thought by writing, terrorism by fashion and the media, events by TV. Things seem only to exist in this strange manner. One wonders if the world itself exists only as a function of the publicity it can be used for in another world.]

Like Barthes in Japan, Baudrillard in America is struck both by the ethnographic and semiological possibilities of discovering and experiencing the hyperreal of 'la société primitive de l'avenir' (1986: 13):

L'Amérique n'est ni un rêve, ni une réalité, c'est une hyperréalité. C'est une hyperréalité parce que c'est une utopie qui dès le début s'est vécue comme réalisée. Tout ici est réel, pragmatique, et tout vous laisse rêveur. Il se peut que la vérité de l'Amérique ne puisse apparaître qu'à un Européen, puisque lui seul trouve ici le simulacre parfait, celui de l'immanence et de la transcription matérielle de toutes les valeurs. Les Américains, eux, n'ont aucun sens de la simulation. Ils en sont la configuration parfaite, mais ils n'en ont pas le langage, étant eux-mêmes le modèle. Ils constituent donc le matériau idéal d'une analyse de toutes les variantes possibles du monde moderne. Ni plus ni moins d'ailleurs que le furent en leurs temps les sociétés primitives. La même exultation mythique et analytique qui nous faisait tourner nos regards vers ces sociétés antérieures nous pousse à regarder aujourd'hui du côté de l'Amérique, avec la même passion et les mêmes préjugés. (1986: 32)

[America is neither a dream nor a reality but a hyperreality. It is a hyperreality in that it is a Utopia that from the start has existed in real terms. Here everything is real or pragmatic but at the same time everything makes one wonder. It may be that the reality of America can only appear to a European since the latter alone is able to find here the perfect simulacrum, that of the immanence and the material transcription of all values. The Americans themselves have no sense of simulation. They are themselves the perfect configuration of it, but they do not speak its language, being themselves the model for it. They constitute thus ideal material for an analysis of all the possible variants of the modern world. No more no less so moreover than were primitive societies in their time. The same mythic and analytic exultation which made us turn our gaze towards earlier societies leads us today to look towards America, with the same passion and the same prejudices.]

This passage reads, indeed, like a résumé of many of the key issues at stake in modern travel writing, raising the question of travel not only into a primitive past, but into a proximate future from which anticipatory images (like the mythical beasts imagined by Renaissance travellers and explorers) have already been projected to saturation point onto European consciousness via film, TV and other media. Such images constitute a hyperreality, both in that sophisticated electronic media make them appear more real than the real, and in that they present a culture in which, from a European perspective, the future is already realised. In this respect America fulfils a European longing that goes back at least to the Renaissance, for a Utopia, in this case one in which the miracle of the materialisation of the ideological has been fully realised (a theme explored in Chapter 4). In this respect, modern America constitutes as fertile a terrain for ethnographic study as so-called primitive early societies. Here Baudrillard anticipates a project also formulated around this time by Marc Augé (1994a, 1997) – the ethnographic analysis of the mythical/epistemic structures governing modern global societies (a theme developed in Chapter 2).

It is the aim, however, of this chapter primarily to focus on the semiotic issues at stake in Baudrillard's experience of American culture – in so far as they can in Baudrillard's writings ever be isolated from other related concerns. For in *Amérique* the whole of the social, psychological and cultural process is re-examined in terms of photography, TV, film or video. In other words, *Amérique* is an essay in which the media are analysed as a paradigm of the sign. First, on the level of the individual, the principle of the hyperreal is applied to the self as well as to cultural processes in general. For the individual understands him/herself less as an object and more as a sign; he/she sees him/herself from the outside like a signifier. Internal mental processes, the activity of the interpretant, increasingly modelled on information technology, are projected outside as if onto the computer and relayed back via the computer screen. The aim here is 'être branché sur son propre cerveau' (1986: 38) ['plugged into your own brain']. Ideas and concepts are thus realised as much in the material terms of audio-visual display as in thought processes, a phenomenon Baudrillard describes as 'la vidéographie des concepts' (1986: 39). Identity, the entry into the symbolic, is as much realised through the computer as through language, leading to a situation in which 'le stade video [remplace] le stade du miroir' (1986: 40). The sign becomes as much an agent of feed-back as an issue onto the real. The ultimate image of this quest for instant knowledge, for immediate epistemological gratification is provided by the Polaroid, the sign as Polaroid image:

l'extase du polaroïd: tenir presque simultanément l'objet et son image, comme si se réalisait cette vieille physique, ou métaphysique, de la lumière, où chaque objet sécrète des doubles, des clichés de lui-même que nous captons par la vue. C'est un rêve. C'est la matérialisation optique d'un processus magique. La photo polaroïd est comme une pellicule extatique qui tombe du réel. (1986: 40)

[this is the ecstasy of the polaroid: to be able almost simultaneously to hold the object and its image, as if were being brought into play the properties of that old physics or metaphysics of light according to which each object secretes its double, or its copy which we are able to capture through vision. It's a dream. It's the optical materialisation of a magic process. The polaroid photo is like an ecstatic film peeling off the surface of the real.]

Moving from the individual to the general, the whole physical and social structure of America is also essentially mediated through the screen image: not only America *as seen on TV* but America *as* cinema:

Ce n'est pas le moindre charme de l'Amérique qu'en dehors même des salles de cinéma, tout le pays est cinématographique. Vous parcourez le désert comme un western, les métropoles comme un écran de signes et de formules. C'est la même sensation que de sortir d'un musée italien ou hollandais pour entrer dans une ville qui semble le reflet même de cette peinture, comme si elle en était issue, et non l'inverse. La ville américaine semble elle aussi issue vivante du cinéma. Il ne faut donc pas aller de la ville à l'écran, mais de l'écran à la ville pour en saisir le secret. C'est là où le cinéma ne revêt pas de forme exceptionnelle, mais où il investit la rue, la ville entière d'une ambiance mythique, c'est là qu'il est véritablement passionnant. (1986: 56–7)

[It is not the least of America's charms that even outside the cinema, the whole country appears cinematographic. You travel across the desert like a western, the big cities like a screen transmitting signs and formulas. You get the same sensation when you leave a Dutch or Italian museum to pass into a town which seems exactly to reflect the paintings just seen, as if it were itself the replica of them, and not the reverse. The American city, it too seems like a living replica of cinema. To get the secret of this, you don't move from city to screen but from screen to city. It's there that the cinema, while taking on no exceptional form, nevertheless invests the street, the whole city with a mythic ambience, it's there that it really becomes totally absorbing.]

Once again, it is the representation through the media rather than the object or 'reality' itself that produces the determining sign or image of America. Of course, in human culture, signs have always preceded objects (and not vice-versa) and late twentieth-century America is no different in this from Renaissance Italy, seventeenth-century Holland (as evoked by Baudrillard) or nineteenth-century Spain as viewed by Gautier. The difference here is that the whole of the signifying process in contemporary America has become subsumed into the cinematographic model which exerts its influence inescapably on all aspects of cultural experience. There is no part of American life that has not been filmed, from electric chair executions and natural disasters to pornographic sex and home movies. Furthermore, each of these mediatised images, like Warhol's screen-prints of movie stars, is susceptible to exponential multiplication. In this way, America becomes simultaneously a gigantic screen that contains millions of other screens, all of which flicker indefinitely, *vingt-quatre heures sur vingt-quatre heures* – in vacant motel rooms, in closed circuit security systems as well as in practically every room, private or public, in every building across the continent.

Travel in America becomes thus for Baudrillard an exercise in movement in many senses of the word. The vast spaces and distances of the continent are explored by driving: the travelling car cruises along endless freeways, the highways and byways, landscapes and cityscapes unfolding like moving bands of celluloid through the car windscreen as on a cinema screen. Baudrillard uses the terminology of film-making, especially the *travelling* shot, to emphasise both the way the eye, like the movie camera, takes in the vast American spaces and the way it re-imposes on them the cinematographic clichés through which they have always already been seen in films and on TV. As in Michel Butor's novel *Mobile* (1962), to which we will return, America is experienced by Baudrillard as a road movie in which he is both actor and director moving through an endless chain of signifiers which tautologically signify America as cinema, cinema as America. America is thus experienced as a fictional and a-temporal space in which the flickering of light, real or artificial, mesmerises consciousness which itself becomes little more than a slim film barely registering surface impressions. The 'voyage sans objectif' across America becomes thus essentially abstract, a 'travelling pur', '[qui] se réalise au mieux dans la banalité extensive des déserts ou dans celle, aussi désertique, des métropoles – jamais prises comme lieu de plaisir ou de culture, mais télévisuellement, comme *scenery*, comme scénarios' (1986: 14) ['which happens most effectively in the banal extents of the desert or in those, quite as arid, of the big cities – which are never taken as centres of pleasure or culture, but are rather perceived televisually, like *scenery*, like scenarios or screenplays'].

The seductions of the American scene, however, only temporarily mesmerise Baudrillard, and the European, and more particularly French, mania for analysis periodically kicks in. It does this to reflect both on the *content* of some aspects of American cultural reality – 'Eux fabriquent du réel à partir des idées, nous transformons le réel en idées, ou en idéologie' (1986: 83) ['They produce the real on the basis of ideas, we transform the real into ideas, or into ideology'] – and – above all – on the *form* of consciousness brought to bear on experience:

Nous avons en Europe l'art de penser les choses, de les analyser, de les réfléchir. Personne ne peut nous contester cette subtilité historique et cette imagination conceptuelle, cela même les esprits d'outre-Atlantique en sont jaloux. [Mais] [n]ous sommes désespérément en retard sur la stupidité et le caractère mutationnel, sur la démesure naïve et l'exentricité sociale, raciale, morale, morphologique, architecturale, de cette société. (1986: 27–8)

[We in Europe know the art of thinking things, of analysing and reflecting on them. Nobody can contest this historic sophistication or this conceptual imagination; even minds on the other side of the Atlantic are jealous of our ability in this respect. (But) (we) are desperately behind when it comes to the stupidity and mutational character of Americans, when it comes to the naïve outrageousness, and the social, racial, moral, morphological, architectural eccentricity of this society.]

Incapable of analysing itself, 'l'Amérique sidérale' must be submitted to 'la mélancolie des analyses européennes' (1986: 31). As I suggested in my introductory chapter, Europe has brought to the globe not so much a wisdom or a real belief system as an intellectual tradition, one based from the seventeenth century, at least, on interrogation and dissent. Although this tradition was one that also had a founding influence on American ideology, especially as encapsulated in the eighteenth century in its post-Independence constitution and bill of rights, thereafter, in escaping from history, from a confrontation of intellectual or religious traditions, the United States lost the habit of, or rather the need for, critical self-analysis. The latter must be supplied by old Europe for whom, according to Baudrillard '[l]a politique et l'histoire restent notre scène primitive' (1986: 75).

Baudrillard's inimitable mixture of ecstasy and analysis, hyperbole and deconstruction also of course profoundly marks the style of *Amérique* which manifests an extraordinary mixture of registers, moods and tones. Once again, it is Baudrillard's exploitation of the signifying aspect of the word as much as its function as fully integral sign (signifier/signified) that helps create the impact of the text – as in this example:

Il y a une sorte de miracle dans la fadeur des paradis artificiels, pourvu qu'ils atteignent à la grandeur de toute une (in)culture. En Amérique, l'espace donne une envergure même à la fadeur des *suburbs* et des *funky towns*. Le désert est partout et sauve l'insignifiance. Désert où le miracle de la voiture, de la glace et du whisky se reproduit tous les jours: prodige de la facilité mêlée à la fatalité du désert. Miracle de l'obscénité, proprement américain: de la disponibilité totale, de la transparence

de toutes les fonctions dans l'espace, qui lui pourtant reste insoluble dans son
étendue et ne peut être conjuré que par la vitesse.
    Miracle italien: celui de la scène.
    Miracle américain: celui de l'obscène.
    La luxure du sens contre les déserts de l'insignifiance. (1986: 13)

[There is a sort of miracle in the blandness of artificial paradises, providing that
they reach the scale of a complete (non)culture. In America, space gives scope even
to the blandness of *suburbs* and *funky towns*. The desert is everywhere, preserving
insignificance. A desert where the miracle of cars, ice and whiskey is daily re-
enacted: a marvel of easy living mixed with the desert's inevitability. A miracle
of obscenity that is truly American: that of the total availability, of the complete
transparency of all spatial functions, in a space however that remains insoluble in
its vast expanses and that can only be exorcised by speed.
    The Italian miracle: that of the stage.
    The American miracle: that of the obscene.
    The lustful profusion of sense as against deserts of insignificance.]

    Here, as throughout *Amérique*, Baudrillard assures the adhesion of his
readers through a strategy of assertion and provocation. First the paradox 'miracle'/'fadeur' which within one sentence is already elevated to the
level of hyperbole: 'à la grandeur de toute une (in)culture'. Simultaneously the play on those seductive but often misleading binary oppositions, beloved of structuralists in the human sciences: 'miracle'/'fadeur';
'grandeur'/'(in)culture', the latter term itself proposing a further binary
opposition – 'culture'/'inculture'. The inclusion of colloquial or picturesque
anglicisms or (American) English terms, which stand out in particular to the
French reader ('suburbs', 'funky towns', 'whiskey') providing a kind of discursive local colour. We are led to accept these paradoxes and oppositions,
not through logical argument but through repetition and enumeration –
'miracle de la voiture, de la glace et du whisky', 'Miracle de l'obscénité [. . .]
de la disponibilité totale, de la transparence de toutes les fonctions dans
l'espace', 'Miracle italien', 'Miracle américain' – and through a profusion of
hyperbole: 'miracle', 'paradis artificiels', 'grandeur', 'fatalité', 'disponibilité
totale', 'transparence'. Parallelism ('Miracle italien'/'Miracle américain')
and rhyme ('scène'/'obscène') are brought in near the end of the passage to
prepare for the final clinching opposition, which turns out to be a tautology, where the quasi-synonym 'luxure' is almost misread as the opposition
luxe/déserts. What Baudrillard presents here is thus as much a shimmering,
fascinating surface of signifiers as a reasoned sequence of signs, a flickering
screen of concepts that is only partly resolved into fully articulated sense.
Baudrillard's alibi here is no doubt that what he is re-creating for the reader

is as much what flashes through the speeding traveller's mind as a dispassionate account of America as object: 'Il ne s'agit pas de faire la sociologie ou la psychologie [. . .]. Il s'agit de rouler pour en savoir plus long sur la société que toutes les disciplines réunies (1986: 55)' ['It's not a question of sociology or psychology (. . .). It's a matter of driving to learn more about this society than you ever would studying all the academic disciplines'].

This chapter concludes with a few brief comments on Michel Butor's novel *Mobile* (1962) which brings together in 'une seule vision anthologique' (Baudrillard, 1986: 68) many of the semiotic issues travel writing raises, and anticipates the aim outlined in the passage from Baudrillard just cited. For *Mobile*, subtitled *Etude pour une représentation des Etats-Unis*, is a synthetic take on America in which the various levels of apprehension – semiotic, sociological, anthropological, historical, natural historical – are expressed as separate but intertwining strands in a text which unfolds like a map before the reader. The *épistémè* underlying modern American culture and society is thus presented as a gradually unfolding archeology, one constituted by Native Amerindian myths, the utopian or pragmatic ideals of the European founding fathers, the traditions and aspirations of Black Americans and the diverse elements that make up the *melting pot* of the European national and racial types. Once again, Butor's primary concern is with difference as experienced through *signs*, and in particular the way the signifier fascinates the foreign traveller. Much of the material of *Mobile* is thus not provided directly by objects but almost always through the intermediary of signs: road signs, car *marques*, petrol-station signs, neon signs, texts (whether Sear, Roebuck & Co. catalogues, historical tracts, or documents relating to American Indians), natural history illustrations (the magnificent plates from John James Audubon's *Birds of America*, 1854), and other visual and written sources. As a whole, the novel constitutes a remarkable anticipation of both the semiotic approach and the thematic orientation of both Barthes's and Baudrillard's travel writings.[12]

So, one of the founding fables the reader encounters in *Mobile,* buried among the systematic indicators of time, space and speed that regularly puncture the text, like entries in the log-book of a rally car, is a reprise, this time in terms of Indian history, of the native discovery of the power of writing, in this case as experienced by the Cherokee Indian Sequoyah:

GREENVILLE, sur la rivière du Goudron, chef-lieu de Pike, CAROLINE DU NORD (. . . only), – . . . des Indiens Cherokees.
  [. . .]
  Un Indien Cherokee nommé Sequoyah, se méfiant de l'enseignement des missionnaires, s'abstint d'aller à leurs écoles, mais étudia leurs livres avec grand soin et décida

d'inventer un système d'écriture. Grande méfiance dans les missions et chez les autres Cherokees. Nouvelle sorcellerie puissante qu'il vaut mieux étouffer dans l'œuf...

Sur la route, une Oldsmobile grise, très endommagée, qui dépasse largement les soixante miles autorisées, 'il faudra prendre de l'essence au prochain Clatex', – les marais des Houx et Sinistre. (Butor, 1962: 30)

[GREENVILLE, on the River Goudron, capital of Pike, NORTH CAROLINA (. . . only) – . . . Cherokee Indians.

(. . .)

A Cherokee Indian named Sequoyah, distrusting the missionaries' teaching, stopped going to their classes; instead he studied their books with great care and decided to invent a system of writing. Great distrust in the mission schools and among the other Cherokees. A new and powerful magic that it would be better to nip in the bud...

On the road, a grey Oldsmobile, badly dented, travelling way above the sixty-mile-an-hour speed limit, 'we must fill up with gas at the next Clatex' – Houx and Sinistre marshes.]

In the sequel (1962: 31, 62, 63–4, 68), Sequoyah is successively persecuted, ostracised and finally welcomed when he returns with an alphabet for his language, which his fellow Indians then learn and for which he is awarded a medal by European missionaries. Thus is recounted, in the space of a few fragments scattered over a few dozen pages, the brutally rapid integration of Indian culture into the European/American system.

Other, and more contemporary signs, however, make their insistent and flickering presence felt to Butor as a European traveller in America. Once again, as with Barthes and Baudrillard, it is the *smile* as sign that flashes its ambiguous promise. First appearing on page 118 – *Souriez!* – it reappears on the same page – *Souriez encore!* – followed by *Continuez à sourire!* (119), *Gardez le sourire!* (127), *Pourquoi ne souriez-vous pas?* (131), *Votre absence de sourire nous brûle* (133), while from page 137 the smile, as in Baudrillard's *Amérique*, becomes a sign of political propaganda – *Regardez comme notre président sourit!*, *Regardez Mrs Kennedy, comme elle sourit!* (138), *Regardez Mr Nixon, comme il sourit!* (140) and so on until the smile image is replaced by a more glamorous incarnation in the form of neon signs of Hollywood stars, the first of whom (of course) is Marilyn Monroe: 'Le visage illuminé de Marilyn Monroe' (162) followed by that of Jayne Mansfield, Rita Hayworth and many other 1950s stars of both sexes scattered between pages 164 and 189. To these are added the omnipresent advertising signs (Coca-Cola, Pepsi-Cola, Lucky Strike, oil companies), together with the modern mythology of American car types, which are not only identified as they pass at regular intervals through the text, but also listed – twenty-four makes (a couple of instances slightly confuse manufacturer and car type: 1962: 121–5). Colour as a signifier is omnipresent, Butor establishing through it a significant pattern of contrast between the synthetic colours – sugar pink, turquoise, lemon yellow, tomato red – of the 1950s and 1960s (cars, clothes, ice-cream, fake jewellery) and the authentic colours of the natural world (birds, flowers, trees, fish).

Indeed the alternation of authenticity and simulacrum is a major leit-motiv of *Mobile*, embracing native culture (authentic Indian life and the drive-in Indian reserves already established by the early 1960s), history (texts and documents) versus theme parks such as Freedomland (293–4), natural history (Audubon's birds as painted in the 1840s, the wild birds of 1960s America), racial issues and geological wonders. Butor produces long citations from Sears, Roebuck & Co. catalogues describing wall-sized facsimile reproductions of natural wonders for mounting on the walls of suburban homes (78–9), various children's toys including 'un déguisement de clochard pour vos enfants' (146) ['a tramp's outfit for your kids'], fake jewels ('Glo' diamonds, 119) and synthetic floor coverings. Such citations are interspersed with extracts from the architect Louis Sullivan's spirited critique of ersatz American architecture, and appreciations of early American patchwork quilts, an art form taken as a creative model by Butor in *Mobile* (1962: 45).

The major innovation of Butor's style in *Mobile*, however, is to express on the level of text itself – in a manner similar to Barthes but much more homogeneously and systematically – the multiple categories and levels of signifiers that he encounters in his American travels. Thus roman capitals express the essential geographical indicators of a trans-American itinerary, pinpointing the names of states and major cities. Text in lower-case roman usually indicates general information of current validity – route directions, petrol stations, cars encountered, territories crossed – while lower-case italics indicate historical and cultural information. This fragmentary, hierarchised presentation of the typographical systems reflects the fleeting impressions of real experience of a strange landscape and the inclusion of chunks of reference texts reflects a traveller's habits of consultation of guide-books, catalogues and other sources of information. Fragments of micro-narrative, of ambiguous status (passing fantasies of the narrator? reconstructions of scenes observed? etc.) add further to the patchwork of discursive strategies.

What the texts by Barthes, Baudrillard and Butor thus show us is the way modern travel writing is as much concerned with taking the sign back to its source as with discovering or fully inhabiting the objective world of the other. The other can only be authentically grasped when the same converts itself into it, a process involving a huge investment of time and effort in linguistic and cultural transformation, the outcome of which inevitably involves a loss of difference since knowledge rings the death-knoll of the exotic. The aim in modern travel writing becomes thus to experience the sign of the other more fully in itself as much as for what it says about its object. Hence the fascination with the signifier; for the fascination of signs lies no longer so much in *what* they represent but in *how* they do it. In an increasingly uniform and democratic world, difference is sought not so much in the objects themselves – jeans, cars, media stars – as in the *signs* through which they transmit or advertise themselves to us; not so much in the concepts or signifieds they propose or suggest – happiness, prosperity, sex appeal – as in the way the signifiers fascinate or seduce, if only momentarily, the consumer. Travel writing thus brings us to the heart of the issues at stake in the signifying process in the modern capitalist and post-industrial world.

Correspondingly, the foregrounded signifier becomes a telling sign of the contemporary world, one in which the sign's real (sacred, magic, religious) link with the object has been broken, leaving either a world of unmotivated and alienating objects or the simulacral world of signs in which meanings may be sought but none can claim ultimate authenticity, a real link with their object. In the early modern world, the authority of the artist was still sufficient to convey the meaning of objects, to impose sign systems that have subsequently become a field of investigation and interpretation for theory and criticism. In the post-modern world, this authority has been lost as the reading, interpretative or signifying process itself becomes recognised as the key component in the semiotic or meaning-producing system. This propensity of the signifier to float free of the signified, of the sign to lose its object, is exacerbated by the electronic media through which signs are increasingly transmitted. For the process of mediatisation – transmission, dissemination – itself becomes a hyper-signifying function into which the signifying function of other signs – words, images, sounds – is absorbed. In such a system, less and less signified gets through, the indexical function of signs is reduced and, as Marshall McLuhan (1962) anticipated, the medium becomes the message. So, for example, TV travelogue, like tourist travel, is a sign of nostalgia for the real, imagined in terms of the exotic other, but ultimately undermines the possibility of real experience of it.

CHAPTER 2

The other as interpretant: from Segalen and Michaux to the ethno-roman

[L]'être conscient (par le mécanisme hindou) se retrouve face à face avec lui-même.

(Victor Segalen, [1908b] 1995, 29)

Si un Européen est interrogé à son retour des Indes, il n'hésite pas, il répond: 'J'ai vu Madras, j'ai vu ceci, j'ai vu cela.' Mais non, il a été vu, beaucoup plus qu'il n'a vu.

(Henri Michaux, [1933] 1967: 121)

Dans le voyage, l'homme est un être pour-autrui.

(Francis Affergan, 1987b: 128)

In Peirce's theory of the sign (Peirce, 1966), the function of the third component in the triad sign/object/interpretant is to activate semiosis by interpreting a connection between the first two elements. An interpretant can read a sign in various ways: most commonly, it refers to its immediate object, that is the object (which can be a thing, an idea or another sign) as represented by the sign; in such an instance the interpretant is itself also *immediate* in that it need grasp no more of the object than is suggested by the sign referring to it. However, the interpretant's relation to the *dynamic* object (a particular idea, thing or person in the world) is more complex in that the object is not fully contained by the sign referring to it: further interpretation is required which calls for a more complex process of semiosis in which 'collateral' experience of various sorts (memory, imagination, prior knowledge) must be drawn on. In such a case the interpretant must itself become *dynamic*, in an effort to deduce through various logical strategies (inductive or abductive as well as the deductive logic of the immediate interpretant) a wider or deeper interpretation of the object than that proposed by the sign. No sign and no activity of the dynamic interpretant can ever fully exhaust the meaning potential of the dynamic object, which, like the real, is not completely knowable in any absolute terms. However, no articulation of meaning is possible without the sign's intervention.

The interest in the context of travel writing of Peirce's theory of the functioning of the interpretant is that it offers a model for the interpretative processes adopted by the subject in relation to the exotic object or Other. For the interpretant, like the sign, always constitutes a *relation* between two differences which it mediates in a two-way dynamic: outwards through the sign to the object, inwards from the sign to the mental processes involved in its interpretation. This two-way dynamic is reproduced in the confrontation of differences that meeting the other entails. Faced by the other as a sign of something different, the subject is struck by a certain resistance or strangeness that elicits a dynamic response. The latter takes the form of a mobilisation of collateral experience or imagination in an effort to grasp the dynamic aspect – the deeper meaning or mystery – of the object encountered. At the same time, if the other is a person,[1] the western subject is aware of the status of the other as also being a subject, a subject for whom the European as a sign of the exotic also requires dynamic interpretation. An exchange of glances between subject and other can thus trigger a double dynamic process in which opposing but complementary chains of interpretants strive to grasp the deeper significance of the situation. The latter is further complicated by the mirroring effect produced in such moments of silent mutual observation. The radical activation of interpretants in the mind of the subject, drawing on intuition, memory, imagination – the deeply embedded impulses mobilised by a mind in a state of sudden jubilation or crisis – sometimes leads to a return of the uncanny, the previously known but long forgotten or repressed. In this sense the self can be recovered by interaction with the other. In this way the other can be seen to act as the interpretant through which the self is able to restore a hitherto unknown or forgotten aspect of itself. The fact that sometimes – as we shall see below in the cases of both Segalen and Nicolas Bouvier (Chapter 3) – the other is a *hallucination*, a projection by the subject of part of itself which is then perceived and interpreted as an exotic object or unknown other in the real world, confirms the interpretant's power and versatility as an agent of both mental projection and reception.

No French travel writer expressed such complex semiotic processes with greater lucidity than Victor Segalen (1878–1919). For this pioneering writer and theorist of the exotic, an important part of exoticism is 'la connaissance que quelque chose n'est pas soi-même' ['the knowledge that something is not oneself'], 'le pouvoir de concevoir autre' (Segalen 1978: 23) ['the ability to conceive of things differently'].[2] In elaborating a critique of exoticism as conventionally (mis-)understood, Segalen points out that it is not so much to be interpreted as a quality, rather as a momentary but deep experience: 'le moment d'Exotisme' is 'l'ivresse du sujet à concevoir son objet; à se connaître différent du sujet; à sentir le Divers' (Segalen, 1978: 24) ['the intoxication felt by the subject in conceiving of the object; in recognising itself as different from the subject; in experiencing the diverse']. Exoticism implies not the passive, touristic consumption of the sign of the other but a strong sense of individuality or subjectivity that will react powerfully in the face of the other's radical difference. Furthermore, unlike the ethnographer, the *exote* does not seek exhaustive knowledge of the other, but that which, in the other, is irreducible to the self or its categories of knowledge. Exoticism as understood by Segalen is thus an intensely personal project: although it relies on the presence of the other, this other in a sense only derives its authenticity to the degree that it enables the subject to access the mystery and unknown lurking within the self.[3] So the aim of the traveller as *exote* is to rediscover, if only momentarily, a certain plenitude of existence in which the other, in *exceeding* its containment within known signs, becomes a dynamic object sufficiently challenging and unexpected to activate the dynamic interpretant and, in the process, to mobilise the full inner resources of the observing subject. It is in such moments of radical semiosis, that is, of intense feeling and heightened intelligence, that the subject experiences a sense of the authentic integrality of self with the world.

In *Chine ou le pouvoir de l'étendue* (Segalen, 1978), in which Segalen records his travels in China, where he made three trips between 1909 and 1918 (on the second of which he made important archeological discoveries concerning Han funeral monuments), certain intense experiences of confrontation with the other emerge that exemplify the processes activated by the 'exotic moment' as theorised in his unfinished *Essai sur l'exotisme*. Two in particular stand out, the first presenting the other as mirror of the self's gaze:

C'est au moment même qu'ayant traversé le fleuve qui en vient, pour, de là, drainer toute la Chine; c'est là, qu'émerveillé, étonné, et repu de tant de paysages minéraux, seul depuis de longs jours avec moi, et sans miroir, n'ayant sous les yeux que les fronts chevalins de mes mules ou le paysage connu des yeux plats de mes gens habituels, je me suis trouvé tout d'un coup en présence de quelque chose, qui, lié au plus magnifique paysage dans la grande montagne, en était si distant et si homogène que tous les autres se reculaient et se faisaient souvenirs concrets. Ma vue habituée aux masses énormes s'est tout à coup violemment éprise de cela qu'elle voyait à portée d'elle, et qui la regardait aussi, car cela avait deux yeux dans un visage brun doré, et une frondaison chevelue, noire et sauvage autour du front.

Et c'était toute la face d'une fille aborigène, enfantée là, plantée là sur ses jambes fortes, et qui stupéfaite moins que moi, regardait passer l'animal étrange que j'étais, et qui, par pitié pour l'inattendue beauté du spectacle, n'osa point se détourner pour la revoir encore. Car la seconde épreuve eût peut-être été déplorable. Il n'est pas donné de voir naïvement et innocemment deux fois dans une étape, un voyage ou la vie, ni de reproduire à volonté le miracle de deux yeux organisés depuis des jours pour ne saisir que la grande montagne, versants et cimes, et qui se trouvent tout d'un coup aux prises avec l'étonnant spectacle de deux autres yeux répondants. (1978: 99)

[It was at the very moment that I crossed the river which from there drains all of China, at that point that, delighted, astonished and filled to a surfeit with so many mineral landscapes, alone with myself for many long days, without a mirror, having only before my eyes the manes of my mules or the familiar landscape of the blank eyes of my travelling companions, I suddenly found myself confronted with something which, linked to the magnificent high mountain landscape, was so distant and so homogeneous as to make all the others recede and become cemented into memories. My sight, used to enormous masses, suddenly became fixated by what it saw close to it, and which was also staring at it, because it also had two eyes in a golden brown face, and a wild fringe of dark hair over the forehead. It was the full face of a native girl, born there, planted on her two stout legs, and which, stupefied less than I was, was watching go by the strange beast that I was, I who, out of pity for the unexpected beauty of the spectacle, did not dare to turn back to look at her again. For a second glance would perhaps have been disastrous. You don't get two chances to see naively and innocently in a stage of a journey, a trip or a lifetime, nor to reproduce at will the miracle of two eyes adjusted for days to seeing only high mountains, slopes and summits, and which suddenly find themselves focussing on the astonishing spectacle of two other eyes in a state of reciprocal observation.]

For Segalen, much of the exotic potential of foreign travel is a function of the defamiliarising impact of strange landscapes, one that is experienced, as we shall see, by many travellers in the jungle as well as in the desert. As the passage just cited shows, the habitual vastness of Chinese perspectives leads Segalen to evoke even the faces of his travelling companions in terms of landscape – 'le paysage connu des yeux plats de mes gens habituels' – a monotony out of which surges, literally like an unmapped site, the chance encounter with the eyes of a Chinese woman. Here, the other is first apprehended as some kind of unidentified object, the mere demonstrative 'cela' only subsequently composing itself into a pair of eyes set in a golden brown, aboriginal face. The power of the encounter is almost exclusively a function of an exchange of glances that express mutual stupefaction at the sight of the other. It is noteworthy that in such confrontations Segalen, like Michaux later, evokes the other (or the self as viewed by the other) in terms of a different species, a strange beast surging from the landscape as if from some mythical text or archeological site. The vital intensity of the confrontation is a function uniquely of the moment at which the glances are exchanged, of the flash of obscure mutual recognition. Segalen deliberately avoids looking back at the Chinese girl and thus converting a moment of mysterious identity into an ethnographic or merely touristic gaze.

The second memorable encounter with the other takes the form of a hallucinatory reincarnation of the (former) self. Once again, the exotic landscape's defamiliarising effect is apparent, exacerbated on this occasion by the detachment of certain signs from their objects, as for example the evening light which has become separated from its source in the sun:

Moi-même et l'autre nous sommes rencontrés ici, au plus reculé du voyage. Ceci, au pied des derniers contreforts des plateaux étalés horriblement à six mille mètres de hauteur, plus désertiques et plus âpres que les pics les plus déchirés de l'autre Europe, ceci m'arrive, après cette étape, la dernière de celles qui prolongeaient la route; la plus extrême, celle qui touche aux confins, celle que j'ai fixée d'avance comme la frontière, le but géographique, le gain auquel j'ai conclu de m'en tenir. C'est ici, dans la contrée frémissante d'eaux et de vents dévalants, c'est ici, après cette journée plus fatigante que toutes les autres – (cependant la fatigue était non pas domptée, mais dépassée, dominée), sans avoir pris de repos, l'affalement douleureux et l'envie de pleurer de détresse, avaient fait place à une inattendue lucidité, – sur la terrasse moins enfumée que l'autre de cette maison tibétaine, dans un crépuscule où le jour prolongé n'a plus semble-t-il de liaison au soleil; la lumière s'exhale des choses; – et j'étais debout, marchant malgré moi un peu plus loin qu'il ne m'était permis. C'est alors que l'Autre est venu à moi. (Segalen, 1978:101)

[Myself and the other met here, at the furthest point in the trip. It was at the foot of the last outriggers of the plateaux extending drearily at a height of six thousand metres, more bitter and deserted than the craggiest peaks of the other Europe, that this happened to me, after the last stage of those that extended the planned route; it was at the extreme limit, touching the confines of the stage that I had decided at the start would be the final frontier, the geographical goal to which I had decided to stick. It was here, in a country trembling with the sounds of water and wind, it was here, after a day more tiring than all the others (my fatigue being not so much defeated as passed beyond, dominated), without having stopped for rest, that a state of nervous collapse, close to tearful distress, had given way to an unexpected state of lucidity – on the less smoky of the two terraces of the Tibetan lodge, in a twilight where the light seemed no longer to be emanating from the sun but seemed rather to be exhaled by things; – and there I was, upright, walking despite myself a bit further than I was permitted. It was then that the Other came to me.]

As the passage continues, the other appears not as a native of China or Tibet, but as a fair-haired young European, dressed in sun-faded khaki, with a glint in his eye despite a slightly bitter expression. Segalen, seemingly recognising the young man, immediately enters into conversation, but his questions remain unanswered and in a moment the silent figure is absorbed back into the exotic mountain landscape from which he appeared:

Cependant j'observais une singulière transparence dans sa personne. Le paysage éteint presque par la nuit, le formidable déboulis de roches et de torrents, et les falaises torturées dans l'ombre par des filons qui étreignaient comme des nœuds, la sève dans le tronc, se montraient à travers lui, l'absorbaient. L'Autre devenait fumée, avant de m'avoir répondu. Cependant, avant qu'il ne disparaisse en entier, j'avais eu le temps non mesurable, mieux: j'avais eu le *moment* d'en recueillir toute la présence, et surtout de le reconnaître: l'Autre était moi, de seize à vingt ans. (1978:102)

[However I noticed that his body was of a singular transparency. The landscape extinguished by night, the tremendous outflow of rocks and torrents, and the cliff-faces tortured in the shadows by veins twisted into knots, the sap in the trunk, showed through him, absorbed him. The Other disappeared into smoke, before he could reply to me. However, before he disappeared completely, I had the time, immeasurable for a moment, or rather, I had the *moment* completely to take in his presence, and indeed to recognise him: the Other was me, at between sixteen and twenty years old.]

Having reached the outer limits of his exotic itinerary, at a moment of extreme fatigue and distress, but also of unexpected lucidity, Segalen literally comes up against himself, projecting, in an ultimate moment of anxiety and fulfilment, an image of his earlier self onto the strange Tibetan landscape. The complete movement of identification with the other and then re-absorption of the other back into the self is accomplished in an exemplary hallucination in which the sign of the other surges opaquely from the real only to become transparent as the interpretant races to identify and thus acclimatise the strange apparition, reintegrating it back into the profound identity of the subject. As we shall see with Michaux, the magical apparition of the other only for it to disappear a moment later like a genie in a puff of smoke, offers Segalen an unexpected insight into his destiny or genius (*génie*) as a traveller and archeologist, that is, as a seeker on the surface and in the depths of the earth of a fully restored and authentic model of life.[4]

The travel-writing project of Henri Michaux (1899–1984), as Malcolm Bowie has already suggested (1973: 63–4), in many ways continues that of Segalen. As the title of *Un barbare en Asie* (1933) suggests, Michaux's aim is in part to reverse the usual role of self in relation to other by setting up the self as far as possible as object of the other's gaze. So whereas the other was traditionally viewed from a European or ethnocentric viewpoint as strange, threatening and different, in a word as a Barbarian (see Kristeva, 1988: 74–83), in *Un barbare en Asie* – especially in the 'Barbare en Inde' section – the westerner is the Barbarian ogled by the native eyes of the other. The aim of Michaux's strategy here is both to relativise the status of the western, ethnocentric gaze and to try to grasp a deeper insight into the other by the resistances offered to it by the (European) self. An attempt is thus made to access the dynamic reality of the foreign object by activating the dynamic interpretant, that is to submit the act of understanding to a more painful and lengthy process of cogitation through collateral experience (induction, abduction – experience, imagination), rather than resort to the readymade templates of the immediate interpretant. The resistance which the other offers in its secondness or dynamic quiddity is thus sought by Michaux, savoured and suffered by him, in a dual process in which both the self as perceived by the other and the other as perceived by the self are experienced as an alluring or repellent reality before being consigned, by final interpretants on both sides, to knowledge or understanding (and thus to relative indifference).[5]

Michaux's approach to the other is elaborated in two contrasting but complementary movements. The first focusses on the difference of the other as exotic, resistant, incomprehensible, exasperating or alluring. Here the other is approached as part of a different *ethnie* to be studied and understood as in ethnographic research, by close and systematic observation and analysis of the ethnic group's social and religious practices.[6] Such a strategy, of course, brings with it all the problems that traditionally beset ethnographic study, in particular the tendency to rationalise a different culture according to western scientific or epistemological schemes and, in the process, excessively to polarise into a series of binary oppositions – 'civilised'/'primitive', rational/magical, scientific knowledge / myth, etc. (see Goody, 1979) – the conceptual frame within which the other society is compared to that of Europe. The second movement adopted by Michaux is one that has much in common with that of Segalen: it focusses on difference discovered within the self in a self-reflexive spiral which is dependent on the mirroring gaze of the other. This sort of movement is much more difficult to rationalise in conventional terms since it involves a marked degree of subjectivity; it is only with considerable difficulty susceptible to scientific scrutiny and does not admit of a knowledge that is conventionally classifiable. On the contrary, it involves a high degree of intuitive, abductive or imaginative reasoning and incorporates a considerable dose of mystery. Perhaps one of its most illuminating characteristics is the challenge it offers to conventional western rationalising processes. Faced with strangeness, mystery or the uncanny – in the self or in the other – the individual becomes sensitised to those problematic aspects of the functioning of recognition and signification that, in more familiar circumstances, would pass unnoticed.

For Michaux, ethnology is not fundamentally different from zoology. This is because the (human) other, if different enough to constitute the Other, is different enough from European man to constitute a different species. For Pierre Sauvage, *Un barbare en Asie* has the makings of a bestiary.[7] Francis Affergan observes a similar resurgence of the animal as intermediary image in sixteenth-century travel accounts: 'le narrateur a besoin d'une médiation animalière pour que la comparaison puisse fonctionner avec le sauvage. L'écart est tellement grand que l'animal intervient comme un intermédiare naturel entre deux cultures, ou bien entre une culture européenne et une nature qui inclut l'Autre et l'animal' (1987a: 95) ['the narrator needs an animal as a mediating device enabling comparisons with the savage to be made. The gap (between white man and native) is so vast that the animal intervenes as a natural intermediary between two cultures, or rather between a European culture and a nature that includes the Other as well as the animal']. Unlike the early Renaissance European writer, this does not imply on Michaux's part any sense of racism or value judgement: for the author of *Un barbare en Asie*, animals are not inferior to humans, but merely different from them. Furthermore, the strong – often totemic – identification of so-called primitive societies with their zoological and botanical environment (see Lévi-Strauss, 1961) naturally suggests a metaphorical extension of the animal image. Furthermore, such a strategy is reversible: just as different or foreign ethnic groups may be viewed as a different species of animal, so also may Europeans in their turn be seen by the other as strange beasts. The advantage of such an approach is that it allows Michaux to explore difference across a range of features without falling so rapidly and inevitably into the kinds of polar opposition that tend to beset more scientific, ethnographic studies. It also enables him to maintain the *strangeness* of the other even as he describes and classifies it. So he is able to record *different kinds of difference* while still maintaining an overall frame of epistemological reference. The (mostly zoological) categories of genera or species used in *Un barbare en Asie* provide the slots to which differences can be pegged and prevent his experience of the Other from schematic polarisation or collapse into relativism.

The coincidence in Michaux's travel writing of the ethnographic and zoological is nowhere better illustrated than in the fable he recounts of the monkey and the horse:

Quand le cheval, pour la première fois, voit le singe, il l'observe. Il voit que le singe arrache les fleurs des arbustes, les arrache méchamment (non pas brusquement), il le voit. Il voit aussi qu'il montre souvent les dents à ses compagnons, qu'il leur arrache les bananes qu'ils tiennent, alors que lui-même en possède d'aussi bonnes qu'il laisse tomber, et il voit que le singe mord les faibles. Il le voit gambader, jouer. Alors le cheval se fait une idée du singe. Il s'en fait une idée circonstanciée et il voit que lui, cheval, est un tout autre être.

Le singe, encore plus vite, remarque toutes les caractéristiques du cheval qui le rendent non seulement incapable de se suspendre aux branches des arbres, de tenir une banane dans ses pattes, mais en général de faire aucune de ces actions attrayantes, que les singes savent faire.

Tel est le premier stade de la connaissance.

Mais dans la suite, ils se rencontrent avec un certain plaisir.

Aux Indes, dans les écuries, il y a presque toujours un singe. Il ne rend aucun service apparent au cheval, ni le cheval au singe. Cependant les chevaux qui ont un tel compagnon travaillent mieux, sont plus dispos que les autres. On suppose que par ses grimaces, ses gambades, son rythme différent, le singe délasse le cheval. Quant au singe, il aurait du plaisir à passer tranquillement la nuit. (Un singe qui dort, parmi les siens, est toujours sur le qui-vive.)

Un cheval donc peut se sentir vivre beaucoup plus avec un singe qu'avec une dizaine de chevaux.

Si l'on pouvait savoir ce que le cheval pense du singe, *à présent*, il est assez probable qu'il répondrait: 'Oh! . . . ma foi, je ne sais plus.'

La connaissance ne progresse pas avec le temps. On passe sur les différences. On s'arrange. On s'entend. Mais on ne situe plus. Cette loi fatale fait que les vieux résidents en Asie et les personnes les plus mêlées aux Asiatiques, ne sont pas les plus à même d'en garder une vision centrée et un passant aux yeux naïfs peut parfois mettre le doigt sur le centre. ([1933] 1967: 99–101)

[When the horse sees the monkey for the first time he observes him carefully. He sees the monkey snatching flowers from shrubs, not just roughly but maliciously; he sees all this. He also sees how the monkey bares his teeth to other monkeys, that he grabs the bananas they are holding, even though he already has as good himself, which he drops; and he sees that the monkey bites the weaker animals. He watches him playing and leaping about. And so he forms an impression of what a monkey is. It is a circumstantial impression but sufficient for him to see that, as a horse, he is quite another kind of beast.

The monkey, even more quickly, notices all the characteristics of the horse which render him incapable of hanging from the branches of trees, of holding a banana in his paws, and in general of indulging in any of the amusing activities characteristic of monkeys.

Such is the first stage of knowledge.

But at a second stage, horse and monkey derive a certain pleasure from each other's company.

In the stables of India, you will almost always find a monkey. It serves no useful visible purpose to the horse, nor vice versa. However, horses that have such a companion work harder and are more amenable than the others. Supposedly, the monkey's grimaces, capers and different rhythm of movement relax the horse. As for the monkey, he is pleased to be able to spend his nights in peace. (A monkey who sleeps among his own, has always to be on the alert.)

A horse then lives far more contentedly with a monkey than with a dozen other horses.

If one could know what the horse felt about the matter *now*, it is probable that he would reply: 'Oh! I really don't know.'

Knowledge does not progress with time. You get used to things. You get to understand things. You take them for granted. This ineluctable law results in long-established residents of Asia and people most in contact with Asians no longer being able to maintain a centred vision of their environment whereas an innocent-eyed stranger can sometimes put his finger straight on the centre.]

The interest of this fable is double. As an allegory, it clarifies what is at stake when the (western) horse observes the (eastern) monkey, or vice-versa: observation is most keen when differences are still new and fresh, when the laws underlying patterns of existence and behaviour have not yet been fully grasped: the naïve can be as prescient as the knowledgeable gaze. The passage is also significant in its departure from the ethnographic approach, that is, in its refusal to submit the other species to an appropriating or rationalising gaze. The monkey's advantage is that it is not a *human*: it does not impose an *ethnocentric* frame on the difference of the other. The difference of the other is merely intuitively recognised, accepted and seemingly enjoyed for what it is. The same is true with the horse. Through this fable Michaux seems to establish a position between the ethnographic and the subjective gaze that allows him to claim a certain general validity for his observations – '[être] exact dans mes descriptions' ([1933] 1967: 99); 'mettre le doigt sur le centre' ([1933] 1967: 101) while still preserving a sense of vital difference.

In adumbrating a zoology of the Indian, Michaux is thus at the same time at pains to stress the realisation, stated early in *Un barbare en Asie*, that the European is perceived by the Other also as some kind of animal, perhaps a pig, whose foul habits might be perceived as objectionable. So, for example, the meat-eating western visitor, wading through the cow dung of India, is surprised to learn that natives – attentive as they are to avoid 'souillures' of every kind – find his breath nauseating, conserving as it does 'l'odeur du meurtre de la victime' ([1933] 1967: 20) ['the smell of the murder of the victim']. If zoology and ethnology may be taken as cognate practices, Michaux's readers soon learn to read them as a two-way process between self and other and as mutually translatable or dependent, as in the following passage: 'Il y a des vaches partout dans Calcutta. Elles traversent les rues, s'étalent de tout leur long sur le trottoir qui devient inutilisable, fientent devant l'auto du Vice-roi, inspectent les magasins, menaçent l'ascenseur, s'installent sur le palier, et si l'Hindou était broutable, nul doute qu'il serait brouté' ([1933] 1967: 22) ['There are cows everywhere in Calcutta. They cross the streets, stretch out on the pavement which becomes completely blocked, shit in front of the vice-regal limousine, wander into the shops, threaten to enter the lift, park themselves on the landing; if Hindus were chewable, there's no doubt they would be chewed up']. The close identification of cow and Indian, sharing as they do the same urban as well as rural environment, even to the remotest recesses, brings about a merging of man and beast that motivates Michaux's consistent recourse – in charting the mutual attraction/repellence, alienation/comprehension of the European/Indian, Indian/European relationship – to animal metaphors. Thus the Hindu is a *bête*, a cow, monkey, cat or elephant (the first two both sacred), calm, self-contained, mysterious, oblivious to the entreaties of those outside itself. Like a cat, the Indian parks his arse 'partout sauf où on s'y attend' ([1933] 1967: 21) ['everywhere except where one would expect it'] and is 'sans élan' except when pursuing his own interests. Birds and animals in India stand out from their surroundings like icons; their primary status is not functional but symbolic: 'Dans les campagnes, il y a des paons, pas de moineaux, des paons, des ibis, des échassiers, énormément de corbeaux et de milans. / Tout cela est sérieux' ([1933] 1967: 24) ['In the countryside, there are peacocks, not sparrows, peacocks, ibises, wading birds, lots of crows and kites. / All this is serious stuff']. These objects are 'serious' in that they are waiting to become totems, to attach themselves to one of the many heterogeneous deities of Hindu religion or to supply character traits to individual Indians. So both animals and Indians present themselves to the stranger as *sui generis*, complete in themselves, un-negotiable, immovable in the dignity of their nature, an integrity that the European sometimes finds deeply exasperating: 'Jamais, jamais, l'Indien ne se doutera à quel point il exaspère l'Européen. Le spectacle d'une foule hindoue, d'un village hindou, ou même la traversée d'une rue, où les Indiens sont à leur porte est agaçant ou odieux. / Ils sont tous figés, bétonnés' ([1933] 1967: 23) ['Not for a moment does the Indian suspect how much he annoys a European. The spectacle of a Hindu crowd, of a Hindu village, or even a street crossing where Indians are lolling in their doorways, is odious or exasperating. / There they all are, stuck in pose, cemented to the spot'].

It is in this symbolic or totemic potential that the fundamental difference of the Indian or Hindu as Other becomes apparent to Michaux. As in most so-called primitive societies, it is the symbolic order that governs the nature and behaviour of the native Indian: it is the function of religion to keep the sign attached to its object, to maintain appearances and essences in a symbiotic relationship. Everything is linked to everything else in a system which does not change and in which the function of ritual is precisely to maintain the status quo. It is a world that to the European is maddeningly homogeneous, allowing no selective purchase or opportunity to re-negotiate: 'L'homme blanc possède une qualité qui lui a fait faire du chemin: *l'irrespect*. / L'irrespect n'ayant rien dans les mains doit fabriquer, inventer, progresser. / L'Hindou est *religieux*, il se sent relié à tout' ([1933] 1967: 25) ['The whiteman has a quality that has enabled him to come a long way: *disrespect*. / Disrespect, having nothing to work on, has to make things, invent and progress. / The Hindu is a *religious* man, he feels himself linked to everything']. Here Michaux underlines the fundamental clash between modern western culture and the immemorial systems of the East: where the 'western' mind is critical and sceptical, constantly seeking new combinations, inventing new methods and instruments, the 'eastern' mind is content to re-assert the primeval dignity of Being. Where post-Renaissance European thinking is critical and analytical, eastern and primitive thinking is magical ([1933] 1967: 26); words for the Indian are like prayers or *mantras* – they can act directly on phenomena and permit entry into their essence: 'Ce ne sont pas des pensées, pour penser, ce sont des pensées, pour participer à l'Etre, à *BRAHMA*' ([1933] 1967: 26) ['These are not thoughts for thought's sake, but thoughts enabling participation in the supreme Being, in *BRAHMA*']. In comparison, western thinking, however scientific its claims, is transitory and precarious, offering hypotheses that are born only to be superseded, a knowledge that is only ever provisional.

Since there are few or no gaps in the Indian conception of phenomena, no critical distance between subject and object, there can be no aesthetics, no Beauty. To be right, phenomena have merely to be themselves, and their richness is a function not of aesthetic paring down but of accumulation. Thus Indian architecture and the attributes of divinities are characterised by the richness or plethora of their constituent elements. The Christian European is annoyed to find that even Christ is easily absorbed into the Indian pantheon ([1933] 1967: 30) where He rubs shoulders with deities representing His diametric opposite. Similarly, the woman, seen primarily as representing Maternity not Femininity ([1933] 1967: 30), is not so much an individual as part of a universal system of sensuality, fertility and fornication.

This uncritical, cumulative, inclusive way of thinking is also shown in Indian numerical, classificatory and taxonomic systems. Where a European divides most commonly into binary or triadic sets, the Hindu observes no arbitrary or schematic limits to his subdivisions – it can be ten, twelve, thirty-two or sixty-four. For an Indian, every object is a taxonomy: a horse is not a just horse but a combination of a plethora of parts: 'Pour lui, un cheval, tout court, n'est pas un cheval, il faut qu'on lui dise cheval à quatre pattes, avec quatre sabots, avec un ventre, un sexe, ses deux oreilles' ([1933] 1967: 50) ['For him, a horse *tout court* is not a horse, you have to say a horse with four legs, four hooves, one stomach, one sexual organ, two ears']. Like Borgès's Chinese encyclopedia or a totemic structure within a 'savage' mind, Indian classifications defy western logic in their desire for inclusiveness, as is illustrated by the venerable Nagarena's inventory of the qualities a disciple should possess:

(1) une qualité de l'âne [ass]
(2) deux du coq [cock]
(3) une de l'écureuil [squirrel]
(4) une de la panthère femelle [female panther]
(5) deux de la panthère mâle [male panther]
(6) cinq de la tortue [tortoise]
(7) une du bambou [bamboo]
(8) une de l'oie [goose]
(9) deux du corbeau [crow]
(10) deux d'un singe, etc., etc. [monkey]
(34) deux de l'ancre, etc., etc. [anchor]
(36) trois du pilote [pilot]
(37) une du mât, etc., etc., etc. [mast]
(61) deux de la semence, etc., etc., etc. [sowing]. ([1933] 1967: 51)

Also like Borgès's encyclopedia, the illuminations recorded by Gautama are capable of englobing relations inconceivable to the western mind: what matters to the Indian is 'l'ensemble, l'enchainement' ([1933] 1967: 37–8).

It is against the backdrop of such a plethora of taxonomies that Michaux will find himself confronting the difference *in himself*. For, as with Segalen, the look of the other is a kind of mirror in which is grasped the strangeness of the self to the other as much as the strangeness of the other to the self. So the 700,000 canons or *chanoines* (a class in which Michaux includes ALL the male inhabitants of Calcutta) are all 'sûrs d'eux-mêmes, avec un

regard de miroir' ([1933] 1967: 20) in which the (foreign) self may glimpse
a bit of itself to which it previously had no access: 'Ils vous regardent avec
un contrôle d'eux-mêmes, un blocage mystérieux et, sans que ce soit clair,
vous donnent l'impression d'intervenir quelque part en soi, comme vous
ne le pourriez pas' ([1933] 1967: 23) ['They look at you with a self-control
and a mysterious absorption that, without it being clear, gives you the
impression that they can enter into parts of yourself that even you cannot
access']. Wherever he goes, Michaux is stared at by 'des yeux de crapaud
qui ne vous quittent pas et dont il n'y a rien à extraire. / Pas méditatifs,
mais collants, ou plutôt collés' ([1933] 1967: 44) ['toads' eyes that don't let
you go and from which you can get nothing. Not reflective, but sticking,
or rather stuck, to you']. The look of the other is exasperating for a number
of reasons. First because it turns the subject's zoological gaze back on itself,
turning him into an object of curiosity: 'Ils vous regardent comme au jardin
zoologique on regarde un nouvel arrivé, un bison, une autruche, un serpent.
L'Inde est un jardin où les indigènes ont l'occasion de voir, de temps à autre,
des spécimens d'ailleurs' ([1933] 1967: 120) ['They look at you as if you were
an animal newly arrived at the zoo, a bison, an ostrich, a snake. India is a
zoological garden where the natives have the chance from time to time to
see specimens from elsewhere']. Second, because this subject, in becoming
object of the other's gaze and a phenomenon of general interest, finds itself
arbitrarily compartmentalised, aspects of its character (age, purpose) being
detached and relayed as objects of curiosity in themselves:

Si l'un d'eux attrappe le moindre renseignement sur vous, que vous n'avez que
trente-deux ans, par exemple, immédiatement, il en informe tout le voisinage,
tous les voyageurs dans la gare, tous les passants dans la ville. D'ailleurs, de loin
on l'interroge. Et il répond triomphalement: 'Il a trente-deux ans. Il vient visiter
les Indes!' Et la nouvelle étonnante se répand comme le feu dans la poudre. ([1933]
1967: 120)

[If one of them finds out the smallest bit of information about you, for example,
that you are just thirty-two, he will immediately inform everyone within hearing
distance, all the passengers in the station, all the passers-by in the street. Moreover
the informant is questioned by people standing quite far away. To whom he replies
triumphantly: 'He's thirty-two. He's visiting India!' And the astonishing news
spreads like wildfire.]

Third, because the intrusiveness of the other's gaze becomes so intense that
it obliterates all alternative perspectives, blocking the subject's view: 'Si
l'Hindou vous parle, c'est nez à nez. Il vous prend l'haleine de la bouche.
Il ne sera jamais assez près. Sa tête envahissante et ses yeux hors de propos

se calent entre l'horizon et vous' ([1933] 1967: 121) ['If a Hindu speaks to you, it is nose to nose. He takes the very breath out of your mouth. He can never get close enough. His invasive head and his popping eyes wedge themselves between you and the horizon']. Fourth, because the other's look, when the excitement caused by the subject's zoological difference has worn off, contains an element that cannot be grasped by its object: 'Ces yeux l'agacent parce que contenant un élément élevé ou pas élevé, mais qu'il ne *saisit pas*' ([1933] 1967: 67, Michaux's italics) ['these eyes annoy him because they contain an element, elevated or not, that he *cannot grasp*'].

This look is most poignantly experienced by Michaux in Orissa where the chance gaze of an old man activates an epiphany in which the whole nature of the subject, like the meaning of the glance of which it is the object, is called into question:

Il y avait dans cette cour un très vieil homme: il me salua, mais j'aperçus le salut trop tard. La musique reprit et je me disais: 'Pourvu qu'il me regarde encore!' C'était un pèlerin, il n'était pas d'ici. Il m'avait semblé qu'il avait de l'amitié pour moi. La musique s'acheva. J'étais transporté. Il se retourna sur moi, m'adressa son regard, et sortit. Dans son regard, il y avait quelque chose pour moi, particulièrement. Ce qu'il m'a dit, je le cherche encore. Quelque chose d'important, d'essentiel. Il me regarda, moi et ma destinée, avec une sorte d'acquiescement et de réjouissance, mais un fil de compassion et presque de pitié y passa et je me demande ce que cela signifie. ([1933] 1967: 93)

[There was a very old man in the courtyard: he saluted me, but I noticed this too late. The music began again and I said to myself: 'I hope he looks at me again!' He was a pilgrim, not from these parts. It seemed to me that he liked me. The music stopped. I was in a state of transport. He turned back towards me, looked at me, and left. There was something special for me in his glance, just for me. What he meant by this I still don't know. But it was something important and profound. He looked at me, and my destiny, with a sort of pleasure and approval, but also with a trace of compassion and pity, and I still ask myself what all this meant.]

In this passage, Michaux appears unconsciously to allegorise what is at stake in the relationship between self and other. At first, among the plethora of exotic objects – a concert in the courtyard of a house in which musicians sing – he misses the sign, 'le salut' (a sign of both recognition and salvation), offered by the venerable pilgrim, an outsider like himself. At the close of the concert, in a state of heightened awareness and lyrical exultation inspired by the music – 'le chant de l'affirmation psychique, de l'irrésistible triomphe du surhomme' ([1933] 1967: 92) ['the song of psychic affirmation, the irresistible triumph of the superman'] – Michaux does not this time miss the sign of recognition constituted by the farewell glance of the old man. For he recognises that the glance of the Other, in interpreting him, Michaux, the young foreigner, is able to penetrate to an essential part of him, to identify his destiny, to acquiesce and indeed rejoice, with pity and compassion, in *his difference*. The radically other is thus paradoxically able to lead the subject to a deeper – if not fully fathomable – understanding of the self. It is a moment which offers no final solutions – 'je me demande ce que cela signifie' – but, in triggering the interactive movement of signs in semiosis, also activates and motivates a new awareness of the signifying process. Michaux thus understands that his destiny is to be *different* not only from the other, but also from the same – himself – anticipating a quest that, for the rest of his life as artist and writer, he will relentlessly pursue.

But in India the European comes up against another form of the other that poses almost insuperable difficulties for the subject: the beggar. Begging is endemic to Indian society, being a function of massive inequalities and the absence of rational structures or social strategies susceptible to the production of a more equitable redistribution of wealth. But begging is not just a social and economic problem: to the European traveller it becomes perhaps the greatest challenge the other can institute, making personal demands on the subject to which he or she is often quite unable to respond. This is in part because of the huge *disproportion* in the weighting of the balance between self and other in a begging situation: the other magnifies the weight of the foreign subject in the hope that redistribution in the form of charity will be forthcoming. The problem for the western visitor – and it is a problem of both social consciousness and moral conscience – is that the terms of the relation are so stretched or exaggerated that the subject cannot recognise itself as occupying the position proposed by the attitude of the other or of being able to respond meaningfully. The gap between the terms of the relation is so distended that no meaning, and thus any sense of social or moral contract, can be attached to it. The other thus in a sense ceases to be human, or at least an adult human, and must be treated as a child, an animal or a joke.

The problem is sufficiently fundamental to give rise to deep reflection on the part of travel writers of both ethnographic and literary tendency; indeed begging poses a conundrum so fundamental to human society that writers such as Lévi-Strauss and Michaux, in differing degrees, bring both an ethnographic and personal response to bear on it. In the chapter devoted to 'Foules' in *Tristes Tropiques* (1955: 151–61), Lévi-Strauss describes the beggars' ballet that greets him every morning as he leaves his Calcutta hotel:

le cireur de chaussures, qui se jette à mes pieds;
le petit garçon nasillard qui se précipite: *one anna, papa, one anna*;
l'infirme presque nu pour qu'on puisse mieux détailler ses moignons;
le proxénète; *British girls, very nice . . .*;
le marchand de clarinettes;
le porteur de New-Market, qui supplie de tout acheter [. . .]: *Suit-case? Shirts? Hose? . . .*
Et enfin, toute la troupe de petits sujets: racoleurs de rickshaws, de gharries, de taxis. (1955: 152)

[the shoe polisher, who throws himself at my feet;
the little nasal-voiced boy who rushes out crying *one anna, papa, one anna*;
the almost naked leper displaying his amputations;
the pimp; *British girls, very nice . . .*;
the clarinet-seller;
the New-Market porter who entreats one to buy everything [. . .]: *Suit-case? Shirts? Hose? . . .*
Finally, a band of little boys touting rickshaws, gharries, taxis.]

Resisting the temptation to laugh or to become irritated at this comic display, the ethnographer cannot but seriously ponder it in terms of 'les symptômes cliniques d'une agonie' (1955: 152), the hunger that inspires such desperate behaviour and the impossibility for the outsider of ameliorating the situation. For, in southern Asia the European finds himself in an impossible bind: that of being 'en deça ou au-delà de ce que l'homme est en droit d'exiger du monde, et de l'homme' (1955: 153) ['in deficit or in excess of what man has a right to expect of the world, and of man']. As Lévi-Strauss goes on to say:

La vie quotidienne paraît être une répudiation permanente de la notion de relations humaines. On vous offre tout, on s'engage à tout, on proclame toutes les compétences alors qu'on ne sait rien. Ainsi, on vous oblige d'emblée à nier chez autrui la qualité humaine qui réside dans la bonne foi, le sens du contrat et la capacité de s'obliger. Des *rickshaw boys* proposent de vous conduire n'importe où, bien qu'ils soient plus ignorants de l'itinéraire que vous-même. Comment donc ne pas s'emporter et – quelque scrupule que l'on ait à monter dans leur pousse et à se faire trainer par eux – ne pas les traiter en bêtes, puisqu'ils vous contraignent à les considérer tels par cette déraison qui est la leur? (1955: 153)

[Everyday life seems permanently to repudiate the notion of human relations. They offer you everything, commit themselves to everything, proclaim all kinds of services when in fact they are capable of nothing. You are thus obliged from the start to deny others the human quality enshrined in such notions as good faith, fair contract and reciprocal obligation. Rickshaw boys promise to take you anywhere even though they know the way even less well than you do. How can one keep

one's temper and – however hesitant one is to climb into their rickshaw and let
oneself be transported by them – how can one not treat them like idiots since they
oblige you to see them as such by their unreasonable behaviour?]

The irreducible inequality that the begging situation gives rise to between
European and native is also a function of a profound ideological difference:
in a deeply religious society, the motor for changing a situation is much less
likely to be reason or economic sense than to be *prayer*. As Lévi-Strauss bril-
liantly shows (1955: 153–5), it is through an attitude or words of supplication
that the native attempts to appeal to the stranger, since such strategies are
as likely to have effect in his conception of the world as the more obvious
or common-sensical ones at the disposal of the westerner. Prayer places
the outsider to whom it is addressed in a position of intolerable moral
responsibility, one to which he is unable to respond, incapable as he is of
rationalising the specific situation in terms of the thousands of others with
which an average day confronts him.

Michaux throws less glaringly pessimistic light on the situation by suggesting that, for Hindus at least, begging is a social strategy that can be
adopted coolly and deliberately. It is a destiny that can sometimes be chosen voluntarily, if not willingly: 'Quand, chez un Hindou, quelque chose
ne va pas, même s'il est riche, marié, père de dix enfants: "Bon, s'il en est
ainsi, je vais mendier". Il confie sa fortune à son neveu et s'en va mendier'
([1933] 1967: 111) ['When things go wrong for a Hindu, even if he's rich,
married, the father of ten children, he simply says: "Right, if that's the
way things are, I'm off begging." He leaves his fortune to his nephew and
goes off begging']. Begging becomes a practice which, like other skills, can
be exercised more or less effectively, depending on the astuteness of the
practitioner and his ability to charm without irritating the object of his
trade. Thus Michaux, in Ceylon, encounters a young man riding a smart
new bicycle, who, despite his obvious prosperity, on spotting the European visitor, holds out his hands claiming '*poor boy, no money*' ([1933] 1967:
112). Seduced as much by the cheek as the charm of the boy, Michaux
willingly pays up. Similarly in Darjeeling, begging is accompanied by such
intense and charming focus on the outsider as a personal individual that it
is impossible for the latter to refuse charity. Alternatively, charity is sought
as a personal favour to which the outsider is deemed more likely to respond
in an egalitarian spirit according to which the favour may – an unlikely but
not impossible eventuality – one day be returned.

By concentrating on a range of *individual* charity-seeking strategies, particularly insofar as they appeal to the foreign subject, Michaux is thus able

to acquiesce with more or less good humour to beggars. By focussing on the wider sociological and ethnographic implications of the problem, Lévi-Strauss, on the other hand, finds himself less able to deal with or accept the moral bind exerted by the begging situation. This difference in response is perhaps symptomatic of a deeper divergence of approach between travel writing and ethnology, one implicitly explored by Francis Affergan in his critique of anthropology as outlined in *Exotisme et altérité* (1987a), in which both the validity and the motivation of ethnology's claim to be scientific are questioned. In placing anthropology in a historical perspective, in particular by tracing it back to its pre-Enlightenment roots in the fifteenth- and sixteenth-century age of discovery, Affergan observes that 'Entre le discours de découverte et celui de l'anthropologie moderne, un glissement s'est opéré entre un niveau *discursif*, où l'altérité était appréhendée, et un niveau *descriptif*, où la différence est mise à plat pour être saisie' (1987a: 12) ['In the discourse of discovery and that of modern anthropology, there has been a certain slippage between a *discursive* level, at which alterity was apprehended, and a *descriptive* level at which difference is levelled out so that it can be grasped']. He goes on to suggest that after the seventeenth century 'L'impulsion exotique se transforme en particulier en pulsion épistémologique et en une différence excessive de la scientificité de l'anthropologie. La prétention scientifique n'étant que la justification *a posteriori* des mêmes motivations que le discours de découverte nous offrent' (1987a: 14) ['In particular, the exotic impulse changes into an epistemological project and into an excessive difference from the scientificity of anthropology. The scientific claim is only an *a posteriori* justification for the motivations that the discourse of discovery offers us']. Affergan's conception of 'discours de découverte' can be related to Foucault's conception of pre-Enlightenment analogical thinking to the extent that it combines in various degrees observation and imagination. It has developed beyond the Medieval practice – that of the age of Marco Polo – in which monsters and strange beasts are discovered in the exotic world of the other as a function not of actual observation but of the imposition of a pre-existing western mythology of the other (1987a: 11–12), but has not yet become the purely rational and scientific project of an Enlightenment *épistémè*. It is a synthetic rather than an analytical model, one that includes a strong dose of subjectivity, and thus offers knowledge of an imaginative rather than epistemological nature.

Two questions arising from this can be asked in relation to the issues just raised: to what extent do nineteenth- and twentieth-century travel writers such as Segalen and Michaux represent a 'discours de découverte' as opposed to the 'discours scientifique' of the anthropologist, and, in the last analysis, which discourse brings one closer to the Other? The first is perhaps easier to answer. As we have seen, the travel writing of Segalen and Michaux is already deeply imbued with the discipline of ethnology – with its focus on the deeper, mythical structures of the target culture and the need to understand the latter as a *system* governed by a rationale, however exotic; at the same time, as writers, for whom travel is a deeply personal project, a strong element of individual motivation and subjectivity is inevitably present in Segalen's and Michaux's texts, becomes indeed an essential part of the fascination they exert. Any absolute distinction between 'discours de la découverte' and 'discours scientifique' is also of course problematised by the subtle transformation in the later twentieth century of the anthropological approach. Here, of course, the impact and influence of Lévi-Strauss has been paramount. For Lévi-Strauss, quite apart from his outstanding contribution to ethnology, in particular his systematic application of comparative structuralist analysis to primitive myth systems, has also tackled head-on the problem of the degree of subjectivity that enters into so-called objective discourse on the other. *Tristes Tropiques* (1955) is exemplary in this respect, combining and transcending as it does both the ethnological and the travel-writing project. So when Lévi-Strauss encounters the beggars of Calcutta he is as deeply aware of the moral problem they pose to him personally as he is of the profound sociological or ethnographic issues their impoverished state raises. Above all what Lévi-Strauss shows more generally (Affergan's argument in *Exotisme et altérité* seems to support this position) is that a purely scientific anthropology is not only not possible but also probably not desirable. This does not mean that ethnology is dead, long live travel writing; rather that the two genres should continue to be pursued but with a fuller understanding of their respective limitations and as a necessary complement to each other. So travel writing and anthropology can be seen to offer different but equally valid routes to the other.

The understanding in the post-modern era of the deep interrelationship between travel writing and ethnology has led to a new interdisciplinary approach to the two genres and indeed to an increasing impulse to *merge* them into new hybrid forms. Segalen's ethnographic novel *Les Immémoriaux* (1907), already discussed in Chapter 1, constitutes a significant antecedent to this development, an area in which the work since the 1980s of the ethnologist Marc Augé is of special interest. In *Le Sens des autres. Actualité de l'anthropologie* (1994a), Augé sets out to take stock of anthropology at the end of the modern period, both in the terms in which Lévi-Strauss and others (such as Affergan) have been re-assessing its traditional scope and intentions, and in terms of the increasing application in the current, post-modern era of ethnographic approaches to contemporary *western* society. So when he writes that 'L'idéal de l'ethnologue, c'est d'être assez distancié pour comprendre le système comme système et assez participant pour le vivre comme individu' (1994a: 44) ['The ideal aim of the ethnologist is to be distant enough to understand the system as a system and close enough to experience it as an individual'], he is summarising the position of modern anthropology as understood by Lévi-Strauss; indeed he goes on to cite a passage from Lévi-Strauss's introduction to the 1966 edition of Marcel Mauss's *Sociologie et anthropologie*: 'Pour comprendre convenablement un fait social, il faut l'appréhender *totalement*, c'est-à-dire du dehors comme une chose, mais comme une chose dont fait cependant partie intégrante l'appréhension subjective (consciente et inconsciente) que nous en prendrions si, inéluctablement hommes, nous vivions le fait comme indigène au lieu de l'observer comme ethnographe' (Mauss, 1966: xxvi) ['Properly to understand a social phenomenon, it has to be grasped *totally*, that is to say from the outside as a thing, but also as a thing of which subjective apprehension (conscious or unconscious) is an integral part, as if we were experiencing the phenomenon, ineluctably human that we are, like the native, as opposed to simply observing it as an ethnographer']. The problem however remains of the dizzying size of the task and the possibility of fulfilling it, as Augé wryly comments: 'On imagine ici le vertige que peut ressentir l'ethnologue à se voir assigner une tâche dont aucun romancier n'oserait mesurer l'ampleur' (1994a: 45) ['It is easy to imagine the vertigo the ethnologist might feel seeing himself assigned a task which no novelist would dare to tackle'].

Augé's solution to the problem is one that has made his name since the mid-1980s, both in ethnological circles and among the wider reading public. As this double audience implies, Augé's project is dual: to solve the problem of being simultaneously inside and outside the culture, society or ethnic group being analysed, let the latter be the ethnologist's native group. To ensure that the project remains an authentic ethnographic – and not merely sociological – venture, let the focus be on the mythological and symbolic systems underlining the society studied – remembering, as Augé tells us, that 'la culture se définit comme un ensemble de systèmes symboliques' (1994a: 17), and that 'La culture en somme, c'est le supplément au social' (1994b: 21). And to make the project of universal interest, let it focus in particular on patterns of behaviour that have become fundamental to the globalised world of the post-industrial age, a world in fact which Augé in *Pour une anthropologie des mondes contemporains* (1994b) prefers, as its title suggests, to refer to in the plural. It is in this way that the theme of travel comes back into its own as a type of social behaviour – individualised but generally prevalent, practised by the Third as well as the First World – worthy of deep study. This does not imply a revival of the exotic which, as Augé remarks, has long been debased by mass tourism – 'la mort de l'exotisme est la caractéristique essentielle de notre actualité' (1994a: 10); rather, as he remarks in *L'Impossible Voyage. Le tourisme et ses images*, a re-learning of what it means to travel: 'Peut-être une de nos tâches les plus urgentes est-elle de réapprendre à voyager, éventuellement au plus proche de chez nous, pour réapprendre à voir' (Augé, 1997: 14–15) ['Perhaps one of our most urgent tasks is to re-learn how to travel, possibly as close to home as feasible, in order to re-learn how to see'].

In anthropological terms, such travel leads Augé to consider the way the modern social practice of tourism and mass communications lead the subject away from rather than towards the other. So, in his essay *Non-lieux. Introduction à une anthropologie de la surmodernité* (1992), he shows how mass movement and communication lead to a commodification not only of the other but also of the travel process itself, as the traveller, passing through the vast non-places of today's airports, motorway systems and commercial outlets, becomes, in every sense of the word, a mere passenger, and, on arrival, a mere tourist. In *L'Impossible voyage* (1997), the 'exotic' is re-discovered in Disneyland or the Center Parcs as a world of virtuality and simulacrum, in which thematisation or disneyfication package and sanitise culture, minimising the scope for individual discovery or authentic experience. As a counter argument, in his *ethno-romans*, Augé attempts to restore a sense of the possibility of the authentic in personal experience while at the same time suggesting the wider ethnographic interest of the banal and everyday.[8] So, in *La Traversée du Luxembourg. Ethno-roman d'une journée française considérée sous l'angle des mœurs, de la théorie et du bonheur* (1985), the everyday habits of a Frenchman are seen to weave themselves into a symbolic universe susceptible to ethnographic analysis, reviving in the process, as the elaborate parodic sub-title suggests, an eighteenth-century literary genre such as the *promenade* or *conte philosophique*. Meanwhile, *Un ethnologue dans le métro* (1986) proposes an inverted ethnology in which subjectivity expressed through the form of writing enters into relation with the Other in many forms, recreating the two-way flow or exchange of interpretants already observed in this chapter in the writings of Segalen and Michaux. At the end of this book, Augé remarks 'Que le sens naisse de l'aliénation, l'ethnologue, entre autres, l'a montré depuis longtemps' (1986: 116) ['That meaning is born from alienation, is something that the ethnologist, among others, has for a long time been showing us']. If we interpret the intercalated phrase 'entre autres' in a sense wider than that consciously intended by its author, it becomes a fair statement, *among others*, both of the position of ethnology over the past 200 years – in relation both to the other and to other forms of writing on the other – and a viable programme for its future interdisciplinary development.

CHAPTER 3

Identity crises: 'Je est un autre' – Gautier, Gauguin, Nerval, Bouvier

Que 'je' soit un autre, l'Afrique des lignages l'a su avant Rimbaud.

(Marc Augé, 1994a: 42)

[Le fou] c'est celui qui s'est *aliéné* dans *l'analogie*. Il est le joueur déréglé du Même et de l'Autre.

(Michel Foucault, 1966: 63)

On ne voyage pas sans connaître ces instants où ce dont on s'était fait fort se défile et vous trahit comme dans un cauchemar.

(Nicolas Bouvier, [1982] 1991: 124)

[C]'est toujours la même chose: une fois libéré, vous êtes forcé de vous demander qui vous êtes.

(Jean Baudrillard, 1986: 48)

Travel as a means of discovering the self also implies a loss of self. As we saw in the last chapter, in the travel writing of Michaux and Segalen, the discovery of a deeper and hitherto unknown or unrecognised self through interaction with the other was often made at a moment of extreme personal vulnerability or exhaustion, a moment of excitement or panic when psychological defences were low and when familiar (western) strategies of identification and control began to lose their purchase on the foreign or alien environment. A loss of self is often brought about by a continuation of the above process whereby the unknown and unsuspected within escapes the conscious control of the subject with the result that the latter eventually becomes absorbed into and virtually indistinguishable from the other from which it can only with difficulty retrieve itself. This other can take the form of another person (as we shall see in Gauguin), a landscape or cityscape (as in Gautier) or the two combined (as in Bouvier). On a semiotic level, this merging or overlapping of self and other manifests itself as a process in which signs are taken for objects or objects taken for signs; or, in other words, in which the real is experienced as imaginary, or the imaginary as real. Such an inversion is similar to that observed by Foucault in his analysis of folly in *Les Mots et les choses* (1966) in which the fool or jester proposes a (controlled) *misreading of signs*, a kind of 'raisonné dérèglement', to use the Rimbaldian terms echoed in the following passage:

Le fou, entendu non pas comme malade, mais comme déviance constituée et entretenue, comme fonction culturelle indispensable, est devenu, dans l'expérience occidentale, l'homme des ressemblances sauvages. Ce personnage, tel qu'il est dessiné dans les romans ou le théâtre de l'époque baroque, et tel qu'il s'est institutionnalisé peu à peu jusqu'à la psychiatrie du XIXe siècle, c'est celui qui s'est *aliéné* dans *l'analogie*. Il est le joueur déréglé du Même et de l'Autre. Il prend les choses pour ce qu'elles ne sont pas, et les gens les uns pour les autres; il ignore ses amis, reconnaît les étrangers; il croit démasquer, et il impose un masque. Il inverse toutes les valeurs et toutes les proportions, parce qu'il croit à chaque instant déchiffrer des signes. (1966: 63)

[The fool, understood not as being mad but as representing a deviance invested in and maintained (by society), as an indispensable cultural function, has become, in western experience, the man of unconventional resemblances. This character, as he appears in the novels or theatre of the baroque era, and as he gradually became institutionalised up to the emergence of psychiatry in the nineteenth century, represents he who is *alienated* in *analogy*. He is the deregulated player in the game of Same and Other. He takes things for what they are not, and mixes people up; he does not seem to know his friends, but recognises strangers; he thinks he is de-masking but in fact is masking others. He inverts all values and proportions because he believes all the time that he is interpreting signs.]

The second incarnation of the fool or jester – 'l'homme des ressemblances sauvages' – in the western tradition as analysed by Foucault is that of the poet, he who, like the anthropologist 'au-dessous des différences nommées et quotidiennement prévues, retrouve les parentés enfouies des choses' (1966: 63) ['beneath the difference named and foreseen in everyday life, rediscovers the hidden connection between things']. The experience of travel writers examined in this chapter, whether poets or artists, seems to confirm this model: like ethnologists, they explore the status and function of signs in the identifying and self-identifying process, interrogating the binary oppositions that are conventionally seen as structuring western experience. At the same time, as writers and artists living in an exotic context, they explore the implications in terms of identity and lived experience of the similarity obscurely lurking beneath the difference of signs, or the difference embedded in the same, and the mobile play between them. So for example, as we shall see, polarities such as male/female, civilised/primitive, are questioned by Gauguin in the light of his experience of life in the

South Pacific, both in ethnographical terms – the androgynous forms of Tahitian or Marquisan natives of either sex, the complex symbolism under-lying their apparently primitive rituals – and in terms of his own experience as man and artist in which interaction with native people causes him to explore both his own sexual ambivalence and the ambiguity of western moral values. In a similar way, certain climactic experiences of the other or the other *place* will lead Gautier to reconsider the dream/reality, art/life polarities, while Nerval's travels in the Orient and Bouvier's trip to Ceylon will involve an experience and an analysis of a complex interweaving of multiple inversions – past/present, fantasy/reality, self/other.

The movement that is an essential constituent of travel also alerts the travel writer to the principle of mobility operative in any construction of the self. Divorced from its habitual world, the self is no longer perceived or experienced as static but as a temporary consensus of shifting relations within an alien environment – physical, social, spiritual. All conventionally defining aspects of the subject, those that appear on passports – gender, nationality, age, even appearance – thus become susceptible to modification or problematisation. This phenomenon is cogently analysed by Marc Augé in ethnographic terms in *Le Sens des autres* in which he observes that in some African ethnic groups, the self is perceived less as a function of conscious rationalisation, more as a function of shifting relations with others:

Ainsi ni le corps, ni l'ancêtre, ni le dieu n'autorisent d'autre définition de l'identité individuelle et de l'existence singulière qu'une définition sans cesse différée, tou-jours asymptotique et soumise à l'épreuve de l'événement – l'événement lui-même s'interprétant comme signe d'un autre, renvoi à un autre dont la singularité reste tout aussi problématique. Ce jeu de renvois ne s'arrête éventuellement que sur la figure du sorcier – individualité dès lors impensable et qu'il convient d'anéantir. Que 'je' soit un autre, l'Afrique des lignages l'a su avant Rimbaud; simplement, ses réponses varient sur l'identification des lieux où chercher la présence des différents autres: celui dont on hérite, celui que l'on épouse, celui que l'on agresse, celui que l'on redoute, celui que l'on salue, celui qui vous salue, etc. Les procédures et les règles de cette identification sont très tôt incorporées; le dressage de l'individu passe par cette éducation; il faut apprendre à jouer le jeu et, très littéralement, à respecter les règles du savoir-vivre, en sorte qu'une culture [. . .] ou une société [. . .] pourrait se définir comme la zone imposée de consensus sur les règles du je (du jeu) – ce jeu de mots s'efforçant maladroitement de suggérer la nécessité d'un point de vue unique sur l'homme singulier/pluriel. (Augé, 1994a: 42–3).

[So neither the body, nor the ancestor, nor the god, authorize any other definition of individual identity or of singular existence than a definition continually deferred, always asymptotic and submitted to the test of eventuality – the event itself being interpreted as a sign of something else, a reference to an other whose singularity also remains problematic. This series of references only eventually stops at the figure of the sorcerer – an individuality that is therefore unthinkable and that must be annihilated. That 'I' should be another was known to the Africa of lineages long before Rimbaud; it is simply that responses vary according to the identification of the places where the presence of these others may be sought: the other from whom one inherits, the other whom one marries, the other one attacks, the other one fears, the other one salutes or who salutes you, etc. The rules and procedures of this practice of identification are soon internalised; the formation of the individual is a function of such an education; each must learn to play the game, and literally learn to respect the rules of savoir-vivre so that a culture (. . .) or a society (. . .) could be defined as the zone imposed by common consent on the rules of the 'I' (of the game) – this word-play attempting clumsily to suggest the necessity of a single perspective on man in his combined singularity and plurality.]

This passage is illuminating with regard to both certain travel issues we have already explored and the identity problem that will be confronted more specifically in this chapter. Thus Michaux's surprise at the way he was viewed or received by the natives he encountered in India was in part a function of his inability, in the first instance at least, to grasp the Hindu conceptual frame that is applied to him as foreigner. For the Hindu, rather than view Michaux as a sovereign subject, complete and integral, conceived of him as a mere *sign* within the other's larger scheme or *jeu*, a sign in the rules or the interpretation of which Michaux, as individual, had little say. Similarly, in the analyses that follow, Gautier, Gauguin, Nerval and Bouvier will be seen to reach a point in their travels at which, under the pressure of the other or exotic, the western individual identity begins to unravel and becomes experienced not as a unified whole but as a series of (mere) *signs*, the *object* or totality of which is never fully known since their organising principle is not fully grasped. So as in Augé's pun, the travel writer reaches a point in experience in which he no longer knows the 'règles du jeu/je'.

Gautier's meditation on the battlements of the Alcazar in Toledo provides a point of departure for an analysis of such experiences:

Accoudé à l'embrasure d'un créneau et regardant à vol d'hirondelle cette ville où je ne connaissais personne, où mon nom était parfaitement inconnu, j'étais tombé dans une méditation profonde. Devant tous ces objets, toutes ces formes, que je voyais et que je ne devais probablement plus revoir, il me prenait des doutes sur ma propre identité, je me sentais si absent de moi-même, transporté si loin de ma sphère, que tout cela me paraissait une hallucination, un rêve étrange dont j'allais me réveiller en sursaut au son aigre et chevrotant de quelque musique de vaudeville sur le rebord d'une loge de théâtre. Par un de ces sauts d'idées si fréquents dans la rêverie, je pensai à ce que pouvaient faire mes amis à cette heure; je me demandai s'ils s'apercevaient de mon absence, et si, par hasard, en ce moment même où j'étais penché sur ce créneau dans l'Alcazar de Tolède, mon nom voltigeait à Paris sur quelque bouche aimée et fidèle. Apparemment la réponse intérieure ne fut pas affirmative; car, malgré la magnificence du spectacle, je me sentis l'âme envahie par une tristesse incommensurable, et pourtant j'accomplissais le rêve de toute ma vie, je touchais du doigt un de mes désirs les plus ardemment caressés. ([1840] 1981: 193)

[Leaning over the gap between the battlements and enjoying a bird's eye view of this town where I knew nobody, where my name was perfectly unknown, I fell into a profound state of meditation. In front of all these objects and forms that I could see and that I would probably never see again, I began to have doubts about my own identity, feeling so distant from myself, transported so far from my sphere, that everything seemed to me to be a hallucination, a strange dream from which I would soon awake with a jump to the sharp and quavering sound of vaudeville music on the edge of a box at the theatre. Following one of those associations of ideas so frequent in reverie, I thought about what my friends could be doing at this time; I wondered whether they noticed my absence and whether, by chance, at the very moment that I was leaning over the battlements of the Alcazar in Toledo, my name was being pronounced in Paris by some loving or faithful voice. Apparently the answer was not affirmative since, despite the magnificence of the spectacle, I felt my soul overcome with a boundless sadness, and yet at this very moment I was fulfilling the dream of a lifetime, I was close to satisfying one of my wildest desires.]

Here, the objects so deeply desired by the subject, fail, when apprehended, to communicate any sign of recognition. In the process, signs to which the self is deeply attached become emptied of their significance. In a corollary movement, the self itself becomes emptied, losing its sense of identity and, with it, any significance. Meaning fails to establish any real link between subject and object: semiosis becomes a play of signifiers or interpretants, with no connection through the sign to the real. The effect of this on the subject is experienced as a hallucination which brings with it a disconcerting series of paradoxes: Gautier feels himself to be absent from himself, and from the exotic environment which surrounds him. He imagines himself to be not in the real setting of Toledo but rather in a fantasy representation of it as in a Parisian theatre or *vaudeville*; in this way, he exactly reverses the fantasy he had nurtured in Paris of visiting Toledo. Moreover, while he imagines himself to be back in Paris, in his real absence from that city, he is not even sure of his presence there in terms of signs being apprehended (no known or loved voice seems to be pronouncing his name). On the point of realising his wildest dreams, immeasurable sadness overwhelms him. The gaze of the familiar, with all that it implies of the known *règles du jeu*, is absent, and the subject, in the face of the other, loses all sense of self, becoming a mere bundle of signs open to multiple and aleatory interpretation. To sum up: in semiotic terms, Gautier in this passage finds himself in a world in which 'il ne voit partout que ressemblances et signes de la ressemblance; tous les signes pour lui se ressemblent, et toutes les ressemblances valent comme des signes' (Foucault, 1966: 63), while in anthropological terms he is temporarily exiled from 'la zone imposée de consensus sur les règles du je (du jeu)' (Augé, 1994a: 43).

For the debonair and cosmopolitan Gautier, this crisis is only momentary, the proposition, made by his travelling companion, of a night-time dip in the Tagus soon leading the disorientated traveller to raise his spirits and plunge back into an unexpected aspect of the real. A similar plunge into icy water will rescue Gauguin from a comparable crisis, one however that will not be as easily washed away as was the case with Gautier.

For Paul Gauguin, like Gautier, travel and art were means through which the so-called civilised westerner could rejuvenate signs and bring the subject back into a vital relationship with the world. In both activities, signs are perceived as having an obscure but motivated link with their object while the subject becomes really modified in the ongoing process of their interpretation and re-creation. So the aim of the voyages to Tahiti (1891–3, 1895–1903), following the shorter trip to Panama and Martinique of 1887, was to maximise for Gauguin the possibilities of exposure to new images and experiences, and of the discovery of new forms of expression of them. In realising this double project, Gauguin consciously set out to rediscover the savage or barbarian within himself and to reconstruct, through his painting, what he imagined to be the savage mind's representation of the primitive world. Combining the two functions – semiotic and artistic/poetic – of the fool as analysed by Foucault in the passage from *Les Mots et les choses* cited above, Gauguin becomes 'l'homme des ressemblances sauvages', his writings (as collected by Daniel Guérin in *Oviri*, 1974) bearing the sub-title *Ecrits d'un sauvage* and expressing the *pensée sauvage* of an exile from western civilisation. Of course, throughout this enterprise, Gauguin is obscurely aware of the potential madness of his project, but his experiences with Van Gogh, with whom he shared a studio in Arles during part of 1888, seem, in alerting him to the risks of insanity, also to have protected him from it. For, following on from the suggestion made by Foucault, Van Gogh's madness seems in part to have been a result of a kind of semiotic schizophrenia. Like the jester in Foucault, Van Gogh takes things for what they are not and signs for other signs: as an artist this enables him to create images of astonishing power and intensity but as a man leads to the devastating consequences with which we are all familiar. So the incident of his

sending to Gauguin a real part of himself (his severed ear) as a souvenir
rather than a conventional sign (such as a sketch or drawing) – 'Voici, dit-il,
en souvenir de moi' (Gauguin, [1892–1903] 1974: 296) – may be taken to
illustrate his confusion of the real with the sign. This does not of course
prevent Van Gogh on most occasions from being aware of this problem, as
is shown when he says on seeing Gauguin's portrait of him: 'C'est bien moi,
mais moi devenu fou' ([1892–1903] 1974: 295) ['It's me alright, but me as a
madman'].

The 'wild' nature of Gauguin's travel writings is of course indelibly tainted
by his civilised background, the creative tension between *civilisé* and *barbare*
being a necessary function of their irreconcilable difference. What
Gauguin aims for thus is new syntheses of the two elements, an unstable
and shifting symbiosis in which he can experience the various permutations
of the 'sauvage civilisé' ([1892–1903] 1974: 220) while at the same time
giving coherent expression to them. The written account of his Tahitian
experiences in his book *Noa Noa* was conceived as a collaboration between
the artist and the Symbolist poet, Charles Morice, the latter unwittingly
entering into (and moreover abusing through an excessive inclusion of text)
a project in which he would be set up as a kind of decadent western stooge –
'civilisé pourri' – to Gauguin's 'sauvage naïf et brutal' ([1892–1903] 1974:
248). Here once again, the anthropological project interacts with the artistic/
poetic vocation. Gauguin is acutely conscious of the rivalry between native
Tahitian and European signs. Whereas western colonising powers consciously
impose the marks of their signs on the very fabric and flesh of
the native culture and body – '(Autrefois, me dit-on, les missionnaires
sévissaient contre la luxure et marquaient quelques-unes à la joue comme
un avertissement de l'enfer, ce qui les couvrait de honte, non la honte du
péché commis, mais le ridicule d'une marque distinctive)' ([1892–1903]
1974: 124–5) ['(In earlier times, I was told, missionaries were up in arms
against native lust and marked the cheeks of some native women as a warning
of hell-fire, which covered them in shame, not for the sin committed
but for the embarrassment of being so singled out)'] – Gauguin will as far
as possible welcome native signs and techniques into his painting. So in
confronting the nudity of Tahitian women and men, Gauguin as a painter
will strive to recreate it as a natural state, not as the lewd subterfuge that
it has become in European academic art: 'Pour faire neuf, il faut remonter
aux sources, à l'humanité en enfance. L'Eve de mon choix est presque un
animal; voilà pourquoi elle est chaste, quoique nue. Toutes [l]es Vénus
exposées au Salon sont indécentes, odieusement lubriques . . .' ([1892–
1903] 1974: 140) ['To make something new one must return to the original

Figure 6 Paul Gauguin, *The Spirit of the Dead Keeps Watch (manau tupapau)* (1892) oil on canvas, 73 × 92 cm

sources, to the childhood of humanity. The Eve of my choice is almost an animal; that is why, even though she is naked, she is chaste. All the Venuses of western art are indecent, odiously lewd . . .']. Similarly, exploring 'le civilisé et le barbare en présence' ([1892–1903] 1974: 265), Gauguin will compare Maori elegance favourably with European triviality ([1892–1903] 1974: 120) and, above all, will attempt to transpose to his paintings a sense of the spiritual beliefs of the natives whose bodies he so lavishly represents. His comments on *Manau tupapau* (*The Spirit of the Dead Keeps Watch*, figure 6) of 1892 are pertinent in this respect, in particular his justification for the inclusion of the stiff little figure in black in the left corner of his canvas as a visual equivalent to the primitive Maori reasoning underlying fear of death: 'Enfin, pour terminer, je fais le revenant tout simplement, une petite bonne femme; parce que la jeune fille, ne connaissant pas les théâtres de spirites français, ne peut faire autrement que de voir lié à l'esprit du mort le mort lui-même, c'est-à-dire, une personne comme elle' ([1892–1903] 1974: 89) ['Finally, to sum up, I paint in the ghost quite simply as a little old woman; because the young girl, never having seen the ghosts that appear in French theatre, can only see death in the form of the dead person, that is, as somebody like herself']. A similar combination of ethnographic and artistic sensibility is evident in Gauguin's description in his notes drawn up in 1903 of his eerie encounters with the remains of barbarian culture in the wild hinterlands of Tahiti and the Marquesas ([1892–1903] 1974: 256–8). Like the Segalen of *Les Immémoriaux* ([1907] 1982), published only four years after Gauguin's death (and reproducing some of Gauguin's Tahitian drawings as illustrations), and Lévi-Strauss's memoirs of South American tribes in *Tristes Tropiques*, Gauguin's last writings offer a poignant record of his awareness of the fragility of the native way of life in the face of western colonisation ([1892–1903] 1974: 324–6).

However, it is as artist/semiologist rather than as ethnologist that Gauguin best illustrates the workings of the 'homme des ressemblances sauvages', and nowhere more so than in that area of central concern to the painter, colour. For colour in painting works not only as *ressemblance sauvage* but also lends itself to a reversible semiology in which qualities can become liberated from their objects, and signs linked with other signs regardless of their attachment to phenomena in the real world. In the same way then that Gautier recognises that the imaginary pink horse in Delacroix's painting *The Justice of Trajan* can be discovered in the real landscape of contemporary Spain, thus transforming the latter's visual significance, so Gauguin, in the resplendent light and corresponding shade of the Tahitian landscape, is free to perceive horses in a range of different hues (see *The White Horse*, figure 7) which, like 'le cheval violet de Delacroix' ([1892–1903] 1974: 139), need have no verisimilar relation to their colour as conventionally construed – the pink perceived by Gautier's becoming in Gauguin's eyes the even more radical and *Fauve*-like violet.[1] So, continuing the logic of folly as adumbrated by Foucault, Gauguin is free to admire in Cézanne 'Les blancs [qui] sont bleus et les bleus [qui] sont blancs' ([1892–1903] 1974: 305) or Marquisian art which shows 'Toujours la même chose et cependant jamais la même chose' ([1892–1903] 1974: 324). The 'Mensonge de la vérité' ([1892–1903] 1974: 176–82) ['lie that is the truth'] – this is Gauguin's term, not, as one might expect, Foucault's – is produced whenever colour appears 'déterminée par son charme propre, indéterminée en tant que désignation d'objets perçus dans la nature' ([1892–1903] 1974: 178), ['determined by its own qualities, rather than by the objects in nature that it designates'] and especially when the sign of the same is somehow elevated to the intensity of difference: 'mettre un vert plus vert que celui de la nature' ([1892–1903] 1974: 177). Colour thus becomes a language – 'La couleur! cette langue si profonde, si mystérieuse, langue de rêve'

Figure 7 Paul Gauguin, *The White Horse* (1898) oil on canvas, 140.5 × 92 cm

([1892–1903] 1974: 159) – uniquely susceptible to expressing savage cultures and in the process becomes correspondingly an instrument in the rediscovery of the 'wild' in western European culture – as in the *Fauves* ('Wild Beasts') colourist school of painting whose development in the first decade of the twentieth century was directly tributary to Gauguin.

It is in a quest to adapt another aspect of native Tahitian culture to his creative project as neo-primitive artist – that of wood carving – that Gauguin experiences a moment of crisis that crystallises a number of the paradoxes inherent in his position as a 'civilised' westerner in Polynesia. Since the experience is complex, the passage describing it will be cited in full:

J'ai un ami naturel, venu près de moi chaque jour naturellement, sans intérêt. Mes images coloriées, mes travaux dans le bois l'ont surpris et mes réponses à ses questions l'ont instruit. Il n'y a pas de jour quand je travaille où il ne vienne me regarder. Un jour que lui confiant mes outils je lui demandais d'essayer une sculpture, il me regarde bien étonné et me dit simplement avec sincérité que je n'étais pas comme les autres hommes et, le premier peut-être dans la société, il me dit que j'étais utile aux autres. Enfant! Il faut l'être, pour penser qu'un artiste est quelque chose d'utile.

Ce jeune homme était parfaitement beau et nous fûmes très amis. Quelquefois le soir, quand je me reposais de ma journée, il me faisait des questions de jeune sauvage voulant savoir bien des choses de l'amour en Europe, questions qui souvent m'embarrassaient.

Un jour je voulais avoir, pour sculpter, un arbre de bois rose, morceau assez important et qui ne fût pas creux.

– Il faut pour cela, me dit-il, aller dans la montagne à certain endroit où je connais plusieurs beaux arbres qui pourraient te satisfaire. Si tu veux je t'y mènerai et nous le rapporterons tous deux.

Nous partîmes de bon matin. [. . .]

Nous allions tous deux nus avec le linge à la ceinture et la hache à la main, traversant maintes fois la rivière pour reprendre un bout de sentier que mon compagnon connaissait comme par l'odorat, si peu visible, si ombragé. Le silence complet, seul le bruit de l'eau gémissant sur le rocher, monotone comme le silence. Et nous étions bien deux, deux amis, lui tout jeune homme et moi presque un vieillard, de corps et d'âme, de vices de civilisation, d'illusions perdues. Son corps souple d'animal avait de gracieuses formes, il marchait devant moi sans sexe.*

De toute cette jeunesse, de cette parfaite harmonie avec la nature qui nous entourait il se dégageait une beauté, un parfum (*noa noa*) qui enchantaient mon âme d'artiste. De cette amitié si bien cimentée par attraction mutuelle du simple au composé, l'amour en moi prenait éclosion.

Et nous étions seulement tous deux.

J'eus comme un pressentiment de crime, le désir d'inconnu, le réveil du mal. Puis la lassitude du rôle de mâle qui doit toujours être fort, protecteur; de lourdes épaules à supporter. Etre une minute l'être faible qui aime et obéit.

Je m'approchai, sans peur des lois, le trouble aux tempes.

Le sentier était fini, il fallait traverser la rivière; mon compagnon se détournait en ce moment, me présentant sa poitrine.

L'androgyne avait disparu: ce fut bien un jeune homme; ses yeux innocents présentaient l'aspect de la limpidité des eaux. Le calme soudain rentra dans mon âme et cette fois je goûtai délicieusement la fraîcheur du ruisseau, m'y trempant avec délices.

– *Toe toe* ('c'est froid'), me dit-il.

– Oh! Non, répondis-je, et cette négation, répondant à mon désir antérieur, s'enfonça comme un écho dans la montagne, avec âpreté.

Je m'enfonçai vivement dans le taillis devenu de plus en plus sauvage; l'enfant continuait sa route, toujours l'œil limpide. Il n'avait rien compris; moi seul portais le fardeau d'une mauvaise pensée, toute une civilisation m'avait devancé dans le mal et m'avait éduqué.

Nous arrivions au but. [. . .]

Plusieurs arbres (bois de rose) étendaient là leurs immenses ramages. Tous deux, sauvages, nous attaquâmes à la hache un magnifique arbre qu'il fallut détruire pour avoir une branche convenable à mes désirs. Je frappai avec rage et les mains ensanglantées je coupais avec le plaisir d'une brutalité assouvie, d'une destruction de je ne sais quoi.

Avec la cadence du bruit de la hache, je chantais:

Coupe par le pied la forêt tout entière (des désirs)
Coupe en toi l'amour de toi-même comme avec la main en automne
on couperait le Lotus.

Bien détruit en effet tout mon vieux stock de civilisé. Je revins tranquille, me sentant désormais un autre homme, un Maori. Tous deux nous portions gaiement notre lourd fardeau, et je pus encore admirer devant moi les formes gracieuses de mon jeune ami, et cela tranquille, formes robustes comme l'arbre que nous portions. L'arbre sentait la rose, *noa noa.*

Nous étions l'après-midi de retour, fatigués. Il me dit:

– Tu es content?

– Oui; et dans moi je redis: Oui. J'étais décidément tranquille désormais.

Je n'ai pas donné un seul coup de ciseau dans ce morceau de bois sans avoir des souvenirs d'une douce quiétude, d'un parfum, d'une victoire et d'un rajeunissement.

[*The following notes by Gauguin appear in the margin of his text.]

1. Le côté androgyne du sauvage, le peu de différence de sexe chez les animaux.

2. La pureté qu'entraine la vue du nu et les mœurs faciles entre les deux sexes.

L'inconnu du vice chez des sauvages.

Désir d'être un instant faible, femme. ([1892–1903] 1974: 111–15)

[I have a native friend who comes to see me every day, casually, without any particular reason. My coloured images and wood carvings interested him and he seems to benefit from my answers to his questions. There is hardly a day passes without him coming to watch me work. One day, handing him my tools, I ask him to start a sculpture; surprised, he looks at me and says simply and sincerely that I was not like other men; he is the first in this native society to tell me that I am useful to others. Child that he is! You'd have to be to think that an artist could be useful.

This young man was perfectly good-looking and we were friends. Sometimes in the evening when I was resting after the day's work, he would ask the sort of questions a young native would ask about love in Europe, questions which often embarrassed me.

One day, I was looking for a certain kind of rose-wood to sculpt, a piece that was quite big and not hollow.

– For that, he told me, you'd have to go up the mountain to a certain place that I know where there are several fine trees that would suit your purpose. If you like, I'll come with you and we can carry the timber back together.

We set off early one morning. (. . .)

We were both making our way up, naked except for a cloth around our loins, each carrying an axe, criss-crossing the stream to follow what remained of the path that my companion seemed to sniff out by smell, it was so overgrown and shaded. The silence was complete except for the water babbling over the rocks, quietly monotonous. And there were just the two of us, two friends, he a young man and me ageing, in body, in soul, in civilisation's vices and in lost illusions. His sinuous animal body was gracefully formed, seeming androgynous as he walked along before me.

All this youth and this perfect harmony with nature which surrounded us exuded a beauty, a perfume (*noa noa*) which enchanted my artist's soul. And this friendship, cemented by the mutual attraction of the simple and the sophisticated, burgeoned in me into love.

And there were just the two of us.

I felt a premonition of crime, of a desire for the unknown, the awakening of evil. And then the tedium of the male's role, always being the strong one, the protective one, with heavy responsibilities to shoulder. Oh to be just for a minute the weaker one who loves and obeys.

I approached the boy, fearless of any law, my head pounding.

The path came to an abrupt end, we had to cross the stream; my companion turned at this moment, to face me.

The androgyne had disappeared: he was just a young man; his innocent eyes reflected the limpid clarity of the water. Calm suddenly returned to my soul and this time I really enjoyed the coolness of the stream, plunging into it with delight.

– *Toe toe* ('it's cold'), he said.

– Oh no! I replied, and this negation, responding to the desire I had just felt, re-echoed through the mountain, with bitterness.

I plunged vigorously into the thicket which was getting more and more dense; the boy continued on his way, still clear-eyed, having understood nothing; it was only I who carried the burden of a wicked thought, a whole civilisation before me had marched along the path of evil and had educated me.

We arrived at our goal. (. . .)

Several rose-wood trees extended their immense branches. Like two savages, we attacked a magnificent tree with our axes; we had to cut it down to get the sort of branch I was looking for. I struck with rage and bloodied hands, chopping with the pleasure of brutality appeased, with the pleasure of destroying I know not what.

Following the rhythm of the axe-strokes, I sang:
Cut the whole forest down to the roots (of desire)
Cut from yourself the love of yourself just as in Autumn
one cuts the Lotus.

Thoroughly destroyed indeed was my old stock of civilisation. Now I was calm, feeling myself to be another man, a Maori. Both of us gaily carried back our heavy load, and I could still admire the graceful form of my young friend in front of me, calmly, the form as strong as the tree we were carrying. The tree smelt of roses, *noa noa.*

On the afternoon of our return, we were both tired. He asked me:
– Are you happy?
– Yes, I replied, saying to myself: Yes I was definitely content from now on.

I have not given one stroke of the chisel to this piece of wood without having memories of quiet calm, of perfume, of victory and of rejuvenation.
1. The androgynous side of the native, the lack of differentiation between the sexes in animals.
2. The purity that the sight of nudity brings and the easy commerce between the sexes.
The fact that the natives seem to have no concept of vice.
The desire for once to be the weaker one, to be a woman.]

The passage begins with the recounting of a male friendship in which a good-looking young native questions Gauguin in relation to both western art and western sexual practices, the latter giving rise to some embarrassment in Gauguin. The native boy agrees to lead the artist to a place in the mountains in which he can find the rosewood he needs for his sculpture. They set off together, axe in hand, naked except for a loincloth. On the trip Gauguin becomes increasingly aware of the androgynous, animal beauty of the boy's body which he follows through the forest paths. From the beginning of his stay in Tahiti, Gauguin – as artist and heterosexual lover – had been struck by the androgynous quality of native Maori women, with their broad shoulders and narrow hips (1974: 325). In drawings such as *Man with an Axe* (1893–4, figure 8) it is sometimes difficult, at first glance at least, to distinguish male from female forms. This ambiguity becomes further apparent to Gauguin in this passage as he marches through the wood behind the glistening male body which, in a moment of perfect harmony with the wild environment (one expressed as a perfume – *noa noa* – that is for Gauguin the symbol of the fragrant natural beauty of Tahiti and to which he refers later in the title, *Noa Noa*, of his account of his life in Tahiti), stimulates (homo-)sexual desire. This places Gauguin

Figure 8 Paul Gauguin, *Man with an Axe* (1893–4) ink and gouache on paper,
39 × 28 cm

in a quandary, obliging him to balance conflicting impulses of desire and guilt: desire for the unknown, desire for the androgynous native body, desire to relinquish the heavy responsibilities of masculinity and become feminine and submissive for a moment, awareness of the naturalness of sexual relations in Tahiti and the innocence of erotic impulses. Against this must be set an intense feeling of guilt, a fear of perpetrating an act that could be construed as criminal, a sense of evil. The desiring impulses seem about to get the upper hand when the native boy, on approaching a stream, suddenly turns towards Gauguin, the ambiguity of his sexuality disappearing as he gazes with innocent eyes at the artist. The plunge into the cold waters of the stream momentarily releases the tension of the experience, but as the continuing narrative makes clear, the profound ambiguity of Gauguin's state is not to be so easily resolved. Gauguin's frustration – both real (that is, sexual) and symbolic (the western Phallus or Law has deprived him of new pleasure and fulfilment) – is violently exorcised on the rosewood tree which with bloodied hands and with the boy's aid he fells, releasing again in the process the sweet perfume, *noa noa*, one of whose connotations must by now include sexual desire. But his frustration is at the same time continued in the bitter *double entendres* of his ensuing dialogues with the boy. Finally, the images of desire are transferred from the body of the young man to the potential of the wood as a medium of sculpture, the *civilisé/sauvage* polarity being re-adjusted in a number of ways in an attempt, never fully resolved, to balance the bundle of conflicting impulses – desire/guilt, male/female, artist/lover, master/pupil – that make up Gaugin's identity at this moment.[2] Such tensions are in turn expressed in Gaugin's paintings, such as *Three Tahitians* (1899, figure 9) in which the object of possible homosexual desire in the form of a young male viewed from behind is juxtaposed with images of heterosexual love in the form of two Tahitian women.

The passage just cited thus shows how the discovery of the other in the outside world can precipitate a deep questioning of the inner world, undermining moral, social and sexual values, and leading to a crisis of identity in which the stabilising signs of the inherited culture are tested to the extreme by the alternative system proposed by the foreign environment. Values begin to detach themselves from the impulses or behaviour patterns to which a strong convention normally succeeds in rooting them, and signs begin to float free of their objects, becoming available for re-attachment in new and unanticipated ways. Another lesson the passage from Gauguin proposes, as does of course, in a more spectacular way, his *œuvre* as painter, is that what is experienced as culture shock, moral or sexual confusion or momentary madness can be recuperated by the travel writer or artist and

Figure 9 Paul Gauguin, *Three Tahitians* (1899) oil on canvas, 73 × 94 cm

reintegrated into new patterns of meaning able to challenge and reward the other that is their future reader or viewer.[3]

To no nineteenth-century travel writer is this view more applicable than to Gérard de Nerval who exemplifies perfectly the predicament of the Romantic writer striving to relate the *analogical* to the *symbolic* and to adapt reality or experience to the demands of the imagination. While the twelve sonnets that constitute *Les Chimères* (1854) give the most concentrated expression in Nerval's writing to the collision of analogical and symbolic, archetypal and autobiographical, *Le Voyage en Orient* ([1851] 1980) provides a more discursive account of what is at stake in the interaction of experience and imagination, though even here the writing process is as much a symptom as a record of the problematic it states. The problem with the travel journal as handled by Nerval is that, despite claims to the contrary – 'ayant l'usage', he says, 'de ne parler que de ce que j'ai pu voir moi-même' ([1851] 1980: II, 356 ['being used only to talking about what I have seen with my own eyes']) – it is never really clear what is the status of any given element, whether relating to the writer, his itinerary, his destinations or the people encountered. As Michel Jeanneret puts it in his introduction to Nerval's *Voyage en Orient*: 'quel est le statut du référent: vécu ou lu? immédiat ou textuel?' ([1851] 1980: 22–3).

The problem is exacerbated in that, perhaps more than any other writer studied in this book, Nerval writes in the light of previous textual responses, real or imaginary, to the East and to the Other. As Gautier already perceptively remarked in 1860, recalling a process very similar to the one he himself experienced twenty years before, as we just saw, on the battlements of the Alcazar in Toledo:

Le pays ne lui apparaît pas avec une nouveauté absolue; il lui revient comme un souvenir d'existence antérieure, comme un de ces rêves oubliés que ravive la rencontre inattendue de l'objet dans la réalité. Les récits des historiens et des voyageurs, les tableaux, les gravures composent au fond de l'âme une sorte de géographie chimérique que contrarie souvent la véritable, et c'est là un des désenchantements du touriste. Il voit crouler, une à une devant lui des villes merveilleuses qu'il s'était créées avec la libre et riche architecture de l'imagination. Mais ici, ce n'est pas le cas; il n'y a pas de déception; la fantastique perspective existe et satisfait à toutes les exigences du mirage. ([1860] 1877: 180–1)

[The country does not appear to him as entirely new: it comes back to him like a memory of a previous existence, like one of those forgotten dreams that is brought alive by an unexpected encounter with an object in reality. Historians' and travellers' accounts, paintings, engravings, all combine to establish deep in the soul a kind of imaginary geography which reality often contradicts; and therein lies a cause of disappointment to the tourist. He sees collapse one by one in front of him the magical cities that he had built up for himself using the rich and varied architecture of the imagination. But this is not the case here; there is no disappointment; the fantastic perspective exists and satisfies all the requirements of a mirage.]

But if, as Gautier claims for Nerval, the fantastic is made real in *Le Voyage en Orient*, it is because the symbolic as text often precedes place or person as real, the latter being adapted to fulfil an analogical function in relation to the former, rather than the other way round. For example, the itinerary of Nerval's journey is itself partly fictive (Nerval never visited Cythera and the excursion to Vienna was part of another trip) and the places, encounters and engagements recounted are often described in terms borrowed or derived from other sources. – Nerval's plagiarism is of course notorious: much of his description of Cairo and its modern inhabitants was lifted from Edward William Lane's *Account of the Manners and Customs of the Modern Egyptians* (1836). But Nerval's text's relation with its intertexts is both complex and multifunctional. The incorporation of the symbolic in the form of more or less borrowed texts – whether the legend of Adoniram, the history of

Solomon, or the *Histoire du Calife Hakem* – functions, apart from the intrinsic interest of the tales, to supplement gaps both in Nerval's literal and spiritual itinerary and in his role as narrator/hero of the travel story.

So, for example, the Biblical texts and stories adapted by Nerval in *Le Voyage en Orient* function in part to bolster the presence, real and symbolic, of Palestine itself, only part of which was actually visited by Nerval who missed out Jérusalem, and spent far more time in Constantinople and Egypt than in the Holy Lands (see Nerval, [1851] 1980). Nerval's negative itinerary in relation to the preceding travel journal intertexts such as those of Chateaubriand (1811) and Lamartine (1835) was also an unconscious strategy aimed at differentiating his version of the East from that of his Romantic predecessors (see Butor, 1974: 24–6). For Nerval, whether by omission or inclusion, geography exists as much to confirm what has already been described or imagined as to provide new experience: it must be able to work on a mythical or archetypal as much as on a real level; Jean-Pierre Richard's development of Gautier's concept of 'géographie' *chimérique* in his essay 'Géographie magique de Nerval' (1955) is illuminating in this context. Furthermore, the symbolic is itself never open to immediate or standard interpretation by Nerval in whose writing the Biblical tradition is modified and subverted by other esoteric or heterodox interpretations involving Islamic, masonic and other sources.

The problem is compounded by a certain symbolic slippage, in which the sign and its interpreting consciousness are both essentially mobile, with the result that meaning or satisfaction risk being infinitely deferred. As Nerval poignantly observes: 'En Afrique on rêve l'Inde, comme en Europe on rêve l'Afrique: l'idéal rayonne toujours au-delà de notre horizon actuel' ([1851] 1980: I, 262) ['In Africa one dreams of India just as in Europe one dreams of Africa; the ideal always beckons to us from beyond the horizon we have in front of us']. In attempting to return to the source of the self (emotional, religious, literary) by returning to sources of European culture in the Middle East, he finds that the Origin he sought in the Orient is also subject to deferral – or does not meet his expectations. As he wrote to Gautier: 'Moi j'ai déjà perdu, royaume à royaume, et province à province, la plus belle moitié de l'univers, et bientôt je ne vais plus savoir où réfugier mes rêves' (August 1843: [1851] 1980: 30) ['I have already lost, kingdom by kingdom, province by province, half of the universe; soon I won't know any longer where to find a safe refuge for my dreams']. A result of this is the uneasy mixture in Nerval's *Le Voyage en Orient* of personal journal and fiction. Nerval's text strives to maintain a subjective, first-person angle on experience but, in doing so, is unable in itself to do justice to the huge symbolic potential of the East as the writer imagines it. Unlike Gautier, Nerval does not, using artistic paradigms as a criterion of authenticity or truth, opt for a primarily aesthetic approach to the reality of the other. His profoundly voluptuous desire to identify with the objects and individuals that constitute the oriental other lead him on the contrary to inscribe himself as hero in his own narrative, even though his comic inadequacy in such a quest is clearly evidenced in his text, in which his experiences (marriages and other models of integration) mostly end in disaster. Hence the recourse to legends with whose heroes (Hakem, Adoniram) Nerval can identify. Fiction and fantasy thus undermine and subvert the supposedly objective truth of the travel journal. So like that of Van Gogh, Nerval's madness, fatal in both its nature and its outcome, is as described by Foucault, partly a result of mistaking or substituting the real for the imaginary, or of conflating the analogical and the symbolic.

This is of course a fundamental conundrum of autobiographical literature, of which the travel journal is just one type of manifestation. Whereas in a work of poetry or fiction, the conflation of personal and mythological provides a source of inspiration as inexhaustible as it is legitimate, in life, or in the autobiographic journal, it creates an untenable situation. The particular originality of Nerval is to risk exploring further than any other French travel writer of the Romantic period the possibility of conflating such opposing tendencies. In the process however he inevitably undermines what is at stake in the conventional travel journal and brings into the foreground the tension between the mythical and the scientific that has in fact always haunted the travel writing form from the beginning of its European inception in the sixteenth century (see Affergan, 1987a). The particular acuteness of Nerval's project in this respect is the degree to which he is prepared to identify with the other, to enter into and identify with difference to the extent that he becomes different from himself and thus opens up a chasm that it became increasingly difficult for him thereafter to bridge. As Jeanneret succinctly summarises it: 'Dissémination dans l'espace, vaporisation du moi, abolition de la différence . . . On sent bien que, derrière sa façade sereine, le récit tout entier – et pas seulement les deux légendes – reconstitue les bribes d'une aventure inquiétante, une aventure toute personnelle où les évidences, soudain, se trouvent mises en question: cet ébranlement des certitudes, peut-être, que l'on est convenu d'appeler la folie' (Nerval [1851] 1980: 26) ['Dissemination in space, vaporisation of the self, abolition of difference . . . One really senses that, behind its serene façade, the entire story – and not just the two legends – brings together the remnants of a disturbing and deeply personal adventure in which appearances are suddenly brought into question, giving rise to an unhinging of certitudes that often passes for madness'].

In many ways, Nicolas Bouvier's travel writing constitutes a reformulation in twentieth-century terms of the Nervalian experience. This is because for Bouvier, as for Nerval, the world exists to be reformulated through writing, just as extensive travel across it exists to make and unmake the subject. What Bouvier adds is perhaps a more fully self-conscious and systematically articulated account of these processes, as the title of his first major book – *L'Usage du monde* (1963) – would seem to confirm. For following in the footsteps (or rather tyre-tracks) of other notable Swiss travel writers such as Ella Maillart,[4] Bouvier, anticipating the Hippies of the 1960s, sees the Afghan trail as a necessary rite of passage to a modern reconstructed individual identity. Like the battered Fiat which takes Bouvier and his artist friend Thierry Vernet across the deserts of Iran and central Asia, the individual subject breaks down under the stresses of travel, is stripped down and reassembled (often exploiting the skills in *bricolage* of a range of different cultures and techniques), the motor at the end of the trip not being quite the same as that which started out from Belgrade eighteen months before. As Bouvier says in his *avant-propos*: 'Un voyage se passe de motifs. Il ne tarde pas à prouver qu'il se suffit à lui-même. On croit qu'on va faire un voyage, mais bientôt c'est le voyage qui vous fait, ou vous défait' ([1963] 1992: 12) ['A trip doesn't need motivations. It doesn't take long to prove that it is sufficient unto itself. One thinks one is going to make a trip, but soon it is the trip that is making, or unmaking, you']. The making and unmaking of the self thus becomes the *motive* of travel writing as Bouvier sees it, and is, as Ella Maillart's book title suggests, a cruel undertaking precisely in the light of the major issue at stake: the integrity (in both senses of the word) of the individual personality.

On the whole, Bouvier's experience as recounted in *L'Usage du monde* is a positive one, no doubt in part owing to the writer's youth and naivety and the fact that he was travelling with a young and stalwart compatriot. Thus the spirit of adventure and the resilience of youthful companionship counteract the potential for existential crisis. So nights spent drowsing or drinking tea under the desert stars or driving, shirt-sleeves rolled, along sweltering sandy tracks, give rise to an elation that is sufficient to counter more desperate moments, such as the losing of several weeks of travel journal and breakdowns in the middle of nowhere. Indeed, the presence of physical and psychological risk is an essential part of the learning experience and satisfaction derived from the rite of passage, the rare instants of elation providing a deeper knowledge of the essence of being than all the

frameworks that conventionally structure an individual identity: 'Finalement, ce qui constitue l'ossature de l'existence, ce n'est ni la famille, ni
la carrière, ni ce que d'autres diront ou penseront de vous, mais quelques
instants de cette nature, soulevés par une lévitation plus sereine encore
que celle de l'amour, et que la vie nous distribue avec une parcimonie à la
mesure de notre faible cœur' ([1963] 1992: 104) ['In the end, what provides
the framework for our existence is neither family, career nor what others
will say or think of you, but certain instants of this kind, raised to our attention by a levitation serener even than that provided by love, and that life
doles out to us with a parsimony commensurate with the feebleness of our
hearts'].

The euphoric buoyancy provided by moments of epiphany in *L'Usage
du monde* is however superseded by a much more sombre experience of
levitation in Bouvier's later sequel to his first Indian trip as recorded in the
Celanese journal *Le Poisson-Scorpion* ([1982] 1991). The unstated aim of this
novel seems to be to explore the 'point zéro de l'existence' ([1982] 1991: 124)
by asking the question: what happens to the individual identity when the self
is emptied to the very bottom, when in solitude, in penury, in a bewitched
island, in an alien culture, all ties – family, sexual, affectionate – are cut
with the distant home base? What then fills the mental or psychological
void? What happens to the *poisson-scorpion* that is the central image of
the book and which may be taken as a plausible metaphor for human
identity? As a many-segmented fish, the *poisson-scorpion* is described by
Michaux on his travels where he saw one in the tiny aquarium at Madras:
'Le *poisson-scorpion* est un poisson pour autant que dix petits parasols unis
à un petit corps peuvent former un poisson, aussi est-il infiniment plus
embarrassé que n'importe quel poisson chinois' (Michaux, [1933] 1967: 98)
['The *scorpion-fish* is a fish inasmuch as ten little parasols attached to a short
body can form a fish; because of this it is infinitely more ill at ease than
any kind of Chinese fish']. Michaux's unconscious intertext provides an
account of the scorpion fish that lends itself as a token for the personality.
It appears to be without any backbone or *ossature* and is susceptible to
deconstruction as each of its ten or so longitudinally articulated segments
become separated – as in a horse-tail fern – leaving only a headless tail or a
tail-less head. In Bouvier's novel the fish becomes doubly symbolic of the
author as it is his birth sign, and he is posted a replica of it in the form of
a tiny gold charm as a souvenir from his former girlfriend on ending her
relationship with him and announcing her marriage to another. Bouvier
receives the same day a letter from his parents in which they express their
complete misunderstanding of his life in Ceylon. The fish thus symbolises

the remains of the narrator's past – personality, family, lover – and his first impulse is to divest himself of it by presenting it to his Cingalese landlord who hangs it around the chubby neck of his lethargic three-year-old son. This symbolic act is followed by a gradual but ineluctable mental breakdown that reaches its term in the following passage:

Si c'était la solitude que j'étais venu chercher ici, j'avais bien choisi mon Ile. A mesure que je perdais pied, j'avais appris à l'aménager en astiquant ma mémoire. J'avais dans la tête assez de lieux, d'instants, de visages pour me tenir compagnie, meubler le miroir de la mer et m'alléger par leur présence fictive du poids de la journée. Cette nuit-là, je m'aperçus avec une panique indicible que mon cinéma ne fonctionnait plus. Presque personne au rendez-vous, ou alors des ombres floues, écornées, plaintives. Les voix et les odeurs s'étaient fait la paire. Quelque chose au fil de la journée les avait mises à sac pendant que je m'échinais. Mon magot s'évaporait en douce. Ma seule fortune décampait et derrière cette débandade, je voyais venir le moment où il ne resterait rien que des peurs, plus même de vrai chagrin. J'avais beau tisonner quelques anciennes défaites, ça ne bougeait plus. C'est sans doute cet appétit de chagrin qui fait la jeunesse parce que tout d'un coup je me sentais bien vieux et perdu dans l'énorme beauté de cette plage, pauvre petit lettreux baisé par les Tropiques.

Il n'y a pas ici d'alliances solides et rien ne tient vraiment à nous. Je le savais. La dentelle sombre des cocotiers qui bougeaient à peine contre la nuit plus sombre encore venait justement me le rappeler. Pour le cas où j'aurais oublié.

On ne voyage pas sans connaître ces instants où ce dont on s'était fait fort se défile et vous trahit comme dans un cauchemar. Derrière ce dénuement terrifiant, au-delà de ce point zéro de l'existence et du bout de la route il doit encore y avoir quelque chose. Quelque chose de pas ordinaire, un vrai Koh-i-Nor c'est certain pour être à ce point gardé et défendu. Peut-être cette allégresse originelle que nous avons connue, perdue, retrouvée par instants, mais toujours cherchée à tâtons dans le colin-maillard de nos vies. (Bouvier, [1982] 1991, 123–4)

[If it was solitude that I came to find here, I had chosen my Island well. As I gradually lost my footing, I had learnt to fit out my memory by polishing it. I had in my head enough places, moments, faces to keep me company, to furnish the mirroring sea and lighten by their imaginary presence the weight of the day. But that night I realised in a moment of inexpressible panic that my inner cinema wasn't functioning any longer. There was nobody there, or only a few faint, tatty and plaintive shadows. Voices and smells had evaporated. Something during the day had demolished them while I was wearing myself out. My money was quietly running out. My only remaining fortune was fast disappearing and beyond this flight I saw approaching the moment when nothing would remain except fear, not even real grief. In vain had I tried to warm over a few defeats, it didn't work any more. There is no doubt that an appetite for grief is a sign of youth because suddenly I felt very old and lost in the enormous beauty of this beach, a poor little man of letters kissed by the Tropics.

There are not really any solid alliances on earth, and nothing really depends on us. I knew this. The sombre lacework of the palm trees, scarcely moving against the deeper shadows of the night, had just reminded me of that. In case I had forgotten.

You can't travel without experiencing those moments when everything you had prided yourself on disappears and betrays you as in a nightmare. Behind this terrifying destitution, beyond the point zero of existence, at the end of the line, there must be something. Something out of the ordinary, a real Koh-i-Nor it must be if it was being so carefully guarded and protected. Perhaps it is that first elation that we used to have, then lost, then rediscovered from time to time, but that we always tentatively sought in the game of blind man's buff that is our lives.]

It seems to be a recurrent, though no doubt unconscious, motive that leads Bouvier, like Gauguin, to search for the other on an island. In French, the *île/il* play on words suggests that the *je* seeks to escape into the *autre* by converting to the third person or *il*, an ambivalence which, according to Buddha as cited by Michaux, is deeply conducive to self-knowledge: *Tenez-vous bien dans votre île à vous* ([1933] 1967: 233) [*Stick Fast to your own island*]. Bouvier will later seek out this effect in both Japan and Aran (see 1989 and 1990). In any case, the palm-fringed shore, oppressive heat and bewitched atmosphere of Ceylon more than do the trick, leaving one evening the 'pauvre petit lettreux baisé par les Tropiques' clutching at the last straws of his identity. Of memory, which constitutes the last bastion of self-recognition, only a few tatters remain, and as the writer's internal cinema flickers to a standstill, the blank screen which he had all along been seeking begins to absorb him. What lies beyond the nightmare realisation of essential void at the heart of the self, what reward beckons at the end of the ascetic journey that is the travel project? Like Mallarmé, Bouvier, in the face of the 'grande déroute vespérale' ([1982] 1991: 122) ['evening's great rout'], wonders how ultimate despair can be transformed into a diamond, the priceless Indian Koh-i-Nor, the jewel in the writer's fictive crown.

In the event, the reward takes the form of a recovery of the self, though transformed, through a series of hallucinatory experiences in which, in an *opéra-bouffe* scenario worthy of Nerval or Gautier's ironic romanticism, the other emerges in the form of Père Alvaro, from the steps of a baroque church, to give an astutely hilarious account of his life as a Catholic priest in India and lessons of wisdom to his bemused listener: 'J'ai cru si longtemps en Dieu, c'est bien son tour de croire en moi . . .'; 'moins on en amène dans l'Ile, moins elle vous prend', etc. ([1982] 1991: 126, 127). The priest then proceeds to levitate in front of the narrator: 'La brise gonflait sa soutane et il flottait maintenant une bonne coudée au-dessus de la dernière marche, l'axe du corps oscillant légèrement sur cette noire corolle, ses bottines de comédie se balançant dans le vide. Il fixait la mer en fumant un de ses infects cigares sans se préoccuper le moins du monde de cette lévitation, d'ailleurs modeste' ([1982] 1991: 128) ['The breeze was swelling his cassock as he floated a good foot above the last step, the axis of his body oscillating slightly around the black corolla of his surplice, his comedian's boots swaying in the void. He gazed at the sea, smoking one of his filthy cigars, without showing the least concern about this levitation, which was in any case only modest']. What then emerges from the depths of the narrator's unconscious is the image of the Father, the Phallus, the Law, those mythic structures that even in an extreme state of 'dénuement terrifiant' return to shore up the western mind in crisis. Alvaro, as a priest, is a *father* in both senses of the word, representing spiritual and emotional love, an origin and a goal, the source of moral guilt and the possibility of expiation ([1982] 1991: 132). For Bouvier, love always implies a certain levitation, as we saw in *L'Usage du monde* cited above ([1963] 1992: 104), and earlier in *Le Poisson-Scorpion* where he writes in a passage offering anticipatory hints of the significance of the Padre Alvaro hallucination: 'Pourquoi dans toutes nos langues occidentales dit-on "tomber amoureux"? Monter serait plus juste. L'amour est ascensionnel comme la prière. Ascensionnel et éperdu' ([1982] 1991: 83) ['Why do we say in all western languages "fall in love"? Rise would be more appropriate. Love, like prayer, is ascensional. Ascensional and frantic']. In psychoanalytical terms, the emergence of Padre Alvaro represents an experience of the uncanny, the return of a previously unknown or only half or obscurely known reality. The narrator will later discover that a real Padre Alvaro did indeed live for a while and then die in Ceylon and that, as with Bouvier himself, the priest 'lui-même [. . .] avait choisi [. . .] de s'exiler dans l'Ile pour une expiation à laquelle personne ne le poussait' ([1982] 1991: 134) ['himself (. . .) had chosen (. . .) to go into exile on the Island to expiate a sin for which no-one had condemned him']. Furthermore, during his chequered and colourful career in India, Father Alvaro had distinguished himself as a linguist and an anthropologist, bringing back to his religious community a grammar of South Dekkan, a little-known Indian tribe among whom he lived for a year with a native woman. So it is through an extraordinary hallucinatory experience of 'ressemblances sauvages' that the narrator of *Le Poisson-Scorpion* is able to reconstruct the components of his identity as person and creative agent, conjuring signs and objects, and the two components, *je* and *autre*, that make up his identity, until a new equilibrium is finally established between them: 'J'aurais voulu ce matin-là qu'une main étrangère me ferme les paupières. J'étais inexplicablement allégé et le bonheur se partage. J'étais seul, je les fermai donc moi-même.

"Comment vais-je? Bien, merci et moi?"' ([1982] 1991: 132) ['I would like to have had a stranger close my eyes that morning. I had inexplicably calmed down and happiness should be shared. But since I was alone, I closed my own eyes. "How was I? Very well, thank you, and how about me?"'].

The heroism of Bouvier's late Romantic project of re-discovering an essential part of himself through further and deeper travel into the real seems of another age in comparison to the post-modern world in which the virtual is increasingly establishing itself as the stuff both of everyday existence and of personal identity. In the light of this, Baudrillard's post-modern take in *Amérique* on the construction of identity provides a striking contrast. For, as we saw in Chapter 1, identity in the capitalist, post-industrial, global world is seen by Baudrillard as being increasingly formed from without and programmed by the all-pervasive media. So to the mobile, unstable, fashion-conscious post-modern mind, travel becomes as much a fantasy programmed by the media, especially cinema, TV and video, as a real activity, and, like surfing the internet, leads to the virtual or simulacral, not to the real. Since such activities affect the human being from his/her earliest years, the growth of individual identity is ineluctably shaped by them and the potential for creative hallucination or epiphany progressively diminishes as fantasy projection becomes a part of everyday life in popular mass culture. In the following passage, Baudrillard explores the implications of this state of affairs for sexual identity in the post-modern world:

Péripétie dans le champ sexuel. Finie l'orgie, finie la libération, on ne cherche plus le sexe, on cherche son 'genre' (*gender*), c'est-à-dire à la fois son *look* et sa formule génétique. On ne balance plus entre le désir et la jouissance, mais entre sa formule génétique et son identité sexuelle (à trouver). Voici une autre culture érotique, après celle de l'interdit [. . .] voici celle de l'interrogation sur sa propre définition: 'Suis-je sexué? De quel sexe suis-je? Y a-t-il finalement nécessité du sexe? Où est la différence sexuelle?' La libération a laissé tout le monde en état d'indéfinition (c'est toujours la même chose: une fois libéré, vous êtes forcé de vous demander qui vous êtes). Après une phase triomphaliste, l'assertion de la sexualité féminine est devenue aussi fragile que celle de la masculine. Personne ne sait où il en est. [. . .]

Mais le problème plus général est celui de l'indifférence, liée à la récession des caractéristiques sexuelles. Les signes du masculin inclinent vers le degré zéro, mais les signes du féminin aussi. C'est dans cette conjoncture qu'on voit se lever les nouvelles idoles, celles qui relèvent le défi de l'indéfinition et qui jouent à mélanger les genres. *Gender benders*. Ni masculin, ni féminin, mais non plus homosexuel. Boy George, Michaël [*sic*] Jackson, David Bowie . . . Alors que les héros de la génération précédente incarnaient la figure explosive du sexe et du plaisir, ceux-ci posent à tous la question du *jeu* de la différence et de leur propre indéfinition. Ces idoles sont des exceptions. La plupart sont à la recherche d'un 'modèle du genre', d'une formule générique, à défaut d'une identité. Il faut trouver un différentiel de singularité. Pourquoi pas dans la mode, ou dans la génétique? Un *look* vestimentaire, ou un *look* cellulaire? [. . .]

A la limite, il n'y aurait plus le masculin et le féminin, mais une dissémination de sexes individuels ne se référant qu'à eux-mêmes, chacun se gérant comme une entreprise autonome. Fin de la séduction, fin de la différence, et glissement vers un autre système de valeurs. Paradoxe étonnant: la sexualité pourrait redevenir un problème secondaire, comme elle le fut dans la plupart des sociétés antérieures, et sans commune mesure avec d'autres systèmes symboliques plus forts (la naissance, la hiérarchie, l'ascèse, la gloire, la mort). La preuve serait faite que la sexualité n'était somme toute qu'un des modèles possibles, et non le plus décisif. (Baudrillard, 1986: 48–9)

[A new development in the sexual domain. The orgy is over, liberation is finished, we are not looking for sex anymore, we are looking for our gender, that is both our look and our genetic formula. We no longer have to choose between desire and its satisfaction, but between its genetic formula and our sexual identity (to be discovered). Here we have another sort of erotic culture: after prohibition (. . .) we now have a questioning of our own sexual status: 'Am I sexed? What sex am I? Do we really need sex? In what does sexual difference lie?' Sexual liberation has left us all in an undefined state (it's always the same: once liberated you have to find out who you are). After the triumphalist phase, the assertion of female sexuality has become as fragile as that of male. Nobody knows anymore where we are. (. . .)

But a more general problem is that of an absence of difference, linked to the decline in the display of sexual characteristics. The signs of masculinity are tending towards zero, just like the signs of femininity. It is at this point that we see new idols emerging. Idols who take up the challenge of sexuality undefined and who play at mixing genders. *Gender benders*. Neither masculine nor feminine, but not homosexual either. Boy George, Michael Jackson, David Bowie . . . Whereas the idols of the preceding generation were symbols of explosive sex and pleasure, these new idols pose for everyone the question of the *play* of difference and their own sexual ambivalence. These idols are exceptions. Most of them are, for want of an identity, in search of a 'gender model', of a generic formula. Some kind of differentiating feature has to be found. Why not in fashion, or in genetics? Why not a *look* based on clothes or one based on cells? (. . .)

In the last analysis, there would no longer be either masculine or feminine, but a profusion of individual sexes based entirely on their own model, each managing itself like an independent company. No more seduction, no more difference, but rather a slide towards another system of values. From this, an astonishing paradox emerges: sexuality could once again become a secondary problem, as it was in most earlier societies, and be overshadowed by different and stronger symbolic systems (birth, social standing, asceticism, celebrity, death). This would prove that sexuality was after all only one possible model, and not the most crucial one.]

Here, it is argued, in the western world of which America represents the apotheosis, identity is constructed *from outside*, around a look or formula designed to be marketed as seductive, like a consumer product, drawing on the multiple glamour icons that increasingly fill both the social and personal (fantasy) space of the modern world. The image of the sex symbol à la Marilyn Monroe continues but this time with sexual ambiguity – or even a range of sexual deviancies – as the new style.[5] The internal dimension to identity is supplied neither by the individual conscience nor by the internalised archetypes of the social group, nor even by the now discredited psychoanalysis, but by genetics. It is the genes that are the multiple unknown within, governing our psychical impulses as much as our physical appearance, and they will soon be modifiable more or less at will. Programming will replace moral taboo. In such a world of 'récession des caractéristiques' and 'indéfinition', difference as *jeu* will replace the 'strong' identities (based on racial, sexual, class and other stereotypes) that have until recently mostly governed role models, whether European, African or other non-western ethnic groups (see Augé, 1994a). The identity crisis of the future will be based less on a perception of the void at the heart of the self or on an agonising selection between strong alternatives, and more on infinite consumerist choice – the nightmare not of less identity but of the virtually infinite choice offered by a plethora of possible identifying images as provided by fashion or by genetic modification. A 'différentiel de singularité' will be acquired not through an effort of personal ascesis but by merely being bought into – not by personal but by financial investment. This implies, as Baudrillard suggests, another system of values, perhaps involving a return to earlier anthropological models of human social organisation in which sexual difference is less important than other symbolic values – such as (media) prestige or (material) spending-power.

The anthropological implications of travel and identity in the postmodern world have also become, as we saw in the last chapter, a major concern of Marc Augé, one of whose main projects as an ethnologist since the mid 1980s has been to analyse the impact on an increasingly globalised human society of changes in the mediatised, post-modern world. In works such as *Non-lieux. Introduction à une anthropologie de la surmodernité* (1992) and *Pour une anthropologie des mondes contemporains* (1994b), Augé argues that post-modernity, or, as he prefers to call it, *surmodernité*, has brought about a triple reconfiguration within modern social experience – 'l'expérience de l'accélération de l'histoire, du resserrement de l'espace et de l'individualisation des destins' (1994b: 145) ['the experience of the acceleration of history, the contraction of space and the individualisation of human

destinies']. This rapid transformation of culture and society has affected
so-called primitive, post-colonial and western societies alike, involving individuals throughout the global village in a fresh confrontation with the issues
of identity and place, in particular through an increasing institution in the
contemporary world of *non-places*. It is Augé's contention that 'la surmodernité est productrice de non-lieux' (1992: 100), that is, spaces of pure utility,
commercialism or transit. Such places – airports, supermarkets, motorways,
metro-stations, refugee camps – are non-anthropological, empty of symbolism in that they speak of neither history, identity nor human relations,
'ni [. . .] identitaire, ni [. . .] relationnel, ni [. . .] historique' (1992: 100),
though, of course, a deeper symbolic and anthropological significance to
such places can always be discovered if they are studied from a wider, scientific angle, as François Maspéro, does for example, in his epic trip from
Roissy to central Paris as recorded in *Les Passagers du Roissy-Express* (1990).
Augé sees such non-places as posing a challenge to the individual in the
post-modern world comparable to that confronted by the Romantic or
early modern travel writer of the sort discussed in this chapter:

Il n'est donc pas étonnant que ce soit parmi les 'voyageurs' solitaires du siècle passé,
non les voyageurs professionnels ou les savants, mais les voyageurs d'humeur,
de prétexte ou d'occasion, que nous soyons à même de retrouver l'évocation
prophétique d'espaces où ni l'identité, ni la relation, ni l'histoire ne font
véritablement sens, où la solitude s'éprouve comme dépassement ou évidement de
l'individualité, où seul le mouvement des images laisse entrapercevoir par instants
à celui qui les regarde fuir l'hypothèse d'un passé et la possibilité d'un avenir. (1992:
111)

[It is therefore not surprising that it should be among the solitary travellers of the last
century – not professional travellers or scientists, but those travellers following their
whims, pretexts or opportunities – that we are able to find a prophetic evocation
of spaces where neither identity, nor relation, nor history really make sense, where
solitude is experienced as a superseding or emptying of individuality, where only
the movement of images permits the occasional perception by the viewer who
watches them slip away, of the hypothesis of a past and the possibility of a future.]

    How is this similarity and continuity to be reconciled with what the post-
modern or *surmoderne* seems to mark as a paradigm shift in modern social
sensibility? Perhaps the answer is that the non-place merely provokes more
readily a form of alienation and identity crisis that in the past people had to
travel further to experience, raising to a level of general awareness what had
hitherto only been confronted privately by perceptive individuals (mostly
artists and writers) of the modern tradition (one which continues to thrive
after Bouvier in the work of Boman, 1989, 1999; Pesquès, 1997; and many

others). The paradox of travel today, under the auspices of modern mass tourism, as analysed by both Baudrillard and Augé, is that the moment of intense alienation is as likely to precede as to follow the encounter with the other. Experienced as a *non-lieu*, increasingly it takes the form of the nightmare of flight delays in over-crowded airports or of traffic jams on motorways – any confrontation, on arrival, with the other seeming less of a problem. In this respect, Jean-Didier Urbain's remark (1986: 43), quoted from Pascal Bruckner and Alain Finkelkraut (1979: 37), that '*le touriste, c'est l'autre*' takes on a new twist! Correspondingly (though there are of course other factors at stake here), travel writing as a sociological/anthropological project increasingly focusses in more recent times – as is the case with François Maspéro in *Les Passagers du Roissy-Express* (1990) and Jean Rolin in *Zones* (1995) – on prolonged experience of the *non-lieu*, one that in both cases is provided by an itinerary that takes the writer no further than the Parisian suburbs. How confrontations with modern social structures as totalities, familiar or foreign, can be experienced as profoundly dystopian will be explored in the next chapter.

CHAPTER 4

Utopias and dystopias: back in the US. Back in the USSR – Gide, Baudrillard, Disneyland

Je pense qu'il n'y a pas, dans le monde civilisé, de pays où l'on s'occupe moins de la philosophie qu'aux Etats-unis.

(Alexis de Tocqueville, [1835] 1951: II, 11)

Les Etats-Unis, c'est l'utopie réalisée.

(Jean Baudrillard, 1986: 76)

Il était donc une terre où l'utopie était en passe de devenir réalité.

(André Gide, 1936–7: 18)

Il faut rendre compte d'un processus unique où le sort de la société humaine est en jeu *en un lieu, dans un pays exemplaire*.

(Jacques Derrida, 1992: 37)

Une utopie dégénérée est une idéologie réalisée sous la forme d'un mythe.

[L]es utopies n'ont jamais été que des livres.

(Louis Marin, 1973: 297, 17)

The problem of identity as explored in Chapter 3 is also implicated in the concept of Utopia, in particular in relation to the ambivalence of Utopia's status as a *place*. First of all, as Lyman Tower Sargent reminds us (Schaer, Claeys and Sargent, 2000: 8), a utopia can be understood to be not only a place or phenomenon but also a word and a literary genre. Louis Marin, writing in the aftermath of the events of May 1968 in Paris, in which a certain 'pratique utopique' ultimately failed to undermine ('déconstruire') existing social institutions, goes so far as to suggest that utopias are and have indeed always been, as spaces, essentially textual (1973: 17). In this chapter, Utopia will be understood primarily as a concept applied or mis-applied by certain French travel writers to real places other to or distant from the France from which they are viewed. In the light of this, a clear distinction is made in what follows between travel writing with a utopian orientation and utopia as a literary genre, one which became increasingly popular in France from the eighteenth to the early twentieth centuries,[1] and one whose science-fiction potential was already widely explored by Jules Verne and others from the second half of the nineteenth century. The countries or places construed to be utopias in the texts studied in this chapter are thus real (Communist USSR, capitalist democratic USA), but nonetheless places invested by the writers on them with a certain exemplary status (see Derrida, 1992: 37). It is the question of the justifiability of this exemplary status that is raised in the utopia/dystopia opposition, one which is of course also implicit in all discussions of utopia since Thomas More's text of 1516. The utopia/dystopia opposition will be used here then primarily as a critical frame within which to explore the contradictions inherent in the idea of *l'utopie réalisée*.

The ambivalence under discussion is of course neatly encapsulated in the word *utopia*, which, meaning 'no-place' (*u-topia*), cannot, logically be taken to exist in the real world, though its meanings can be explored in terms of text. Utopia can also be interpreted as happy place, or *eu-topia*, one in which the trials and tribulations of the real world can become resolved. But utopia as a no-place may also be seen to relate to the non-place (*non-lieu*) that, as we saw in the last chapter, is increasingly asserting its dystopian presence in the real post-modern world. For if, in the light of Augé's analysis, a non-place is one synonymous with an absence of recognisable temporal, spatial and individual links, then utopia is also a model for such a place, being predicated precisely on a break with history, space and identity. Absence is therefore built into the very concept of Utopia as place, whether viewed as real or as an idea. This point becomes central to Derrida's discussion of Gide's *Retour de l'URSS* in the context of his visit to the USSR after the collapse of the Berlin Wall in 1989, as recorded in *Moscou aller-retour* in which he underlines the *non-lieu/avoir lieu* paradox: 'L'Utopie, le non-lieu, était sur le point ou en train d'avoir lieu sur cette "*terre*"' (1992: 64).

A further paradox central to utopias is their relation to signs: utopias, like all fantasy or imaginary projections, are born precisely of the possibility of signs being separated from their object in the real world, and explored on the level of ideas or concepts. In this sense, every book is potentially a utopian project. The dystopian obverse of this liberating potentiality is the virtual impossibility of putting those signs back to work again in the real world. This difficulty is in part a function of a utopian tendency to empty signs of their cruel or violent symbolic content, for utopias are essentially anti-sacred, iconoclastic texts. Such characteristic tendencies are already, as we shall see, evident in Sir Thomas More's *Utopia* of 1516, but will be given a radical turn in Baudrillard's discussion of simulacra in *Amérique* (1986).

The re-emergence of models of utopia in the early Renaissance period in Europe seems in part to have been a function of a humanist desire, inspired by the rediscovery of ancient Greek writing, to move beyond the medieval world of cruel signs (Baudrillard, 1976) and the semiotics of analogy (Foucault, 1966) into a transparent and rational universe. In a pre-utopian state, the world of signs was understood to be immovably grafted to the world of things and woe betide anyone who attempted to prise them apart: 'Un interdit protège les signes et les assure une clarté totale: chacun renvoie sans équivoque à un statut. Pas de contrefaçon possible dans le cérémonial – sinon comme magie noire et sacrilège, et c'est bien ainsi que le mélange des signes est puni: comme infraction grave à l'ordre des choses' (Baudrillard, 1976: 78) ['A prohibition protects signs and ensures that they are perfectly clear: each refers unequivocally to a statute. No part of any ceremonial can be counterfeited – except as black magic or as sacrilege, and it is indeed in this way that any mixing of signs is punished: as a grave infraction of the order of things']. So Thomas More's model of utopia, in offering the early modern age the possibility of a different social world, also proposed a different semiology. For one aim of More's concept of utopia seems to have to been to empty signs of cruelty, to abolish or minimise hierarchies and the violence that accompanies them, and to shift from an analogical to a rational model in relation to human knowledge and social organisation. This involved de-mythologising religious and other belief systems, the reduction of the iconic potential of signs and a focus on the signified (idea, concept, moral value) rather than the signifier (insignia of office, symbols of power). It also led to a radical reduction of *difference* on every level of social and individual interaction, creating a world of uniformity – all in Utopia wear throughout their lives the same natural wool-coloured clothes (More, [1516] 1965: 75) – and transparency – 'they use a great deal of glass there' ([1516] 1965: 74) – as opposed to the violent contrast and pageantry of the medieval world.

Violence was of course an ever-present reality of More's world and in the form of *war* becomes one of his central concerns. For war was, and is, the apotheosis of the real, experienced as cruelty, pain, violence and death. So in his *Utopia* More tries to minimise the impact of war by elaborating various strategies. Violence and war also of course represent an aspect of the cruel semiology of a pre-rationalist world in which difference and disagreement would be resolved through violence (on an individual as well as a group or national level) rather than through rational negotiation. The physical aspect of violence provided the 'real' dimension that validated the meaning or sign-value of an action or a moral position. Capital punishment, another major preoccupation of More in Book One of *Utopia*, is a case in point, one whose symbolic potential was to take an inaugural reversal in following centuries in which capital execution was turned against the absolute monarchs of both England and France, becoming in the process a prologue to the modern state. The instrument of state violence in the feudal system, the king, was himself executed, be-headed, thus enabling, in theory at any rate, the cruel link between sign and object to be severed once and for all. (This fate was, ironically, also to befall Thomas More himself for refusing to bow to the violent ideological pressure exerted on him by Henry VIII in the light of the king's break with Roman Catholic hegemony in the Christian Church.) The reduction of violence in a rationalist world brought with it a reduction of the cruelty of the sign, which lost its necessary link with its object and became open to wider interpretation. At the same time the analogical link between sign and object was proportionately weakened, and with it the sign's purchase on the real.

An important exception to this rule in *Utopia* is the observation that Utopian priests' costumes are decorated with *symbolic* patterns of feathers:

> The congregation is dressed in white, and the priest wears multicoloured vestments, magnificent in workmanship and design, but made of quite cheap materials – for instead of being woven with gold thread, or encrusted with rare jewels, they're merely decorated with the feathers of various birds. On the other hand, their value as works of art is far greater than that of the richest material in the world. Besides, the feathers are arranged in special patterns which are said to symbolize certain divine truths, and the priests are careful to teach the meanings of these hieroglyphics, since they serve to remind worshippers of God's favours towards them, of their duty towards Him in return, and their duty towards one another. (More, [1516] 1965: 127)

This passage then signals a return to an analogical model of symbolisation, one that, despite the priest's commitment to explain it to his congregation, is by its nature ambivalent and open to interpretation by the individual. Does the use of feathers here reflect More's awareness of early ethnographic science that was beginning to record the symbolic and ritual significance of the native Indian cultures being discovered at this time in north and south America? Whatever the case may be, the value of the colourful and exotic as a source of reverie additional to any specific or denotative meaning of the sign, clearly prefigures post-Enlightenment Europe's fascination with the semiotic systems of the other, which were to provide a valuable incentive to both scientific ethnography and Romantic travel writing as it developed in the nineteenth century. In addition, the valorisation of such signs as *works of art* in their own right further anticipates the conscious *aestheticisation* of the meaning process that follows the sign's detachment from the real.

More's *Utopia* is of course most commonly read as inaugurating a theory of communist social practice. Based on values of equality, rationalism, materialism, the utopian model set out to impose a rational ideology on the real world. In practice, however, a revolution was in some cases needed to bring such a transformation about. Despite the regicidal violence that characterised both the English revolution of 1649 and the French of 1789, neither were able to sustain the momentum necessary to impose in the longer term the Commonwealth or egalitarian model of society. It was only perhaps in the nineteenth century that theories of history (such as that on which Marxism is based) provided the ideological justification for the selective elimination of historical past on which any realisation of utopia would necessarily depend – though both Marx and Engels were ambivalent in their attitude to utopianism, 'social utopianism' becoming for them a pejorative term (see Geoghegan, 1987). Despite this, however, communist utopias still seemed doomed to fail in practice, as Gide foresaw in his *Retour de l'URSS* (1936). This is because the real world is mobile; it is not answerable to the determinist view of history adopted by Marxism, which does not sufficiently allow or account for change and difference – either in the real world or in the individual desires of members of the community. Cultural, social, political and ideological values all in their turn become fixed, harden into cruel signs which are not negotiable by individual or community. So, in the Stalinist USSR, difference – on individual, creative, political, ideological and even racial levels – was wiped out through state violence: 'Tous ceux dont le front se redresse sont fauchés ou déportés l'un après l'autre' (Gide, 1936: 118) ['all those who stick their head above the parapet are cut down or deported one after the other'].

Such values or categories – individual, social, political, ideological – are of course all still operative in modern capitalist democratic society, but are generally interpreted with much less cruel precision. Western party politics for example are a ritualistically programmed display of insignificant policy differences, in which, as Baudrillard shows in contemporary America, the real and the historical disappear into the merely televisual (1986: 99). But this is not perceived as a problem provided they supply motions and images allowing sufficient energy for *play*, for individual or group fantasy projection or desire. If Baudrillard is able to view present-day United States as a realisation of Utopia as (social) practice, this is because the rational and real as values established in Enlightenment Europe are also experienced as *entertainment*, as fantasy. In the modern USA, images return, but not as the cruel signs of a pre-utopian world, nor even the rational signs of the Enlightenment, but as fantasies having an ambivalent relation with the reality of everyday life. Signs are no longer to be feared or even interpreted but merely *consumed*. In the capitalist post-modern world, focus is on the signifier; the inauthenticity of the sign – its lack of real connection with an object in the real world or with a coherent idea – is perceived as a positive quality and enjoyed by the receiver in mass society. So in the 'Pax Americana' following the atom bomb and the end of the Second World War, even war, like other forms of violence, becomes recycled as *entertainment* or fantasy, like other previously real or cruel components of western society. In comic strips, film, video, video games, war games, war and violence move into the realm of the virtual, and become (mere) entertainment, even when they pretend to be real, as in the US 'Star Wars' project. Even unanticipated real acts of violence, such as the terrorist attacks in 2001 on the World Trade Center in New York, are absorbed by the media and vicariously experienced by a vast public in constantly repeated TV replay. The exemplary model of Utopia becomes thus realised in the United States, and in the globalised world that it increasingly influences, in the form of mass entertainment, and Disneyland becomes a major preoccupation of post-modern ethnology (Augé, 1997), semiotics (Marin, 1973) and sociology (Baudrillard, 1986, 1996).

But there is another aspect of More's inaugural utopian model that needs preliminary discussion before some subsequent misapplications (in more recent French writing) are explored in this chapter, and that is the problem of language. Surprisingly, in the light of subsequent history and ethnographic observation, the arrival of western visitors to More's *Utopia* does not immediately bring about a collapse of the utopian language or other sign systems. This is not only because More's Utopia is fictive rather than real but also because the Utopian language, it is suggested, is only superficially different from western languages and may indeed have its origin in Greek ([1516] 1965: 100). More takes the trouble to invent a Utopian alphabet that looks very like Greek, which he presents at the very beginning of his text (figure 10), and he even cites by way of epigraph an example of Utopian poetry:

> Utopos ha Boccas peu la chama polta chamaan.
> Bargol he maglomi baccan soma gymnosophaon
> Agrama gymnosophon labarembacha bodamilomin.
> Volvala barchin heman, la lavolvola dramme pagloni.
>
> ([1516] 1965: 25)

VTOPIAE INSVLAE FIGVRA

Figure 10 Frontispiece, Thomas More, *Utopia* (1516)

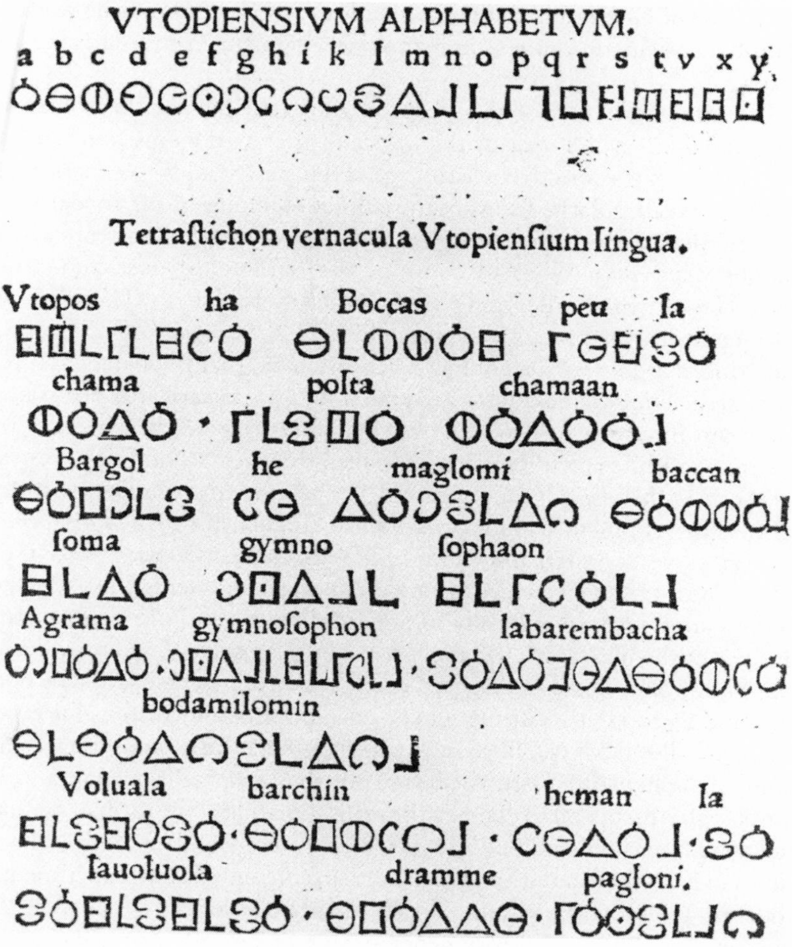

VTOPIENSIVM ALPHABETVM.

Figure 10 (*cont.*)

Utopians, we are told, are able to learn Greek quickly; they are interested in and sympathetic to the Greek texts they are shown. Thus More subtly or ironically shows how the Utopian system is in fact obscurely based on Greek ideas and models. In this way, the difference between Utopian and European systems is significantly reduced, enabling a relatively easy flow of ideas and concepts between them. This fact also of course has important consequences for any polemical and ideological aims More may have had in writing *Utopia*. For if the latter's value systems are seen to be contiguous

with those of Greek- and Latin-based culture, they could thus be read as a
plausible anticipation of real humanist development in sixteenth-century
Europe.

The aim of the rest of this chapter will be to explore the contradictions inherent in the idea of the *utopie réalisée* as demonstrated in two
key French texts respectively focusing on the 'new worlds' – America and
Russia – which polarised European political thinking in the modern and
early modern periods. So, following Derrida's cue, when, attempting in
Moscou aller-retour (1992) to confront the tensions of post-communist
Russia, he cites the Beatles' song 'Back in the US. Back in the USSR', it will
be along the east–west axis constituted by Gide's *Retour de l'URSS* (1936–7)
and Baudrillard's *Amérique* of half a century later, that the paradox of real
utopian societies will be explored. Both Gide's and Baudrillard's books have
important intertexts in two early nineteenth-century works which, in the
aftermath of the French Revolution, looked to America and Russia respectively as possible models, one democratic, the other reactionary, for future
political development in Europe: Alexis de Tocqueville's *De la démocratie
en Amérique* ([1835] 1951) and Astolphe de Custine's *La Russie en 1839* ([1843]
1990). The former is of particular interest in that it represents one of the first
modern attempts systematically to test an existing political system against
the ideal or theoretical criteria applied to a utopian society, and provides an
exemplary political and sociological reflection on democracy. Cited by both
Gide and Derrida, it constitutes a key reference in Baudrillard's *Amérique*.

Tocqueville (1805–59), like Custine (1790–1857), was an aristocrat sufficiently enlightened to learn the lessons of the French Revolution and its
complex aftermath and to come to the realisation that some form of democracy would inevitably establish itself within future European political systems. For him, the United States of America represented a real experimental
model of a democratic system, already highly developed. What were the
conditions – relating to history, geography and identity – that had enabled
the United States to realise a quasi-utopian model of social and political
organisation? Firstly, because America's founding fathers had been able, in
a sense, to step out of history and establish a new community in a virtually
virgin territory, thus escaping the pressures of the traditional structures still
shaping the political system of the home country. This was possible in part
because of the New World's distance from the old continent of Europe, and
its vastness as a territory. Like some mythical antecedents of Utopia, such
as the Atlantis of Greek mythology, America could be imagined to have
surged from the sea, a new and self-contained world to which it would be
possible to apply a new model of human society: 'La démocratie, telle que

n'avait point osé la rêver l'antiquité, s'échappait toute grande et tout armée [*sic*] du milieu de la vieille société féodale' ([1835] 1951: I, 34)² ['Democracy, as Antiquity had not dared imagine it, escaped fully grown and fully armed from the midst of ancient feudal society']. Secondly, in relation to identity, although America's founding fathers were primarily Anglo-Saxon, the subsequent influx of colonists from all over Europe and the Middle East brought about the 'melting pot' situation in which new cocktails of identity and religious belief could be created. Finally, the problematic transition from an old to a new model of social and political structure is achieved *without* violence or revolution. So although Tocqueville avoids applying the term 'utopia' specifically to the United States, he is nevertheless able to announce such a miracle in the following phrase that, in modified form, will recur in subsequent utopian travel texts: 'Il est un pays dans le monde où la grande révolution sociale dont je parle semble avoir à peu près atteint ses limites naturelles [. . .] ce pays voit les résultats de la révolution démocratique qui s'opère parmi nous, sans avoir eu la révolution elle-même' ([1835] 1951: I, 11; see also II, 14) ['There is a country in the world where the great social revolution of which I was speaking seems more or less to have reached its natural limits (. . .) this country now enjoys the results of the democratic revolution that we are undergoing, without itself having suffered such an upheaval'].

However, that Tocqueville is far from being a utopian is shown by his preoccupation in both volumes of *De la démocratie en Amérique* with the possible consequences of the development of democratic systems in a 'classless' society. He is concerned in particular with the moral incentives in a non-authoritarian and therefore potentially (spiritually) anarchic society and the problem of the hegemony of public opinion in a society without hierarchical class divisions: '[Q]uelles que soient les lois politiques qui régissent les hommes dans les siècles d'égalité, l'on peut prévoir que la foi dans l'opinion commune y deviendra une sorte de religion dont la majorité sera le prophète' ([1835] 1951: II, 19) ['Whatever the political laws governing men in the egalitarian age, one foresees that faith in public opinion will become a sort of religion of which the majority will be the prophet'].

To some extent, however, the founding fathers' combination of deep belief with religious toleration provided a basis both for moral values and for liberty: 'Les fondateurs de la Nouvelle Angleterre étaient tout à la fois d'ardents sectaires et de novateurs exaltés [. . .]. Loin de se nuire, ces deux tendances en apparence si opposées, marchent d'accord et semblent se prêter un mutuel appui'([1835] 1951: I, 42; also II, 14)['The founders of New England were at the same time ardently sectarian and enthusiastic innovators (. . .). Far from working against each other, these two apparently opposed tendencies, are in accord with each other and seem to support each other']. Another problem is that of the materialism consequent to the establishment of a new classless society in a vast country with huge physical and economic resources. Once again, the problem finds a uniquely American solution in the unprecedented rapidity and mobility of the circulation of wealth: 'Je ne connais [. . .] pas de pays où l'amour de l'argent tienne une plus large place dans le cœur de l'homme [. . .]. Mais la fortune circule avec une incroyable rapidité' ([1835] 1951: I, 50)['I do not know (. . .) a country in which love of money occupies a larger place in men's hearts (. . .). But this money circulates with incredible rapidity'].

Such checks and balances are mentioned here both because they are of interest *per se* as original and unanticipated developments in a new society and because they underline the importance of an empirical, scientific approach to the study of social and political structures. The originality of Tocqueville lies precisely in his realisation, notwithstanding his knowledge of a long tradition of utopian thought in 'La docte et littéraire Europe' ([1835]1951: II, 42), that 'Il faut une science politique nouvelle à un monde tout nouveau' (I, 5). For, as he says: 'Ceux qui cultivent les sciences chez les peuples démocratiques craignent toujours de se perdre dans les utopies. Ils se défient des systèmes, ils aiment à se tenir très près des faits et à les étudier par eux-mêmes' (II, 46) ['Those who cultivate the sciences among democratic peoples always fear to lose themselves in utopian fantasies. They distrust systems, preferring to stick as close as possible to the facts and to study them closely themselves']. In this way, Tocqueville's *De la démocratie en Amérique* provides both new themes (economic materialism, social mobility, realism in the arts) and new models (scientific observation, comprehensive documentation, historical contextualisation) for subsequent writers in the newly developing social sciences – anthropology, sociology, politics. Such resources will be of particular value to travel writers of the following century such as Baudrillard and Gide who seek to investigate if not to resolve the tension between utopian and scientific approaches to the exploration of other cultures.

As a European sociologist and semiotician travelling in the United States, Baudrillard is in a position to offer a provocative rereading of Tocqueville. In the 150 years which elapsed since the latter's visit, little, in Baudrillard's view, has fundamentally changed, either in the structure of the American politico-social systems or in the analytical strategies employed in their apprehension:

Il est d'ailleurs extraordinaire de voir combien les Américains ont peu changé depuis deux siècles, bien moins que les sociétés européennes prises dans les révolutions politiques du XIXe siècle, alors qu'eux ont gardé intacte, préservée par la distance océanique qui est l'équivalent d'une insularité dans le temps, la perspective utopique et morale des hommes du XVIIIe, ou même des sectes puritaines du XVIIe siècle, transplantée et perpétuée à l'abri des péripéties de l'histoire. Cette hystérésie puritaine et morale est celle de l'exil, c'est celle de l'utopie.(1986: 88)

[It is moreover extraordinary how little Americans have changed over the last two centuries, much less so than European societies caught up in the political revolutions of the nineteenth century; preserved by the Atlantic Ocean that is the spatial equivalent of temporal insularity, they have kept intact the moral and utopian outlook of the eighteenth century, or even of seventeenth-century Puritans, transplanted and sheltered from the episodes of history. Moral and Puritan hysteresis is a result of exile, of a utopian society.]

The one difference is the much greater insistence in Baudrillard on the *utopian* quality of the American *expérience* (in both – French – senses of the word). However, Baudrillard's stress on the total originality / extreme banality dualism characterising American egalitarianism, that he sees as having an essentially utopian character, is itself based on a paradox, the recognition of which he attributes to Tocqueville: 'C'est autour d'elle [l'égalité] que se redessine le paradoxe de Tocqueville, à savoir que l'univers américain tend à la fois vers l'insignifiance absolue [. . .] et vers l'originalité absolue – aujourd'hui plus encore qu'il y a cent cinquante ans' (1986: 88)['It is around (equality) that Tocqueville's paradox is redrawn, that is to say that American society tends both towards absolute insignificance (. . .) and towards absolute originality – even more so today than a hundred and fifty years ago'].

In what sense then according to Baudrillard is it possible, even more today than in Tocqueville's time, to view America as an essentially utopian society? And to what extent is the utopian dimension also nuanced by dystopian tendencies? Many aspects of the utopian potentiality of the United States were of course, as we saw, already observed by Tocqueville: escape from history, geographical distance from Europe, immense material resources, a social ethos characterised by a unique combination of sectarian and democratic tendencies. Tocqueville was also already acutely aware of the brash self-confidence and self-sufficiency of the Americans, combined, however, with a need for praise and recognition by the old world ([1835] 1951: II,179– 82 – 'Pourquoi les Américains ont si peu de susceptibilité dans leurs pays et se montrent si susceptibles dans le nôtre'). What makes the United States a utopian system for Baudrillard is however something that Tocqueville, writing only at the dawn of the modern, technological, world, could not really have anticipated: the development and mass dissemination of media capable of both simulating reality and projecting fantasy on a scale and with a verisimilitude unimaginable before the invention of photography and the cinema. For it is the symbiosis of the real and the phantasmic, the glorification through mythologisation of contemporary everyday life, the Hollywoodian cult of American celebrity or stardom, that enables America to perceive itself as a utopian society – that is, one in which its ultimate values and desires become realisable in the present. So for Baudrillard it is 'cette conviction intime et délirante d'avoir matérialisé tous leurs rêves' (1986: 77) ['the intimate and delirious conviction that they have realised all their dreams'] combined with 'la consécration phantas-matique de tout cela par le cinéma' (1986: 77) ['the phantasmic conse-cration of all that by the cinema'] that assures the utopian status of the American experience. Of course this would not have been possible *with-out* the general characteristics – historical, geographical, psychological – of utopias also being uniquely attributable to the American situation, enabling thus an 'opérationalis[ation de] l'idéal que les autres cultivent comme fin dernière et secrètement impossible' (1986: 77) ['operationalisation of the ideal that others cultivate only as a final and ultimately impossible aim']. Americans, in other words, are able – something Europeans will never achieve – to live in the present of their dreams, to have utopia now.

To have utopia now, however, inevitably brings with it a certain dystopian fall-out, one that is of course only really perceptible to the critical, Euro-pean outsider in whose world, unlike that of America, negativity and con-tradiction are still real possibilities: 'Nous vivons dans la négativité et la contradiction, eux vivent dans le paradoxe (car c'est une idée paradoxale que celle de l'utopie réalisée)' (Baudrillard, 1986: 78). From a European per-spective, then, the utopia/dystopia relation is essentially symbiotic; for part of the paradox of utopia actually realised is the necessary concomitance of dystopian elements, born through the very accident of its realisation, though they may not be visible to the happy utopians inhabiting their ideal world. The internal uniformity that is a hallmark of utopias at least from the time of Thomas More's brings with it a marked disincentive to com-pare critically, to explore radical *difference* that becomes, by pointing to a world *outside*, a threat to the utopian ideal. Difference in contemporary America, whose society was founded on a *brassage* (1986: 89) of many racial and cultural types (that by the late twentieth century even includes native Indian components), is consumed *internally*, is part of an ongoing process of absorption and cultural homogenisation; any threat difference might pose if it comes from without is either wiped out by military action abroad or neutralised by a processing or packaging that enables it, if not to be ignored, then to be consumed as entertainment or exoticism. The absence of an outside perspective on the ideal world is also, as we shall see – though in different terms – necessary to sustain the illusion of utopian progress in the USSR visited by Gide in 1936, as also tsarist Russia as analysed by Custine in 1839.

A corollary of utopian Americans' refusal or inability to confront external difference is also manifested in an American characteristic, noted already by Tocqueville a century and a half before – 'Je pense qu'il n'y a pas, dans le monde civilisé, de pays où l'on s'occupe moins de la philosophie qu'aux Etats-unis' ([1835]1951: II, 11). For the American reluctance to engage in theoretical or speculative thinking in relation to political and social matters is a deeply utopian tendency. As Baudrillard argues: 'Le principe de l'utopie réalisée explique l'absence, et d'ailleurs l'inutilité, de la métaphysique et de l'imaginaire dans la vie américaine. Elle crée chez les Américains une perception de la réalité différente de la nôtre. Le réel n'y est pas lié à l'impossible, et aucun échec ne peut le remettre en cause' (1986: 83) ['The principle of a utopia made real explains the absence, and moreover the uselessness, of metaphysics and imagination in American life. It gives rise among Americans to a perception of reality that is different from our own. The real is not linked to the impossible, and no failure can ever cast doubt on it']. From this follows the profound American aversion to Marxism or any other radical conception of political economy or development. As Baudrillard jokingly comments, 'L'histoire et le marxisme sont comme les vins fins et la cuisine: ils ne franchissent pas vraiment l'océan' (1986: 79) ['History and Marxism are like fine wines and haute cuisine: they don't travel well across the Atlantic']. The American primal scene, moral and utopian, has nothing in common with the historical and intellectual model that determines European reflection and action. This variance results in a totally different approach to reality – in America, to be apprehended, a thing must be translatable in terms of the real in the present or immediately foreseeable future: ideas and concepts are there to be translated, otherwise they make no sense. And the privileged term of translation for the Americans is of course that of the *cinema*: any thing, idea or concept that can be realised cinematographically has reached its perfect form of being or expression – 'Car la matérialité des choses, bien sûr, c'est leur cinématographie' (1986: 83). And nowhere is this truer than in the case of the human being: stardom and celebrity are the ultimate forms of utopian existence, implying an ideal world of glamour and photogenic perfection. Everything is real – even the other – if it is seen *as on TV*. Hence the encroachment of TV and home movie into all aspects of everyday American life, leading to the narcissistic self-obsession that, from the outside, is perceived, no less nightmarishly than the telescreens in George Orwell's anti-utopian novel *Nineteen Eighty-Four*, as a deeply dystopian tendency.

But as befits a semiotician, the ultimate take by Baudrillard on America as a utopia of the hyperreal is also that of America as a dystopia of signs. For America is a place in which it is impossible to pin signs to objects in the real world or to elaborate a logic of the relations between them. For signs are always moving, always in a state of translation or transition from one media to another or in a state of feed-back or of action re-play. Nowhere is this more evident than in the culture of the car, the ultimate object of American materialism. Deeply invested with myth and glamour, the Mustang and the Camaro, the Transam and the Thunderbird, are framing devices not only for viewing landscape and cityscape – exemplifying to perfection the American love of panoramic glass – but also for simulating freedom and egalitarian adventure. In its transparency and candour, car travel as movement becomes an essential mode of American utopianism for which space and time exist purely to measure and facilitate. The American continent is divided into different time zones with the result that different times can be simultaneously the right time across the USA – a phenomenon exerting a fascination as acute for Butor in *Mobile* as for Baudrillard in his *sideral* America. The view of time receding through the rear-view mirror as the car cruises along an endless freeway implies both the apotheosis and the occultation of the image, a process in which the sign becomes infinitely extended and emptied through movement. And since 'passing thru' and the road movie are essential models for American experience, the meaning of life itself becomes simultaneously expanded and evacuated. But Baudrillard puts all this much better himself, as in the following passage in which his lyricism is more jubilant even than the utopian vision it purports to evoke:

L'Amérique sidérale. Le caractère lyrique de la circulation pure. Contre la mélancolie des analyses européennes. La sidération immédiate du vectoriel, du signalétique, du vertical, du spatial. Contre la distance fébrile du regard culturel.

La joie de l'effondrement de la métaphore, dont nous ne portons chez nous que le deuil. L'allégresse de l'obscénité, l'obscénité de l'évidence, l'évidence de la puissance, la puissance de la simulation. Contre notre virginité déçue, nos abîmes d'affectation.

La sidération. Celle, horizontale, de l'automobile, celle, altitudinale, de l'avion, celle électronique, de la télévision, celle géologique, des déserts, celle, stéréolytique, des mégalopoles, celle transpolitique, du jeu de la puissance, du musée de la puissance qu'est devenue l'Amérique pour le monde entier. (1986: 31)

[Astral America. The lyrical quality of pure movement. As against the melancholy of European analysis. The astral immediacy of vectors and signals, of the vertical and the spatial. As against the febrile distance of the cultural gaze.

The joy in the collapse of metaphor, over which we in Europe are still mourning. The exhilaration of obscenity, the obscenity of obviousness, the obviousness of power, the power of simulation. As against our disappointed virginity, our abysses of affectation.

Sideral vectors – horizontal in the case of the car; altitudinal in that of aircraft, electronic in TV, geological in the deserts, stereolithic in the great conurbations, transpolitical in the power game, the museum of power that America has become for the whole world.]

The marquis de Custine's substantial study *La Russie en 1839*, though a less trailblazing enterprise, from both a methodological and ideological point of view, than that of Tocqueville's *De la démocratie en Amérique* with which it is almost exactly contemporary, nonetheless articulates certain intuitions that will subsequently be corroborated by the experience of later travellers to the vast domains of Russia, both pre- and post-revolutionary. Once again any attempt at rational analysis of such a distant and different culture confronts the outsider with paradoxes. So, for Custine, the barbarism of institutional structures must be set against the nobility of the people; the immense potential – political and economic – of the state against the still feudal management structure of large tracts of the country; the inertia of many parts of the system against the vitality of many individuals within it:

Ce que fait la Russie l'Etat le plus curieux du monde à observer aujourd'hui, c'est qu'on y trouve en présence l'extrême barbarie favorisée par l'asservissement de l'Eglise, et l'extrême civilisation importée des pays étrangers par un gouvernement éclectique. Pour savoir comment le repos ou du moins l'immobilité peut naître du choc des éléments si divers, il faut suivre le voyageur jusque dans le cœur de ce singulier pays. ([1843]1990: I, 19)

[What makes Russia the most curious State in the world to observe today is that one finds oneself there in the presence of extreme barbarity brought about by the enslavement of the Church, and ultimate civilisation imported from foreign countries by an eclectically minded government. To understand how rest or at least immobility result from the impact of such diverse elements, you have to follow the traveller right into the heart of this strange country.]

Les Russes ne seront pas satisfaits; l'amour-propre l'est-il jamais? Cependant personne n'a été plus frappé que moi de la grandeur de leur nation et de son importance politique. Les hautes destinées de ce peuple, le dernier venu sur le vieux théâtre du monde, m'ont préoccupé tout le temps de mon séjour chez lui. Les Russes en masse m'ont paru grands jusque dans leurs vices les plus choquants; isolés, ils m'ont paru aimables. ([1843] 1990: I, 21)

[Russians will not like this: is self-love ever satisfied? However nobody was more struck than I was myself by the greatness of their country and its political importance. The noble destiny of this people, the last to step onto the world's old stage, preoccupied me all the time I spent there. Russians as a group struck me as being great even in their most shocking vices; as individuals they seemed to me to be very likeable.]

The greatest paradox of all however, one that Gide, in his turn, though for different reasons, will be obliged to confront on his return from the USSR, is that the writer comes back from what he imagines is a state exemplary in its fulfilment of the aims of a certain political model with the conviction that it may in fact produce the antithesis of what it promised, either in terms of its own realisation or in terms of the expectations to which it gave rise. As Custine is obliged ruefully to admit: 'J'allais en Russie pour chercher des arguments contre le gouvernement représentatif, j'en reviens partisan des constitutions' ([1843] 1990: I, 20) ['I went to Russia looking for arguments against representative government; I return a partisan of constitutions'].

Once again then is raised, this time in the context of Russia, not only the issue of the markedly different ways utopia or dystopia are experienced, depending on whether they are viewed from within or from without, but also the more general problem of the logical reversal of categories as applied by the rational mind to radically different cultural situations. Interesting light is shed on this question by Derrida, as one might suspect, in *Moscou aller-retour* in which the problematic of expectation and reward or anticipation and disappointment is set in the context of differing cultural points of view (1992: 65–72). (Derrida, for example, is surprised to find young Russian intellectuals translating *Perestroïka* as *déconstruction*.) So the *paradoxe de Tocqueville* as explored by writers on American utopia such as Baudrillard is paralleled or supplemented in writers on Russia such as Gide and Derrida by what one might call the *paradoxe de Custine*, that is the paradox of the *aller-retour*. For not the least interesting aspect of Custine's text is his awareness of how positions change in relation to different situations; he writes: 'je m'aperçois que je parle ici comme les radicaux parlent à Paris; démocrate en Russie, je n'en suis pas moins, en France, un aristocrate obstiné' ([1843]1990: I, 237) ['I realise that I speak here in the style of Parisian radicals; a democrat in Russia, I am nonetheless obstinately reactionary in France']. He goes on to say later 'j'ai passé en Russie un été terrible [. . .]. J'espérais arriver à des solutions, je vous rapporte des problèmes' (II, 440). In this way is raised the question of the extent to which the logical oppositions 'là-bas' and 'ici', 'fort' and 'da', the same and the different, can ever be, if not assimilated to each other, then at least comprehended as supplements within an alternating and reciprocal frame.

This *aller-retour* bind, already present in Custine, becomes pervasive in Gide's travel writing, both in the Congo journals – *Voyage au Congo* and *Retour du Tchad* (1927–8)– and in the report on the Russian trip of 1936: 'Je ne connaissais point tout ceci lorsque j'étais en U.R.S.S., non plus que je ne connaissais le fonctionnement des grandes Compagnies Concessionnaires lorsque je voyageais au Congo. Ici comme là, je constatais des effets désastreux, dont encore je ne pouvais pas bien comprendre les causes' (1936–7: 135) ['I didn't know any of this when I was in the USSR, any more than I knew how the big colonial Concessionary Companies operated when I was in the Congo. Here, as there, I observed the disastrous effects of which I was still unable to understand the causes']. In relation to the later trip, it is visible in the very structure of *Retour de l'URSS* (1936) with its accompanying supplement *Retouches à mon retour de l'URSS* (1937) and the *Témoignages* that further supplement the volume. These divisions precisely reflect the different perspectives brought to bear on the question of the nature of the communist revolution in the USSR. These are viewed first with an initial and unprejudiced enthusiasm by Gide; second with a more critical and sceptical gaze; third, on the return, in an attempt to assess and balance not only the positive and negative qualities of the Soviet revolution but also the different interpretations to which they could be submitted, both by Gide himself and by other commentators in France, whether pro- or anti-communist, and to answer the criticisms Gide's text elicited on publication; finally, adapting a tactic already used by Custine a century before, additional *témoignages*, mostly unsolicited, are added further to widen the basis of judgement and assessment. In addition, Gide includes in Chapter 5 of his text some speeches to deliver in the USSR that he had written *before* his departure for Russia. The reader of Gide's text is thus as much confronted with the *aller-retour* of different critical and ideological perspectives as with the *aller-retour* of the journey itself.

Far, then, from clarifying or confirming a theory or its political realisation, travel deepens Gide's confusion in relation to the utopian/dystopian status of Stalinist USSR, where he is confronted, not with answers but with further questions, not with resolutions but with paradoxes: like Custine, in seeking solutions, he is merely confronted with further problems. And Gide's awareness that the uncritical seeker will tend to find what he seeks does little to solve the problem of arriving at a balanced overall assessment:

Parfois le pire accompagne et double le meilleur; on dirait presque qu'il en est la conséquence. Et l'on passe du plus lumineux au plus sombre avec une brusquerie déconcertante. Il arrive souvent que le voyageur, selon des convictions préétablies, ne soit sensible qu'à l'un ou qu'à l'autre. Il arrive trop souvent que les amis de l'U.R.S.S. se refusent à voir le mauvais, ou du moins à le reconnaître; de sorte que, trop souvent, la vérité sur l'U.R.S.S. est dite avec haine, le mensonge avec amour. (1936–7: 17)

[Sometimes the worst accompanies and matches the best, one might almost say that it was the consequence of it. One passes from the brightest to the most sombre with a disconcerting abruptness. It often happens that the traveller, following well-established convictions, is aware of only one or the other. All too often, friends of Russia refuse to see or at least to acknowledge the bad; with the result that, too often, the truth about the USSR is revealed with hatred, while the false is recounted with love.]

It is partly of course a semiotic problem and is attributable to the diverging ambitions of travel writer and scientific analyst: the former to a certain extent may be permitted to enjoy signs for their own sake while the latter is primarily concerned with the more objective responses of recognition and interpretation. For Gide, unreserved sympathy is possible only where there is minimal or no exchange of signs. Gide's poor understanding of the Russian language, like Barthes's inability to read Japanese (as admitted in *L'Empire des signes*), clearly facilitates this: 'Aussi bien nulle part autant qu'en U.R.S.S. le contact avec tous et n'importe qui ne s'établit plus aisément, immédiat, profond, chaleureux. Il se tisse aussitôt – parfois un regard y suffit – des liens de sympathie violente' (1936–7: 27) ['In the same way, nowhere as much as in the USSR is contact with anybody – immediate, warm, profound – made more easily. Deep friendships are quickly made – sometimes a glance suffices to establish a profound rapport']. But as other travel records of visits to communist countries as part of an official delegation confirm – for example, that of Michel Leiris in his 1955 *Journal de Chine* (published posthumously in 1994) – such sympathy is often based not only on intellectual exchange but also on cultural goodwill. Criticism – political, ideological – is a function of the interrogation of signs and is readily forthcoming in the case of Gide as soon as the distinction is made between the personal warmth of the Russian people and the Soviet system under which they live.[3]

The lack of critical reflection on the part of the inhabitants of the putative utopia – 'l'esprit critique (en dépit du marxisme) y fait à peu près complètement défaut' (1936–7: 44) – is a characteristic we have already observed in Baudrillard's analysis of America and is a point noted in Russia by Custine. For when the latter writes in 1839, 'Les pauvres gens se croiraient heureux si nous autres étrangers nous ne les qualifions imprudemment de victimes' ([1843] 1990: I, 156) ['The poor devils would consider themselves happy if we foreigners didn't inadvisedly judge them to be victims'], and observes that 'Le dédain de ce qu'ils ne connaissent pas me paraît le trait dominant du caractère des Russes. Au lieu de tâcher de comprendre, ils tâchent de se moquer' (II, 255)['A disdain for what they don't know seems to me to be the dominant trait of the Russian character. Instead of trying to understand, they only mock'], he anticipates the paradox, also identified by Tocqueville, that Gide in turn is obliged to confront in his realisation that utopian happiness is always in part a function of ignorance. 'Leur bonheur est fait d'espérance, de confiance et d'ignorance' (1936–7: 43) he observes and goes on to show that the maintenance of this ignorance is a key aim of Soviet propaganda: 'Le citoyen soviétique reste dans une extraordinaire ignorance de l'étranger. Bien plus: on l'a persuadé que tout, à l'étranger, et dans tous les domaines, allait beaucoup moins bien qu'en U.R.S.S. Cette illusion est savamment entretenue; car il importe que chacun, même peu satisfait, se félicite du régime qui le préserve de pires maux' (1936–7: 44) ['The Soviet citizen remains incredibly ignorant of what is going on outside the country. Furthermore, he has been persuaded that everything in foreign countries, in every domain, is much worse than in the USSR. This illusion is cleverly maintained; for it is important that each citizen, even if dissatisfied, should feel grateful to the regime which preserves him from worse evils']. The function of *Pravda*, the leading Soviet newspaper, thus is not to give a broad insight into events in the world inside or outside Soviet Russia, but rather to mouth government policy or the Communist Party's interpretation of events: 'Chaque matin la *Pravda* leur enseigne ce qu'il sied de savoir, de penser, de croire' (1936–7: 43). In a recent article in *Le Débat*, Orlando Figes, in stressing the 'vision utopique de la Russie' historically projected both from within and without the country, argues that this historic power of government in Russia is in part founded on a (mis)apprehension resulting from a confusion of the words *pravitelstrvo* ('government') and *pravda* ('truth and justice'). In the mind of the masses, Figes argues, 'la seule forme du gouvernement authentique était l'administration de la *pravda*' (2001: 159). The institution of this ambiguity in the leading organ of the Russian communist press, *Pravda*, thus underlines not only the extreme difficulty of articulating from within Russia a critical approach to government or an alternative view of the world, but also the fact that, in utopias, power and truth, government and information, tend towards synonymity.

But it was not only this paradox that in the end spelt the death knoll for Gide of any hope of a realistic claim by Stalinist USSR to be an *utopie réalisée*. In addition there was to be confronted the flagrant disparity between Marxist theory and Soviet practice whereby the radical *difference* that logically constituted utopia was becoming progressively undermined, beneath the communist propaganda, by a stealthy return of the *same* in the form of

bourgeois values (1936–7: 51). The 'dictature du prolétariat' was in its turn
being hijacked by Stalin's personal dictatorship (1936–7: 61) while internal
forces of counter-revolution were being further surreptitiously encouraged
by political expediency in the light of the threat posed by the fascism and
the belligerence of Hitler's Germany (1936–7: 60).[4] Most seriously of all
for Gide, however, is the elimination (through silencing or through exile
or execution) of difference within Soviet society in the area of the intel-
ligentsia and the arts, sections in which individual creativity and critical
reflection were most likely to reinvigorate and renew the potential realisation of utopian aims. It is noteworthy how in the following passage,
difference is judged by Gide to be in itself a value of primary importance:
'Ceux qui disparaissent, que l'on fait disparaître, ce sont les plus valeureux;
peut-être pas comme rendement matériel, mais ce sont ceux qui diffèrent,
se diversifient de la masse et celle-ci n'assure son unité, son uniformité,
que dans une médiocrité qui tend à devenir toujours plus basse' (1936–7:
144)['Those who disappear, or who are made to disappear, are the most
valuable people; perhaps not in the material return they offer, but rather
in the way they are different from and add diversity to the masses. The
masses themselves are only unified and uniform to the extent that they
share a mediocrity that is getting progressively more dire']. The risk that
general mediocrity would be one of the by-products of egalitarian levelling
in democracies, a risk that Tocqueville had anticipated and that Baudrillard
was, a century and a half later, to confirm, is thus also seen by Gide as being
run in communist Russia of the 1930s, just as it had prevailed in tsarist
Russia as observed by Custine in 1839.[5]

The problem of utopia for Gide thus hinges, as it does for Baudrillard,
on the reality/fantasy relation. If utopia is to realise itself it cannot do so
in terms of the universal logical and scientific values that have become the
criterion for truth in Europe since the Enlightenment. So utopia confronts
us with another paradox: as a modern project, it is only conceivable within
a framework of European enlightenment values – equality, tolerance, etc. –
but, at the same time, it is unable to stand the test of such criteria being
applied to it on its putative realisation. Possible as a concept, utopia is
impossible as a reality unless it is assessed in terms of values (fantasy, irra-
tionality) that run counter to those according to which it was originally
conceived. So, for Gide, communist Russia of the 1930s fails above all
because it is incapable in reality of accommodating the difference of the
multiple individualities, with their multiple fantasies, that constitute it.
On the other hand, America, for Baudrillard, can be construed as *utopie
réalisée* if that realisation is judged not only in rational, scientific terms but

also – as he argues is the case – in terms of fantasy projection and hyper-reality. For utopia to be realised in general terms then, it can only be done within a logic of *aller-retour* that includes *imaginative* as much as rational displacement.

This logical bind leaves (pseudo)cultural projects such as Disneyland as the only possible realisation of utopia in the modern western world and thus as subject to serious semiotic and ethnographic investigation – in Augé (1997), Baudrillard (1996) and Marin (1973) – as any other form of cultural or social construct. For Augé, in 'Un ethnologue à Disneyland', Disneyland seems to offer a solution to some of the problems of *utopie réalisée* as posed by Gide in *Retour de l'U.R.S.S.* In the first place, the Custine paradox or *aller-retour* bind is resolved in that Disneyland offers 'un spectacle en tout point semblable à celui qu'on nous avait annoncé' (1997: 23): the silhouette of Sleeping Beauty's castle against the sky corresponds exactly with the images of it promoted in Disney publicity material, a correspondence that is maintained throughout the rest of the visit. Secondly, the disparity between inside and outside perspectives on the utopian scene is resolved by a double narcissism that characterises both the object itself and the individual's experience of it. In the first place, Disneyland is the spectacle of a spectacle, the reversion back to the (pseudo)real of the cinematographic or televisual images in which the myths and fantasies of American experience found their originary expression. In the second place, the viewer him/herself becomes as much an object of observation as the scene itself: nearly all visitors, Augé included, come with cameras or camcorders, and thus become as much stars in their own movies as Mickey Mouse or the Swiss Family Robinson. Finally, Disneyland as a utopia is able to resolve the problem of cruel signs to the extent that it is able to present objects that are fully real and yet which are completely emptied of real significance. In this way Disneyland succeeds in being both contiguous with and yet apart from the real world – or, as Augé puts it, it represents 'le monde d'aujourd'hui, dans ce qu'il a de pire et de meilleur: l'expérience du vide et de la liberté' (1997: 33). The emptiness or 'vide' is a function of the essential inauthenticity of the experience it offers, 'la gratuité absolue d'un jeu d'images' (1997: 33); the experience of liberty results from the multiple possible trajectories on offer, all of which however are 'sans objet, sans raison, sans enjeu' (1997: 33). As a utopia, Disneyland thus offers not only 'la quintessence du tourisme', in which it is 'real' images rather than the real world that are consumed, but also the quintessence of modern consumer society. To confirm this point, in another essay, 'Une ville de rêve' (1997: 173–85), Augé proposes a utopian vision of Paris in 2040 in which the entire main part of the city has been handed over to Disney to manage as a tourist attraction in which the town's various historic districts are re-programmed and re-labelled – 'Paris historique', 'Disney Belle Epoque' (the 'grands boulevards'), 'Disney Beaux-Arts' (Montmartre), 'Disney-Louvre' – for the delectation and consumption of our descendants.

Baudrillard, in his essay 'Disneyworld Company' (1996), imagines a similar transformation by Disney 'Illimited' of part of New York, in which the whole of the 'hot' stretch of 42nd Street, that 'haut lieu de la pornographie' (1996: 169) becomes a branch of Disneyworld, and thus doubly a 'haut lieu de l'imaginaire' (1996: 170). More radically still, Baudrillard suggests, following on from his famous essays 'La Guerre du Golfe n'aura pas lieu', 'La Guerre du Golfe a-t-elle eu lieu?', 'La Guerre du Golfe n'a pas eu lieu' (1991), that Disney might also buy out from CNN the televisual options on the Gulf War, that anomalous latter-day recrudescence of feudal violence and of the cruel sign, and turn it into an 'attraction mondiale' (1996: 170). In this way 'la pure logique baroque de Disneyland' (1986: 99) could be applied to the whole of reality, following a logic that Baudrillard had already seen at work in the America of the 1980s. For beyond 'la disparition de l'esthétique et des valeurs nobles dans le kitsch et l'hyperréalité [. . .] tout comme la disparition de l'histoire et du réel dans le télévisuel' (1986: 99) that Baudrillard had already observed in *Amérique*, it is, in the later essay, in the *structural* modifications Disneyfication exerts on culture and apprehension of the truth, as much as in thematic content, that it reveals its most alarming and dystopian tendencies. For, Baudrillard argues:

Disney est gagnant sur un autre plan encore. Non content d'effacer le réel en en faisant une image virtuelle à trois dimensions, mais sans profondeur, il efface le temps en synchronisant toutes les époques, toutes les cultures dans le même travelling, en les juxtaposant dans le même scénario. Il inaugure ainsi le temps réel, ponctuel, unidimensionnel, lui-même sans profondeur: ni présent, ni passé, ni futur, mais synchronie immédiate de tous les lieux, de tous les temps, dans la même virtualité intemporelle. (1996: 172)

[Disney is a winner on yet another level. Not content to efface the real by making of it a virtual image – in three dimensions yet without depth – it abolishes time by synchronising all epochs, all cultures into the same travelling shot, by juxtaposing them in the same setting. In this way it inaugurates a real time, specific, one-dimensional, without depth: neither present, nor past, nor future, it offers an instant synchronisation of all places and times in the same virtual atemporality.]

In this way, for Baudrillard as for Augé, Disneyland is able to resolve the issues at stake in any realisation of Utopia – coming and going, present and future, real and sign, freedom and community – but at the price of a radical reformulation of the conceptual frames operative within the western mind:

Disney réalise *de facto* cette utopie intemporelle en produisant tous les événements, passés ou futurs, sur des écrans simultanés, mixant inexorablement toutes les séquences – telles qu'elles apparaîtraient, ou apparaîtront, à une autre civilisation que la nôtre. Mais c'est déjà la nôtre. Car il nous est déjà de plus en plus difficile d'imaginer le réel, d'imaginer l'Histoire, la profondeur du temps, l'espace à trois dimensions – tout aussi difficile qu'il était jadis, à partir du monde réel, d'imaginer l'univers virtuel ou la quatrième dimension. (1996: 173)

[Disney brings into being this atemporal utopia by simultaneously screening all events, past or future, inexorably mixing all the sequences – as they would appear, or will appear, to a civilisation other than our own. But it is already our civilisation. For it is more and more difficult for us to imagine the real, to imagine History, the depth of time, three-dimensional space – quite as difficult as it used to be before to imagine, on the basis of the real world, a virtual universe or a fourth dimension.]

The analyses of Disneyland as utopian scene by Augé and Baudrillard as just cited are prefigured in Louis Marin's magisterial essay 'Dégénérescence utopique' in *Utopiques* (1973: 297–324) where, after a visit to the Los Angeles Disneyland (the first to be constructed), he writes:

Mais, parce que toutes les pressions idéologiques, toutes les formes et tous les aspects de l'aliénation capitaliste et impérialiste moderne sont représentées, parce que Disneyland est la représentation de la représentation constitutive de l'idéologie contemporaine, parce que le lieu est une scène et un espace de projection où nous pouvons voir et expérimenter l'idéologie de la classe dominante de la société américaine, nous pouvons penser que le monde réalisé de Walt Disney remplit la fonction idéologique-critique que nous reconnaissons à la production utopique. (1973: 298)

[But because all ideological pressures, all forms and aspects of modern capitalist and imperialist alienation are represented, because Disneyland is the representation of the representation that constitutes contemporary ideology, because the place is a stage and a projected space in which we can see and experience the ideology of the dominant class of American society, we have grounds to believe that the world as reproduced by Walt Disney fulfils the ideological–critical function that we recognise in utopian production.]

In fact, however, as Marin is quick to assert, Disneyland offers only a degenerate form of utopianism, one in which the vital critical/comparative aspect of utopian thinking is lacking. For although, as we have seen, Disneyland seems to solve many of the problems any realisation of utopia might be expected to bring in its train, it does not, for all its exuberant fantasy and technological sophistication, in fact provide the cues that would stimulate critical or creative engagement with the 'réalité de l'imaginaire' (1973: 306) that it substitutes for everyday reality. This is because the fantastic return of reality does not in fact bring a version of the latter that is anything like rich enough to provoke profound reverie, or complex enough to stimulate a re-vision, and possible consequent enrichment of reality itself. Disneyland, according to Marin, in another paradox of ideological reversal, is thus too *totalitarian* in its programming of the imaginary world it proposes to satisfy the criteria of a utopia within the European intellectual tradition:

D'où la violence exercée dans l'imaginaire par le fantasme de ce district de Disneyland [le 'Monde fantastique']: l'autre de la réalité apparaît – et en cela, le 'Monde fantastique' est le lieu utopique privilégié de Disneyland – mais il apparaît comme la réalité des images banalisées, routinisées, des films de Walt Disney, signes pauvres d'une imagination homogénéisée par les mass-media; cet autre est bien le leurre où le désir se prend, mais ce leurre est la forme collective, totalitaire, que l'imaginaire d'une société a reçue et où elle s'est contrainte dans le face-à-face assimilé, digéré et caricaturé de sa propre image. (1973: 306)

[From this follows the violence exerted on the imaginative realm by the phantasm of this district of Disneyland (the 'Fantastic World'): the other of reality appears – and in this way the 'Fantastic World' is the privileged utopian site of Disneyland – but it appears like the reality of the common-place and routine images of Walt Disney's films, the weak signs of an imagination homogenised by the mass media; this other is the decoy by which desire is taken in, but this decoy takes the collective, totalitarian form that has been imprinted on a society's imagination and by which that society is constrained when it comes face to face with the fully assimilated, pre-digested caricature of its own image.]

In this way the potential violence of the real, the cruelty of signs that used to have a sacred relation with their object, are re-instated in the purely imaginary terms of the Disney scenario in which an ideology – that of capitalist democracy – invisibly exerts its coercion on the sign-reading process. So, instead of stimulating creative engagement, Disneyland, as Marin pointedly indicates, invites not only passive consumption of the scenarios presented, but also investment in the only form of real activity the governing capitalist ideology acknowledges, that of shopping. So the visitor to Main Street USA, 'l'espace réel de la marchandise' (1973: 309) – the central axis of the amusement park – is above all invited to extend his or her fantasy involvement to the realm of the real by spending, and thus to act out their duty as a consumer within the capitalist system.

In this mechanism we also see exemplified the ideology underlying the souvenir industry: a real object – such as a plastic Mickey Mouse – is marketed to stand metonymically as a sign for another object of so-called mythic or cultural significance (the character Mickey Mouse) which refers its purchaser or receiver to the sign (Mickey Mouse) without any enrichment (except financial, and that to the company marketing the object) accruing to the semiological circuit: no revalorisation or re-exploration of memory (*souvenir*) is activated in the process, the mental construct being reduced to a stereotypical object. In this way the semiological process is drastically short-circuited, consisting merely of an exchange and consumption of tautological signs in which no new meaning or significance accrues to any of the participants. The message of such souvenirs, thus, like that of Disneyland's utopian centre, Main Street USA, as analysed by Marin, is merely that '*la vie est un échange constant et une perpétuelle consommation*' (1973: 319).

To summarise, despite the presence of numerous utopian components, Disneyland in the end offers a degenerate or dystopian model of a possible ideal society. This is because of fundamental weaknesses in the area of semiotics, aesthetics and intellectual challenge. So although Disneyland supplies a plethora of images in unanticipated juxtaposition, it does not provide, as Marin has convincingly shown (1973), any new patterns of combinatory articulation. It merely presents another myth: 'Une utopie dégénérée est une idéologie réalisée sous la forme d'un mythe' (1973: 297). Nor, as Baudrillard has pointed out (1986: 99), does it explore the possibility of a new aesthetics, every one of its scenarios being a realisation of a previous cinematographic, illustrative or textual model: most Disney graphics date back at least half a century. Finally, despite the totality of the experience it offers, it provides little nourishment for intellectual or creative impulses; on the contrary, it ultimately satiates or infantilises the visitor with the banality of its propositions. Disneyland does however have one indisputable critical value in that in offering in the here and now a bland and manipulative vision of a future world it also acts as a warning. For the narrow, circumscribed model it proposes is what will become of our world if culture continues to be subjected to thematisation rather than interrogation, to mediatisation rather than critical evaluation. It also shows, as Baudrillard points out (1996: 172–3), how the current intensive technological mediatisation of cultural experience, of which Disneyland offers a paradigm (and in doing so fulfils its most original critical function), is in the process of fundamentally transforming the categories we apply in relation to our perception and understanding of time, space and continuity. Disneyland as *utopie réalisée* is thus to be read – like all utopias, real or textual – essentially as a cautionary tale.

Despite the multiple and no doubt irresolvable paradoxes attached to the idea of utopia or utopia realised, utopianism remains an essential component of all travel writing. Consciously or unconsciously it insinuates itself into motivations for travel whether in relation to the discovery of new political, moral, sexual or aesthetic values, or in the more general domain of cultural comparison. Thus ethnography and ethnology – drawing their origins in part from the desire to test scientifically the concept of the noble savage, a project dating back at least to the eighteenth century – are as strong in utopian motivation as the religious and other ideological pilgrimages – individual or group – that have since the Renaissance become integral to the western cultural agenda. This utopianism is further visible in the tendency to mythologise both the travel itinerary or voyage experience itself and the country of destination. So, as we shall see in the next two chapters, the Jungle and the Desert are themselves perceived and explored by both nineteenth- and twentieth-century writers as quasi-utopian constructs. Like all utopias, however, they become correspondingly susceptible to dystopian transformation, as will be the case with the jungle in both Michaux and Gide. The desert, on the other hand, though seemingly promising an arid and dystopian scenario, in the event is widely experienced by Chateaubriand, Fromentin, Loti and Baudrillard, in each case for different reasons, as a utopian scene, albeit one that sometimes has to struggle to project its sombre and religious glow into the future rather than the past. A lesson that utopianism will thus continue to teach is that the other – whether landscape, culture, society or individual – always contains the potential to be exemplary, if only in its *difference*.

CHAPTER 5

Signs in the desert: from Chateaubriand to Baudrillard

Le désert paraît encore muet de terreur.

(François René de Chateaubriand, [1811] 1968: 255)

Desert views are eminently suggestive; they appeal to the Future, not to the Past.

(Richard Burton, [1855] 1893: I, 148–9)

Le ciel sans nuages, au-dessus du désert sans ombre.

(Eugène Fromentin, [1854] 1938: 10)

Le désert est une forme sublime.

(Jean Baudrillard, 1986: 70)

The fascination of the desert for travellers in the western tradition is – to use Foucault's distinction as cited in my Introduction (1966: 44–5) – both hermeneutic and semiological. On the hermeneutic level the desert at first seems to offer unpromising materials: appearing as a virtually blank sheet, an empty landscape, it offers little purchase to interpretation.[1] However, its vacant contours are soon imagined to be pregnant with hidden significance. For the wilderness is replete with mythical and/or (Christian) religious associations; it is the theatre of initiatory, expiatory or visionary experiences. It is the site of recollection of or communication with otherwise unheard or forgotten voices, inner or supernatural. It gives access to the deeper self or to the divinity. By drastically reducing the proliferation of phenomena, it can elicit insight into a whole cultural or mythical trajectory – as in the following passage from Chateaubriand's *Itinéraire de Paris à Jérusalem* (1811) in which a dribble of a stream in a Grecian desert suffices to conjure up the glorious exploits of Alexander the Great:

Quelle est donc la magie de la gloire? Un voyageur va traverser un fleuve qui n'a rien de remarquable: on lui dit que ce fleuve se nomme Sousonghirli; il passe et continue sa route; mais si quelqu'un lui crie: C'est le Granique! il recule, ouvre des yeux étonnés, demeure les regards attachés sur le cours de l'eau, comme si cette

eau avait un pouvoir magique, ou comme si quelque voix extraordinaire se faisait
entendre sur la rive. Et c'est un seul homme qui immortalise ainsi un petit fleuve
dans un désert! Ici tombe un empire immense: ici s'élève un empire encore plus
grand; l'océan Indien entend la chute du trône qui s'écroule près des mers de la
Propontide; le Gange voit accourir le Léopard aux quatre ailes, qui triomphe au
bord du Granique; Babylone que le roi bâtit dans l'éclat de sa puissance, ouvre ses
portes pour recevoir un nouveau maître; Tyr, reine des vaisseaux, s'abaisse, et sa
rivale sort des sables d'Alexandrie. ([1811] 1968: 200)

[Such is the magic of fame: a traveller is about to cross an unremarkable river;
somebody tells him it's called the Sousonghirli; he crosses over and continues on
his way. But if someone shouts out: It's the Granicus! He steps back, opens his
eyes in astonishment and remains glued to the spot watching the water flow past
as if it had a magic power, or as if some supernatural voice could be heard on the
opposite bank. And it is just one man who can thus immortalise a little rivulet
in the desert! Here a great empire falls; here an even greater one supplants it; the
Indian Ocean hears the crash as a throne falls crumbling by the Propontic Sea;
the Ganges sees the four-winged Leopard pounding towards it, spurred on by its
victory on the banks of the Granicus; Babylon built by a king at the peak of his
power, opens its gates to welcome its new master; Tyre, queen of vessels, is abased,
and her rival rises from the sands of Alexandria.]

Just as the quasi-superhuman energy of an Alexander is able to make the
towers of Alexandria rise from the desert, similarly the hermeneutic process,
activated by interpretation or imagination, can draw from the sands of a
wilderness the epic exploits of a mythical/historical human destiny.

On a semiological level, the desert proposes a similarly enticing paradox,
for it is simultaneously a pure sign, what, as we shall see below, Peirce refers
to as a *qualisign* – a pure quality (colour, heat, distance), an abstraction –
and an elaborated symbolic matrix, a 'vision anthologique du monde' as
Baudrillard calls it, a synthesis of all that the earth (and man) ever was
and ever will be. Not only that, the desert also offers an unusually acute
experience of the *sign as a sign*, a special insight into semiosis, that is
the way signs work in activating and structuring the signifying process.
Desert experiences may be construed as semiotic in this way because signs
in the wilderness tend to be reduced to a minimum; like voices in the
wilderness, they elicit both rapt attention and extraordinary interpretative
dynamism. As we shall see, the semiotic nature of the desert experience
will be consciously recognised by later twentieth-century writers such as
Baudrillard, but the whole process is already identified and articulated
in 1855 by Sir Richard Burton in that part of his *Personal Narrative of a
Pilgrimage to Al Madinah and Meccah* that describes his crossing of the
Sinai Desert:

It is strange how the mind can be amused by scenery that presents so few objects to occupy it. But in such a country [the Sinai Desert] every slight modification of form and colour rivets observation: the senses are sharpened, and the perceptive faculties, prone to sleep over a confused mass of natural objects, act vigorously when excited by the capability of embracing every detail. [. . .] To the solitary wayfarer there is an interest in the Wilderness unknown to the Cape seas and the Alpine glaciers, and even the rolling Prairie, – the effect of continued excitement on the mind, stimulating its powers to their pitch. ([1855] 1893: I, 148–9)

This chapter aims to trace both the hermeneutic and semiological implications of French travellers' encounters with the desert. This implies a particular focus on the semiological aspect, that is, both the way the meagre signs of the desert are transformed into symbols of encyclopedic richness, and the writer's increasing consciousness of the semiotic process itself as it structures and enriches such transformations. In order to clarify the movement from minimalist abstraction to intense figuration, from qualities and icons to symbols and propositions, I refer to the sign categories adumbrated by Charles S. Peirce, whose three trichotomies offer an illuminating framework for such an analysis.

The basis of Peirce's semiotic model is a triad which clarifies the link between sign or representamen (first), object (second) and interpretant (third). To paraphrase Peirce, one could say that the representamen (or first) is a sign in so far as it presents itself, and that the interpretant (as shown below) refers it to the object it represents. The object (or second) is everything or anything – real or imaginary – to which the interpretant refers the sign. The interpretant (or third) is not the interpreter of the sign but rather a sign which refers a representamen to its object (Peirce, 1966).

Each component of this triad is broken down by Peirce into three trichotomies. The First Trichotomy, which embraces the three terms *qualisign – sinsign – legisign*, relates to the sign or representamen, clarifying the nature of its construction. A *qualisign* is a quality that is a sign (colour, form, temperature, etc.); strictly speaking, it is not semiotic until *embodied* in a phenomenon or thing of some kind. For example, the colour blue is a qualisign that will recur in desert descriptions that will be studied below. A *sinsign* is a thing or event that is a sign; it includes a *qualisign*. For example, a blue sky is a sinsign that will frequently figure in desert narratives. A *legisign* is a law that is a sign, that is, a conventional sign, repeated as a replica. So, in the texts analysed below, a blue sky will consistently signify African or Arabian desert scenery, as in Eugène Fromentin's 'le pays céleste du bleu' (*Un été dans le Sahara*, [1854] 1938: 7).

The Second Trichotomy, which embraces the three terms *icon – index – symbol*, relates to the object, clarifying the nature of the sign in relation to it. An *icon* is a sign referring to an object in terms of likeness or resemblance. So a schematic sketch of a palm tree stands as a sign of a real palm tree. An *index* is a sign referring to an object as an extension of that object; though not itself a *qualisign*, it includes one or more qualities of the object it denotes, and it involves an icon. So a palm tree is an index of an oasis since it points to water in the desert. A *symbol* is a sign referring to an object by virtue of a law or convention; a symbol is always interpreted as referring to an object. So a palm tree marked on a map is a conventional cartographic sign, signifying an oasis.

The Third Trichotomy, which embraces the terms *rheme – dicisign – argument*, relates to the interpretant, that sign in the mind that processes the representamens it encounters in any signifying process. A *rheme* is a sign of essence or of qualitative possibility – a concept of an object, or idea. It represents its object only in terms of its characteristics. So the verbal sign 'palm tree' conjures up in the mind the qualities or features associated with a palm tree. A *dicisign* or *dicent sign* is a sign of actual existence, an object or idea articulated. So as a *dicisign* the phrase 'This palm tree' signifies or indicates the existence of a palm tree. An *argument* is a sign of an individual; it represents its object in its character as a sign, that is, what is inferred from the sign, as in the proposition 'Palms are trees that grow in oases', or, to cite Burton once again: 'Desert views are eminently suggestive; they appeal to the Future, not to the Past: they arouse because they are by no means memorial' ([1855] 1893: I, 148–9).

Using another triadic model, Peirce also sets out to outline the dynamic structures according to which the interpretant explores the significance of the signs it encounters. For Peirce, neither the object itself (whether thing in the real world, idea, concept or sign) nor the interpretant (whether idea, sign or some other mental operation or phenomenon) is simple and monolithic, but rather double or multiple. Taking the object first, Peirce underlines the difference between the object as indicated by a sign (what he calls the *immediate object*) and the object as it actually exists in reality or as it might exist (the *dynamic object*). So, for example, when someone says the word 'palm' we envisage the object palm in general terms as implied in the sign or word which stands for it. The actual reality of a specific palm tree, or of all the palms in existence, cannot of course ever be completely known and for no individual will the palm as *dynamic object* ever be identical (even if the same tree is referred to). This is because, although the sym-bolising or semiotic processes of a given culture are by definition agreed in practice – without this there would be no possibility of language, culture or communication – in each specific case of *semiosis* (creation or communication of meaning), the individual response will also be a function of multiple, subjective processes. So, just as Peirce envisaged the object as both immediate and dynamic, the interpretant, that sign in the mind which recognises the sign in the world and links it with its object, is also both immediate and dynamic. For example, when the word 'palm' is heard, the immediate interpretant recognises the acoustic sign or signifier and, through the final interpretant, immediately refers it to the object 'palm' in the real world and/or to the concept 'palm' in the mind. If however the word 'palm' is used not literally but metaphorically, to refer to a prize as in the French phrase, 'palmes académiques', the immediate interpretant is not sufficient to interpret the sign; the dynamic interpretant has to be called upon.

The dynamic interpretant is a semiotic mechanism which seeks a plausible interpretation of the sign by exploring its factual context, what Peirce refers to as the logical process of *abduction*. If the word 'palm' is used in a context of academic recognition, then it may be read metaphorically as referring to an award, as in 'palmes académiques', (dynamic interpretant 1). If it is used in the context of the Christian calendar, as in the phrase 'Palm Sunday', then it will be interpreted accordingly by dynamic interpretant 2; in this latter case, 'palm', by drawing on what Peirce refers to as 'collateral experience', is grasped through an *inductive process* depending on specialist knowledge. If the dynamic interpretant cannot grasp the context of the word, it will be unable to understand it and meaning will not be produced. In both the above cases, the Final Interpretant, through a process of abduction or induction, refers the sign to its object. There is also a third interpretative mechanism, that of logical deduction (Final Interpretant 3) which, since it depends on reason and logic, does not need to draw on collateral experience or on the mechanism of the dynamic interpretant. In this case, the sign as reflected by the immediate interpretant is immediately referred to its object.

The peculiarly semiotic quality of desert travel experience is a function of the way it can take the interpretant through the whole range of sign categories from qualisign to argument, in a trajectory whose increasing interpretative complexity follows the hierarchy of signs as set out in Peirce's three trichotomies. Pure qualities or *qualisigns* are generally the first signs perceived. Their semiotic status – pure qualities of colour, heat, extent, etc. – allows the interpretant to experience their vivid, sensuous impact in all their primeval, all-encompassing and incomparable power before being referred for further processing according to the categories of the Second and Third Trichotomies. These qualisigns are embodied in desert scenery so seamlessly with the pure expanses of sand or sky that their conversion to *sinsigns* is scarcely perceived, So, for example, in a passage that will be returned to more fully later, Fromentin's use of the term 'le bleu' already suggests a quality (*qualisign* – blue), a thing (*sinsign* – the sky), and a *legisign* (the Saharan sky), an ambivalence that is resolved later in the same phrase into a complete landscape: 'le pays céleste du bleu' ([1854] 1938: 7). The whole process of interpretation of qualisigns in the desert is vividly spelled out by Pierre Loti in the following passage from his Moroccan travel book *Au Maroc* (1889), with its specifically semiotic terminology ('indication', 'indique', 'représente') and its series of phrases expressing qualisigns:

Dans ce pays sans arbre, on voit toujours à d'extrêmes distances; d'ailleurs, presque jamais de maisons ni de villages, rien qui vienne rompre cette immense monotonie verte ou brune; alors l'œil s'habitue à fouiller les grandes lignes des horizons, à y découvrir du premier coup, comme sur les plaines de la mer, tout ce qui s'y passe d'anormal, tout ce qui est une indication de mouvement ou de vie, même à des degrés d'éloignement tels que, dans notre pays, on ne distinguerait plus. Sur le flanc de quelque colline déserte bleuâtre à force de distance, lorsque des points blancs apparaissent, on se dit, s'ils restent immobiles: ce sont des pierres; des moutons, s'ils se déplacent. Une réunion de points roux indique un troupeau de bœufs. Et enfin, une longue traînée brunâtre, qui s'avance avec une lenteur ondulante, avec un chenillement incessant et tranquille, nous représente tout de suite une caravane, dont nous dessinerions même par avance les nombreux chameaux à la file, balançant leur long cou avec un dandinement de sommeil. ([1889] 1927: 47–8)

[In this treeless country, the eye can scan extreme distances. Moreover, since there are practically no houses or villages, nothing to break the monotonous plains of brown or green, the eye gets used to searching the vast horizons, and discovering at first glance, as it does when sweeping across the sea's expanses, every irregularity, every indication of life or movement, even at distances so great that, in our country, you would not be able to see anything. On the slope of some deserted hill, wrapped in distance's blueish haze, when white spots appear, one takes them, if they do not move, for rocks; if they move, for sheep. A group of red marks indicates a herd of cattle. Finally, a long brownish line, undulating slowly as it advances, with a calm but incessant caterpillar-like movement, is immediately taken to be a caravan, of which one can make out well in advance the number of camels in the troop, swaying their long necks as if nodding off to sleep.]

The flooding of the desert scene with such pure signs tends at first to blind the interpreting consciousness to their possible metaphorical associations, but, with repeated exposure, these latter gradually emerge and are, as it were, retrospectively *re*-cognised in the scene. So, in the first paragraph of the following passage from Chateaubriand's *Itinéraire de Paris à Jérusalem*

(1811), the embodiment of qualities in objects and their evocation in terms of apparently innocent metaphors is followed by a certain symbolisation which will subsequently refer the interpretant back to a range of possible figurative interpretations. The whole art of Chateaubriand in this passage becomes in fact an effort to delay through the writing process the unfolding of the connotations embedded in the qualisigns and sinsigns of his description of the desert of Judea. In this way, the deep symbolic significance of the scene only gradually dawns on the reader who, like the desert traveller, must experience a range of semiotic transformations before he or she is able to grasp its full meaning:

La chaîne du couchant appartient aux montagnes de Judée. Moins élévée et plus inégale que la chaîne de l'est, elle en diffère encore par sa nature: elle présente de grands monceaux de craie et de sable qui imitent la forme de faisceaux d'armes, de drapeaux ployés, ou de tentes d'un camp assis au bord d'une plaine. Du côté de l'Arabie, ce sont au contraire de noirs rochers à pic qui répandent au loin leur ombre sur les eaux de la mer Morte. Le plus petit oiseau du ciel ne trouverait pas dans ces rochers un brin d'herbe pour se nourrir; tout y annonce la patrie d'un peuple réprouvé; tout semble y respirer l'horreur et l'inceste d'où sortirent Ammon et Moab.

La vallée comprise entre ces deux chaînes de montagnes offre un sol semblable au fond d'une mer depuis longtemps retirée: des plages de sel, une vase desséchée, des sables mouvants et comme sillonnés par les flots. Ça et là des arbustes chétifs croissent péniblement sur cette terre privée de vie; leurs feuilles sont couvertes du sel qui les a nourries, et leur écorce a le goût et l'odeur de la fumée. Au lieu de villages, on apperçoit les ruines de quelques tours. Au milieu de la vallée passe un fleuve décoloré; il se traine à regret vers le lac empesté qui l'engloutit. On ne distingue son cours au milieu de l'arène, que par les saules et les roseaux qui le bordent: l'Arabe se cache dans ces roseaux pour attaquer le voyageur et dépouiller le pèlerin.

Tels sont ces lieux fameux par les bénédictions et les malédictions du ciel: ce fleuve est le Jourdain; ce lac est la mer Morte; elle paraît brillante, mais les villes coupables qu'elle cache dans son sein semblent avoir empoisonné ses flots. Ses abîmes solitaires ne peuvent nourrir aucun être vivant; jamais vaisseau n'a pressé ses ondes; ses grèves sont sans oiseaux, sans arbres, sans verdure; et son eau, d'une amertume affreuse, est si pesante, que les vents les plus impétueux peuvent à peine les soulever.

Quand on voyage dans la Judée, d'abord un grand ennui saisit le cœur; mais lorsque, passant de solitude en solitude, l'espace s'étend sans bornes devant vous, peu à peu l'ennui se dissipe, on éprouve une terreur secrète, qui, loin d'abaisser l'âme, donne du courage, et élève le génie. Des aspects extraordinaires décèlent de toutes parts une terre travaillée par des miracles: le soleil brûlant, l'aigle impétueux, le figuier stérile, toute la poésie, tous les tableaux de l'Ecriture sont là. Chaque nom renferme un mystère: chaque grotte déclare l'avenir; chaque sommet retentit des accents d'un prophète. Dieu même a parlé sur ces bords: les torrents desséchés, les rochers fendus, les tombeaux entrouverts attestent le prodige; le désert paraît encore muet de terreur, et l'on dirait qu'il n'a osé rompre le silence depuis qu'il a entendu la voix de l'Eternel. ([1811] 1968: 253–5)

[The chain on the sunset side forms part of the mountains of Judea. Lower and more irregular than the eastern chain, it is also different in its nature: it consists of great heaps of chalk and sand which look like stacks of arms, of folded banners, or of tents in a campsite at the edge of the plain. On the Arabian side, on the other hand, there are black crags that spread their shadow over the waters of the Dead Sea. The smallest bird descending from the sky would not find among these rocks a blade of grass to eat; everything there affirms that this is the land of a condemned people; everything seems to exude the horror and incest from which Ammon and Moab emerged.

The surface of the valley enclosed by these two mountain chains is like that of a sea that long ago receded: beaches encrusted with salt, stretches of dried-up mud, moving sands rippled as if by the movement of water. Here and there a few sickly shrubs eke out a feeble existence in the lifeless earth; their leaves are covered in the salt that nourishes them; their bark has the smell and taste of smoke. No villages, just a few ruined towers. In the middle of the valley flows a bleached and faded river, dragging itself regretfully towards the poisoned lake that swallows it up. Its course through the middle of the plain is only made visible by the reeds that border it: Arabs hide in these rushes, ready to attack the traveller and despoil the pilgrim.

Such are these sites made famous by the benedictions and maledictions of heaven: the river is the Jordan, the lake the Dead Sea; it seems to shine but the guilty cities it hides in its breast seem to have poisoned its waters. Its solitary abysses nourish no living thing; no vessel ever plies its way through its waves; its banks are without birds, trees or verdure; its water, appallingly bitter to the taste, is so heavy that even the most impetuous winds can barely raise a ripple.

When one travels in Judea, one feels at first a deep feeling of ennui; but soon, moving from solitude to solitude, space stretches out before you and gradually, as the tedium is dissipated, one feels a secret terror which, far from being dispiriting, in fact gives one courage and raises the spirits. The scene in all its extraordinary aspects announces a land transformed by miracles: the burning sun, the impetuous eagle, the barren fig-tree, all the poetry, all the scenes of the Bible are there. Each name contains a mystery; each cave foretells the future; each summit resounds with the voice of a prophet. God himself has spoken on these banks: the dried-up torrents, the split rocks, the gaping tombs all attest to prodigious events; the desert itself is struck dumb with terror; seemingly not daring to the break the silence since it last heard the voice of the Eternal.]

In the above passage, the withholding of names of places or tribes – incidentally mentioned in the first paragraph, only fully indentified and *indicated* in the third – 'ce fleuve est le Jourdain; ce lac est la mer Morte' – marks the shift from the First to the Second Trichotomy, from a semiosis of qualities to a semiosis of icons, indexes and symbols. At this stage, the interpreting consciousness moves into a realm of geographical and historical specificity and can situate itself in a field of fixed references: *names* are symbolic signs that *indicate* particular objects, a realm of denotation in which both the traveller and the reader are able to orientate themselves. The scene thus is no longer just a sensual and painterly landscape but a map or *icon* on which the interpretant can plot real geographical and historical links.

The final stage of semiosis – that where the interpretant explores the potentially infinite ramifications of signs in terms of concepts, ideas, arguments or propositions – is embedded most fully in the final paragraph of the passage from Chateaubriand in which he becomes fully cognisant of the Biblical, mythological and moral status of the desert scene before him. Both a recapitulation and an ultimate transformation of his evocation of the desolate wilderness surrounding the Dead Sea and the mountains of Judea, Chateaubriand's text becomes simultaneously an evocation of reality in terms of qualities and objects and an interpretation of the scene's multiple connotations. So the *sign* Judea is first experienced as a quality – solitude; as a feeling of intense oppression – ennui; as well as an object or geographical location. Next it is interpreted as inspiring a secret terror, a response which interpretation through collateral experience or specialist knowledge (religious education) refers to the historical, Biblical past of the area whose momentous events are still *indicated* to the viewer through the signs engraved on the landscape. Here, Chateaubriand's predilection for tripartite groupings – the named places, the caves and the summits; the dried-up torrents, the split rocks and the opened tombs – echo or anticipate Peirce's triadic structures in their quasi-seamless shift between semiotic categories. Finally the terror of the individual is transferred to the scene as a whole as the former's voice, like that of the landscape, is silenced by that of God, who is in this passage the final interpretant, the sign at first hidden but then finally revealed, which gives ultimate meaning to both the desert scene and the text describing it. In this process, the last paragraph also retrospectively semiotises earlier stages of the passage, imbuing with religious, historical and moral significance motifs at first presented as mere qualities or objects. So the geological and geographical features pinpointed in the first paragraph become retrospectively re-interpreted as *signs* of the opposing forces – Good and Evil, Blessed and Cursed, Jew and Arab – for whose confrontation the desert has provided the battleground. The passage thus contrives to be a parable both of the semiotic process and of the divine message the scene holds for Chateaubriand.

Chateaubriand's aim in this passage, as indeed in the *Itinéraire de Paris à Jérusalem* as a whole, is to try to re-impose on the secular, post-revolutionary consciousness of early modern France a sense of the sacred and the profound in which the image is restored to something like the power and prestige it enjoyed in pre-rational times. His journey back through the mythical sites of Greece and the Holy Lands of Palestine is then not only a scientific enterprise (archeological, historical, geographical, etc.), but also a semiotic excursion into an analogical world where signs in the landscape bespeak real past events and possible future action, as well as the present. Chateaubriand's preference for *indexical signs*, that is, those that point to and have what Peirce describes as a 'a real connection' with their object, is revelatory in this respect. The souvenirs that he brings back with him from his trip, for example, are not only his impressions and their transformation into the symbolic through his writing, but also the fragments of objects themselves that he picked up along the way, objects which, like sacred icons, *represent* their Object with an almost tangible intensity: fragments of marble from the Parthenon, bottles of water from the Nile or the Dead Sea, etc. ([1811] 1968: 147). However, as Chateaubriand's reference to such objects as 'bagatelles' ('trifles') makes clear, he realises that, in the scientific world of the nineteenth century, indexical signs no longer exert the power they wielded in the pre-rational world of mythical and religious societies. When collected and displayed in a museum, like the Parthenon frieze acquired by the British Museum from Lord Elgin, they would become a valuable source of historical and cultural reference, but no longer gave direct access to any absolute or all-encompassing Truth. They were mere signs in a world in which any sacred link between representamen and object had been irrevocably severed.

In the light of this severance, French travel writers in the nineteenth century were increasingly to adopt a more ethnocentric, anthropological approach to desert scenery, seeking not so much first-hand evidence of the divine presence but rather that of archetypal *man*. Thus the Arab in Chateaubriand's *Itinéraire* who, in the passage just cited, lurks among the reeds of the River Jordan's desolate banks awaiting his moment to attack the Christian pilgrim, emerges into the desert glare of Fromentin's *Un été dans le Sahara* to exhibit himself in two archetypal forms. Single and on foot, he displays the manners and characteristics of his ancestors of Biblical times, inhabiting an environment hardly changed during two millennia – he is a figure made for history painting; mounted, he becomes the man of the Sahara, ancient and contemporary, and so a candidate for genre painting:

L'Arabe à pied, drapé, chaussé de sandales, est l'homme de tous les temps et de tous les pays; de la Bible, si tu veux, de Rome, des Gaules, avec un trait de la race orientale et la physionomie propre aux gens du désert. Il peut figurer dans quelque scène que ce soit, grande ou petite, et c'est une figure que Poussin ne désavouerait pas. Le cavalier, au contraire, debout sur son cheval efflanqué, lui serrant les côtes, lui rendant la bride, poussant un cri du gosier et partant au galop, penché sur le cou de sa bête, une main à l'arçon de la selle, l'autre au fusil, voilà l'homme du Sahara; tout au plus, pourrait-on le confondre avec le cavalier de Syrie. Il a moins de style que le premier et plus de physionomie. Au surplus, il ne s'agit point de préférer l'un à l'autre: l'un est l'histoire, l'autre le genre; et la *Noce juive* a bien son prix, même après les *Sept Sacrements*. Que suis-je venu chercher ici, d'ailleurs? qu'espérais-je y trouver? Est-ce l'Arabe? est-ce l'homme? ([1854] 1938: 158–9)

[The Arab on foot, clothed, wearing sandals, is a man of every time and every place: Biblical, if you like, Roman, Gallic, with a touch of the oriental and the physiognomy you would expect from an inhabitant of the desert. He can appear in any scene, big or small, and is a figure that Poussin himself would not disdain. The horseman, on the other hand, standing in the stirrups of a raw-boned horse, gripping its flanks, giving free rein, letting out a deep-throated cry as he gallops off, leaning on the neck of his beast, one hand on the pommel, the other brandishing a gun, that is the man of the Sahara; at most could he be confused with a Syrian horseman. He has less style than the first but a more distinctive physiognomy. Moreover, it is not a matter of preferring one to the other: one represents History, the other Genre; the *Jewish Wedding* is still an important work, even after the *Seven Sacraments*. In any case, what am I looking for here? What did I come here to find? Was it the Arab, was it Man?]

As this passage and others in *Un été dans le Sahara* (1854) reveal, Eugène Fromentin (1820–76) is a painter and art critic as well as a travel writer and manifests a correspondingly acute concern with the forms and modes of visual representation. Whereas Chateaubriand as a writer was fundamentally orientated towards scenes of Greek myth or the Bible, subjects worthy of history painting, with its traditionally mythological, religious or historic subject matter, Fromentin is more attuned to the potential of genre-painting with its focus on the contemporary, regardless of whether or not the subjects proposed be symbolically loaded. So, in the following passage, the essence of the Sahara walks out towards Fromentin in the form of a young woman carrying a water jar, her precocious youth and richness of clothing contrasting with the premature age of the old man escorting her. The 'étonnante vision' the scene constitutes for Fromentin corresponds exactly to the 'vision anthologique' that French travel writers from the nineteenth century to Baudrillard would seek in the desert environment:

Les palmiers, les premiers que je voyais; ce petit village couleur d'or, enfoui dans des feuillages verts et déjà chargés des fleurs blanches du printemps; une jeune fille qui venait à nous, en compagnie d'un vieillard, avec le splendide costume rouge et les riches colliers du désert, portant une amphore de grès sur sa hanche nue; cette première fille à la peau blonde, belle et forte, d'une jeunesse précoce, encore enfant et déjà femme; ce vieillard abattu, mais non défiguré, par une vieillesse hâtive; tout le désert m'apparaissant ainsi dans toutes ses formes, dans toutes ses beautés et dans tous ses emblèmes, c'était pour la première, une étonnante vision. ([1854] 1938: 7)

[Palm trees, the first that I had seen; a little village bathed in golden light, buried in green branches already laden with spring blossom; a young girl walking towards us in the company of an old man, wearing the splendid scarlet dress and elaborate necklaces of the desert, carrying a stone water-jar on her bare hip; the first girl I had seen, fair-skinned, handsome and strong, precocious in her youth, still a child yet already a woman; and the old man, worn down but not disfigured by an early old age; the whole desert appearing to me thus in all its forms, in all its beauty and in all its signs, as a first glimpse, it was an astonishing vision.]

The point about the lyrical accumulation of emblems in the last part of this passage is not so much, as would have been the case with Chateaubriand, their interpretative potential as their very vividness and multiplicity. It is the presence of signs as 'formes', 'beautés', or 'emblèmes' as much as agents of semiosis that is of importance to Fromentin here. It will correspondingly lead him to adopt a more purely aesthetic and abstract approach to representing signs in the desert and in doing so will mark a significant step in French travel writing. The promotion of qualisigns in Fromentin's writing will become thus both more systematic and more conscious than in Chateaubriand's, the sign's symbolic reverberations inviting much less urgent interpretation. In this way, Fromentin aims to maximise the reader's/viewer's immersion in and enjoyment of the sign regardless of its ultimate symbolic importance.

It is for this reason that Fromentin's text *Un été dans le Sahara* is as much a meditation on qualisigns as an account of his travels in the desert. Whereas among the wilderness and ruins of nineteenth-century Sparta, Chateaubriand, by shouting 'Leonidas' at the top of his voice, tries to conjure up and restore all that that name implies in terms of symbolic importance ([1811] 1968: 99), Fromentin interrogates the peculiar silence of the desert, discovering in it qualities as valuable to the artist as any symbolic connotations:

Le silence est un des charmes les plus subtils de ce pays solitaire et vide. Il communique à l'âme un équilibre que tu ne connais pas, toi qui as toujours vécu dans le tumulte; loin de l'accabler, il la dispose aux pensées légères. On croit qu'il représente l'absence du bruit, comme l'obscurité résulte de l'absence de la lumière: c'est une erreur. Si je puis comparer les sensations de l'oreille à celles de la vue, le silence répandu sur les grands espaces est plutôt une sorte de transparence aérienne, qui rend les perceptions plus claires, nous ouvre le monde ignoré des infiniment petits bruits, et nous révèle une étendue d'inexprimables jouissances. ([1854] 1938: 67)

[The silence is one of the subtlest charms of this solitary and empty country. It communicates to the soul an equilibrium you, who have always lived in tumult, cannot understand; far from overpowering the mind, it stimulates lively thoughts. People think that silence means absence of sound, just as darkness is a function of absence of light; it's not the case. If you compare the sensations of hearing and seeing, the silence spread across the great spaces of the desert is like a kind of aerial transparency that renders perceptions more distinct, opening up to us an unknown world of infinitely faint noises, and thus revealing to us expanses of inexpressibly pleasurable sensations.]

Like other English and French painters who were drawn to the unique visual experience offered by desert scenery, Fromentin will of course primarily focus on the visual aspect of qualisigns such as colour, light and shade. Thus shade in the desert (figure 11), like silence, when attentively analysed, reveals layers of suggestiveness undreamed of in a more populated or cultivated environment:

Cette ombre des pays de lumière, tu la connais. Elle est inexprimable; c'est quelque chose d'obscur et de transparent, de limpide et de coloré; on dirait une eau profonde. Elle paraît noire, et, quand l'œil y plonge, on est tout surpris d'y voir clair. Supprimez le soleil, et cette ombre elle-même deviendra du jour. Les figures y flottent dans je ne sais quelle blonde atmosphère qui fait évanouir les contours. ([1854] 1938: 152)

[You are already familiar with the effect of shadow in radiant climates. It is inexpressible; it is something that is both obscure and transparent, limpid and coloured; like deep water. It seems black but when the eye plunges into it, it is surprised how clearly it can see. Eliminate the sun, and this shadow itself becomes light as day. Figures in it float in a kind of blond atmosphere that bleaches out all contours.]

A similar depth and multiplicity of sometimes infinitesimal associations is to be found in colour, the desert sky becoming like a magical palette on which are displayed infinite variations of qualities and tones (see [1854] 1938: 7). But perhaps the most enduring lesson Fromentin as painter and writer learns from the desert is that it brings together qualisigns in patterns of unimaginable profusion and simultaneity. Once again, it is the sky and the various effects of weather that provide the signs that organise themselves into patterns of harmony and contrast that seem simultaneously to

Figure 11 Eugène Fromentin, *A Street in El-Aghouat* (1859) oil on canvas, 142 × 103 cm

exhaust any further potential for representation. So in the following passage, colours, weather patterns, seasons, geological formations, coalesce and intermingle seamlessly, constantly deferring any impetus for final interpretation:

Tout ce côté du ciel était sombre et présentait l'aspect d'un énorme océan de nuages, dont le dernier flot venait pour ainsi dire s'abattre et se rouler sur l'extrême arête de la montagne. Mais la montagne, comme une solide falaise, semblait le repousser au large, et, sur toute la ligne orientale du Djebel-Sahari, il y avait un remous violent exactement pareil à celui d'une forte marée. Derrière, descendaient lugubrement les trainées grises d'un vaste déluge; puis, tout à fait au fond, une montagne éloignée montrait sa tête couverte de légers frimas. Il pleuvait à torrents dans la vallée du Metlili, et quinze lieues plus loin il neigeait. L'éternel printemps souriait sur nos têtes. ([1854] 1938: 8)

[All this part of the sky was dark and looked like a great sea of clouds, whose last wave crashed and rolled so to speak over the furthest edge of the mountain. But the mountain, like a solid cliff, seemed to push the cloud back out, and all along the eastern side of Djebel-Sahari, there were violent eddies exactly like those created by a high tide. Behind descended the lugubrious grey streaks of a vast deluge; then, in the far distance, a mountain showed its head white with frost. There was torrential rain in the valley of the Metlili, and fifteen leagues away it was snowing; meanwhile eternal spring was smiling above our heads.]

This deferral of final interpretation becomes both an ethical and an aesthetic issue for Fromentin in his desert writings. Whereas, as we saw, Chateaubriand will systematically explore the unfolding spectrum of signs of desert scenery, submitting it to a complete and inclusive hermeneutic investigation, Fromentin, almost fifty years later, is more semiological in his approach to interpretation. As an artist, he is concerned above all with the *dynamic* aspect of both the object and interpretant, that is, with the aspect that is not fully expressed in the word or symbol that represents it. He is, for example, concerned by the inadequacy of the word 'yellow', a sign standing for a quality, to express the vivid ambiguity of the colour or qualisign of desert sand. For although the latter, in its subtle tones of fawn, provides a completely new sensation, the word to describe it (and perhaps even the colour to paint it) appear to be lacking:

C'est bizarre, frappant; je ne connaissais rien de pareil, et jusqu'à présent je n'avais rien imaginé d'aussi complètement fauve, disons le mot qui me coûte à dire, d'aussi jaune. Je serais désolé qu'on s'emparât du mot, car on a déjà trop abusé de la chose; le mot, d'ailleurs, est brutal; il dénature un ton de toute finesse et qui n'est qu'une apparence. Exprimer l'action du soleil sur cette terre ardente, en disant que cette terre est jaune, c'est enlaidir et gâter tout. Autant vaut donc ne pas parler de couleur et déclarer que c'est très beau; libre à ceux qui n'ont pas vu Boghari d'en fixer le ton d'après la préférence de leur esprit. ([1854] 1938: 28)

[It is bizarre and striking, I have never seen the like of it, and until now I had never imagined anything as completely fawn, or to use a word that I would rather avoid, as yellow. It would be regrettable if this word were latched on to, for the thing has already been much abused; the word moreover is crude; it denatures what is the finest of tones and is indeed only an appearance. To express the effect of sunlight on this ardent earth by describing it as yellow is to make it ugly and to spoil everything. It might be better not to speak of colour at all and simply to declare that the effect was very beautiful; let those who have never seen Boghari decide on a tone according to their preference.]

Here, the failure of the sign 'jaune', which too readily calls up an immediate interpretant of a crude yellow colour, to account for the dynamic aspect of the object – 'l'action du soleil sur cette terre ardente' – leads Fromentin to consider an appeal to the *dynamic interpretant*, that is to the imagination or collateral experience of the reader or viewer for whom the sign 'beau' is sufficiently imprecise to elicit a more vivid and subjective response. The moral implications of a wrong or crude choice of sign are clearly understood by Fromentin for whom to render ugly ('enlaidir') is not just an aesthetic but also an ethical issue; for, in semiotic terms, ugliness is tantamount to a failure of semiosis, a failure to communicate true meaning.

A similar difficulty is encountered by Fromentin in *Une année dans le Sahel* (1858) in relation to the word 'silence'. Although, as we saw above, for Fromentin the silence of the desert was a state pregnant with infinitesimal but real sensations or impressions, the word 'silence' itself expresses only the immediate object; it does not express the dynamic reality of the experience: 'Il n'y a malheureusement qu'un seul mot dans notre langue pour exprimer à tous les degrés imaginables le fait très complexe et tout à fait local de la douceur, de la faiblesse et de l'absence totale des bruits' ([1858] 1991: 62) ['There is unfortunately only one word in our language capable of expressing to every imaginable degree the very complex and highly localised fact of the softness, tenuousness and total absence of sounds']. This difficulty is exacerbated when it comes to suggesting a religious interpretation of desert scenery. Although the immemorial desert scene peopled by the equally timeless Arab suggests a landscape unchanged since Biblical times, Fromentin sees no justification for using it as a backdrop for Biblical history painting or for using details of the present desert scene to add realism or local colour to a painting of a Biblical subject: 'Costumer la Bible, c'est la détruire; comme habiller un demi-dieu, c'est en faire un homme. La placer en un lieu reconnaissable, c'est la faire mentir à son esprit; c'est traduire en histoire un livre antéhistorique' ([1854] 1938: 56) ['To clothe the Bible

Figure 12 Eugène Fromentin, *Horse by the River Nile* (1871) oil on board, 27 × 35 cm

is to destroy it, just as to dress a demigod is to reduce him to a man. To set the Bible in a recognisable place, is to falsify its spirit; it is to translate into history a book that is a-historical']. So if Fromentin eliminates Biblical subjects as an authentic option for a contemporary painter of the desert he does so since the inclusion of the Biblical signs would falsify the reality of the desert as dynamic object. The Arab and the desert do not exist to evoke the Bible. Although they cannot fail to make a western, Christian artist or writer, to a greater or lesser extent, 'involontairement et souvent penser à la Bible' ([1854] 1938: 56), Fromentin, unlike Chateaubriand, does not travel with the Bible in one hand, or even Homer's *Odyssey* in the other. For Fromentin, the sign in the desert is not a legisign, 'la Bible', but a qualisign, 'la grandeur'. It is a sign that appeals to the dynamic as opposed to the immediate interpretant and must therefore be represented through other qualisigns, such as beauty and simplicity, rather than through symbols or arguments (see [1854] 1938: 57, and figure 12). It is in this sense that for Fromentin, to modify slightly Sir Richard Burton's phrase, desert signs 'appeal to the Future, [as well as] the Past', mobilising abductive or imaginative as well as inductive or recollective interpretants.

This focus by French painters and writers of the desert from Fromentin onwards on the qualisign will lead to an increasingly scientific analysis of it and ultimately to a problematisation of the status of the sign as representation of exotic reality. This undermining will be a function of both the hermeneutic richness and the semiological ambivalence of signs in the desert. Thus for a desert traveller such as Pierre Loti (1850–1923), writing towards the end of the nineteenth-century period in France, the very name of the West African Desert (Maghreb), a single word or symbol, latent with connotations – *Maroc, Arabe, Mahomet, la Mecque, Afrique* – is full to bursting point with possibilities of hermeneutic or encyclopedic interpretation:

Il y a pour moi une magie et un inexprimable charme, dans les seules consonances de ce mot: le Moghreb . . . Moghreb, cela signifie à la fois l'ouest; le couchant, et l'heure où s'éteint le soleil. Cela désigne aussi l'empire du Maroc qui est le plus occidental de tous les pays d'Islam, qui est le point de la terre où est venue mourir, en s'assombrissant, la grande poussée religieuse donnée aux Arabes par Mahomet. Surtout, cela exprime cette dernière prière, qui, d'un bout à l'autre du monde musulman, se dit à cette heure du soir; – prière qui part de la Mecque et, dans une prosternation générale, se propage en traînée lente à travers toute l'Afrique, à mesure que décline le soleil – pour ne s'arrêter qu'en face de l'Océan, dans ces extrêmes dunes sahariennes où l'Afrique elle-même finit. ([1889] 1927: 196)

[There is an inexpressible magic and charm for me in the mere sound of the word Maghreb . . . Maghreb means at the same time the west, the place of the setting sun and the time of sunset. It also stands for the Moroccan empire which is the most westerly of the Islamic states, and is the point at which, in a darkening mass, the great religious impulse given to the Arabs by Mahomet comes to die. In particular, it signifies the last prayer of the day, that, from one end to the other of the Moslem world, is pronounced at this hour of the evening; – a prayer which, starting out in Mecca and following a general act of prostration, progresses slowly across the whole of North Africa, following the setting sun – eventually only stopping at the Ocean's edge, along the last dunes of the Sahara, at the very limit of Africa itself.]

At the same time Loti can query the semiological status of qualisigns, calling into question the semantic stability of qualities of form and colour: 'Grises, toutes ces terrasses, incolores plutôt, d'une nuance neutre et morte, indifférente, qui change avec le temps et le ciel. Jadis blanchies, reblanchies de chaux jusqu'à perdre leur forme sous ces couches amoncelées; puis recuites au soleil, calcinées par les brûlantes chaleurs, ravinées par les pluies, jusqu'à devenir presque noirâtres' ([1889] 1927: 192–3) ['All these terraces are grey, colourless rather, of a dead and neutral shade, indefinable, that changes with the time of day and the light. Formerly white, whitewashed with chalk so often that they have lost their shape beneath the many layers of paint; then fired in the sun, scorched by the burning heat, furrowed by rain, until they appear almost blackish'].

As well as his own experience of the radically different or other acquired through foreign travel to the South Pacific and China, it was in taking stock of the experience of predecessors such as Chateaubriand, Fromentin and Loti, that Victor Segalen was led in the uncompleted drafts of his *Essai sur l'exotisme* (1908) to attempt the scientific analysis of the exotic with which his name is now irrevocably associated.[2] By the beginning of the twentieth century, the association of the exotic with the 'tropical' and with a panoply of symbols, including the 'Cocotiers et ciels torrides' ([1908b] 1995: 13) that, as we have seen, figured prominently in earlier travel writing of the desert, was a phenomenon that was for Segalen ripe for deconstruction. In attempting to retain a vital and authentic meaning for the term 'exotic' in the colonial world of the early modern period, Segalen felt obliged to separate 'Exotes' from the 'pseudo-Exotes' among whom, perhaps over-hastily, he includes Loti, along with tourists and other 'Proxénètes de la Sensation du Divers' ([1908] 1995: 34) ['Pimps of the Sensation of the Diverse'].[3] Although this separation is arbitrary – all travel writers, Segalen included, have their touristic moments – there is no doubt that the verbal facility of some nineteenth-century travel writers was increasingly held as suspect – as was the proliferation of 'Déjà-Vu' ([1908] 1995) in books of 'Souvenir[s] de voyage' or 'Impressions' (26). For *l'exotisme* to remain authentic in the twentieth century, a critical 'dépouillement' or paring-down even more radical than that proposed by Fromentin needed to be undertaken.

In the event, as I hope to show in the next chapter, such an exercise will be pursued most completely by French writers of the Jungle such as Gide and Michaux. But to conclude this chapter, it is necessary to turn to a critique not just of exoticism but also of signs. For, although certain voices, such as that of Théodore Monod (1902–2001), managed, in books such as *Maxence au désert. Un Voyage en Mauritanie* (1935) to maintain an authentic note in the face of the challenges of the North African desert, it is paradoxically in a book that constitutes one of the most radical critiques of signs that the desert will receive its final consecration. Thus Baudrillard's *Amérique* (1986) not only explores the decay of the sign and the disneyfication of culture in the society of radical simulation that is the present-day United States, but also discovers in such desolate sights as Death Valley a mystique similar to that found in the deserts of Islam (1986: 68–9) and a problematisation of visual and aural signs that directly recalls the preoccupations of Fromentin and Loti.

As for his nineteenth-century precursors, the desert for Baudrillard is perceived primarily as a world of qualisigns:

La couleur y est comme subtilisée et détachée de la substance, diffractée dans l'air et flottant à la surface des choses – d'où l'impression spectrale, *ghostly* et en même temps voilée, translucide, calme et nuancée des paysages. De là l'effet du mirage, mirage du temps aussi, si proche de l'illusion totale. Les roches, les sables, les cristaux, les cactus sont éternels, mais aussi éphémères, irréels et détachés de leur substance. [. . .] Par contre, la lumière, elle, est substantielle, pulvérisée dans l'air, elle donne à toutes les teintes cette nuance pastel caractéristique qui est comme l'image de la désincarnation, de la séparation de l'âme et du corps. Dans ce sens on peut parler de l'abstraction du désert. (1986: 70)

[Colour there seems to have evaporated from matter, becoming diffracted into the air, floating on the surface of things; the result of this is landscapes that appear ghostly and at the same time veiled, translucent, peaceful and subtle. A mirage effect is produced, one which also affects time, and comes very close to total illusion. The rocks, sand, salt crystals and cacti are eternal, but they are also ephemeral, unreal, detached from any substance. (. . .) On the other hand, the light has substance, is powdery in the air, giving to all colours a characteristic pastel shade that is like an image of disincarnation, of the separation of soul from body. In this sense, one can speak of the abstraction of the desert.]

Here the signs of the desert, whether they are mineral, vegetable, light- or time-related, are perceived both as icons or qualisigns – signs of essence and of quality – and as sinsigns – signs of reality and presence. They can detach themselves from their objects, sensual films or wraiths that bear their imprint while seeming to float, or they can solidify into their objects, like chemical precipitates: light becomes *tangible*, objects ethereal. The essential quality of desert signs is their *undecidability*, an undecidability that throws the whole nature of experience and of semiotic representation into doubt. Hence the recurrence of such terms as 'mirage', 'spectre' and 'ghost'. This fluidity of categories and qualities leads not to a world of stable objects to which signs or labels can be attached, but to a world of abstractions, one suggesting an aesthetic of qualisigns that in the twentieth-century American tradition finds its realisation in that school of painting, the obverse of and complement to Pop Art, that is abstract expressionism.

An equivalent ambivalence characterises the aural qualisigns of the desert. So, in the silence of Death Valley, Baudrillard experiences a semiotic complexity similar to that recorded by Fromentin in the Sahara:

Mais rien n'égale, dans un autre sens, et sous le sceau du silence, la tombée de la nuit sur la Vallée de la Mort, sur la véranda devant les dunes, dans les fauteuils du motel, épuisés, transparents. La chaleur ne tombe pas, seule la nuit tombe, trouée de quelques phares d'automobiles. Le silence est inouï, ou plutôt il est tout ouïe. Ce n'est pas celui du froid, ni de la nudité, ni de l'absence de vie, c'est celui de toute la chaleur sur l'étendue minérale devant nous, sur des centaines de miles, celui du vent léger sur les boues salées de Badwater, et qui caressent les gisements métalliques du Telephon Peak. Silence intérieur à la Vallée elle-même, silence de l'érosion sous-marine, en dessous de la ligne de flottaison du temps comme en dessous du niveau de la mer. Pas de mouvement animal, rien ne rêve ici, rien ne parle de rêve, chaque soir la terre y plonge dans les ténèbres parfaitement calmes, dans le noir de sa gestation alcaline, dans la dépression bienheureuse de son enfantement. (1986: 70–1)

[But, in another sense, nothing compares, under the seal of silence, with nightfall in Death Valley, as one sits on the veranda in front of the dunes in the motel armchairs, bleached and transparent. The temperature does not fall, only the night, stabbed by a few car headlights. The silence here is unheard-of, or rather all-hearing. It is not the silence of cold, of nudity or of absence of life but rather that of the heat stretching across the mineral expanses in front of us, over hundreds of miles, that of the light wind blowing over the salt marshes of Badwater, and which caresses the metallic strata of Telegraph Peak. A silence that is internal to the Valley itself, the silence of underwater erosion, below the waterline of time, as it is below the level of the sea. No animal movements, nothing dreaming here, nothing talking of dreams; every evening the earth plunges calmly into perfect darkness, into the blackness of its alkaline gestation, into the felicitous hollow of its engendering.]

In recording here his impressions of nightfall over Death Valley, Baudrillard adopts a tone as elegiac as that used by Fromentin in his visual renderings of desert scenes, the subtle tones of the latter finding their equivalent in Baudrillard's text in the whispering play of assonance, alliteration and repetition. Baudrillard here constructs a linguistic network in which, just as in the desert certain qualities seem to become detached from their objects, so adjectives detach themselves from their nouns, the words 'épuisés, transparents' left floating in apposition after the noun 'fauteuils' in such a way that the qualities these words suggest become available for reattachment to other objects in the passage, to which, indeed, their semantic content seems as plausibly to relate them.

But the chief challenge Baudrillard faces in the Arizona desert is that of attempting to reconcile the hermeneutic and the semiological, the 'vision anthologique' and the 'signe pur', to equate a 'paysage [. . .] dépositaire de tous les événements géologiques et anthropologiques, jusqu'au plus récents' (1986: 69) with the hyperreal or simulacral. The problem is eloquently posed in the following passage from *Amérique*:

[L]a Death Valley a quelque chose de mystérieux *en soi*. Quelque beauté qu'offrent les déserts de l'Utah et de la Californie réunis, celui-ci est autre chose, et de sublime. La brume de chaleur surnaturelle qui l'enveloppe, sa profondeur inverse, au-dessous du niveau de la mer, la réalité sous-marine de ce paysage, avec les surfaces de sel et les *mudhills*, l'encerclement des hautes montagnes, qui en fait une sorte de sanctuaire intérieur – un lieu initiatique, qui tient de la profondeur géologique et des limbes, doux et spectral. Ce qui m'a toujours frappé, c'est *la douceur* de la Vallée de la Mort, le pastel de ses couleurs, le voile fossile, la fantasmagorie brumeuse de son opéra minéral. Rien de funèbre, ni de morbide: une transverbération où tout est palpable, la douceur minérale de l'air, la substance minérale de la lumière, la fluide corpusculaire de la couleur, l'extraversion totale du corps dans la chaleur. Un fragment d'une autre planète (d'avant toute espèce humaine en tout cas), porteur d'une autre temporalité, plus profonde, à la surface de laquelle vous flottez, comme sur une eau lourde. Ce qui engourdit les sens, l'esprit et tout sentiment d'appartenance à l'espèce humaine, c'est d'avoir devant soi le signe pur, inaltéré, de cent quatre-vingts millions d'années, et donc l'énigme impitoyable de votre propre existence. C'est le seul endroit où il soit possible de revivre, en même temps que le spectre physique des couleurs, le spectre des métamorphoses inhumaines qui nous ont précédés, nos devenirs successifs: minéral, lumière, chaleur, tout ce que la terre a pu être, toutes les formes inhumaines par où elle est passée, réunies en une seule vision anthologique. (1986: 67–8)

[There is something mysterious about Death Valley *in itself.* However beautiful the combined deserts of Utah and California may be, this is something else, something sublime. The haze of supernatural heat that envelops it, its inverse depth (it is below sea level), the underwater appearance of the landscape with its salt flats and mud hills, the circle of surrounding mountains, create the effect of an inner sanctuary, an initiatory site, which reflects the geological depths and the soft and spectral limbo of the scene. What struck me above all is the *softness* of Death Valley, its pastel colours, its fossil veil, the hazy phantasmagoria of its mineral opera. There's nothing funereal or morbid here, just a transverberation where all is palpable, the mineral softness of the air, the mineral substance of the light, the corpuscular fluidity of colour. A fragment from another planet (or at least from an epoch before human life), the bearer of another, deeper, temporality on the surface of which you float as if on briny waters. What numbs the senses, the mind and all feeling of belonging to the human race, is to have before you the pure sign, unalterable, of one hundred and eighty million years, and thus the implacable enigma of your own existence. It is the only place where it is possible to relive, alongside the physical spectre of colours and the spectre of the metamorphoses that preceded us, our successive potentialities: the mineral, light, heat, everything that has been, all the inhuman forms that matter has taken, brought together in one anthologising vision.]

It is interesting to compare this passage with Chateaubriand's evocation of the Jordan Valley and the Dead Sea, cited towards the beginning of this chapter. The geographical similarity of the two places – hot, arid valleys below sea level – is striking, as is the hallucinatory clarity with which they are perceived. The difference lies in the way they are interpreted. As we saw, for Chateaubriand, the final interpretant of Judea, even in a post-revolutionary nineteenth century, was the Christian God; for Baudrillard,

Death Valley offers an experience of the virtually pre-semiotic. No collateral experience (except that of a Martian or other extra-planetary consciousness) could cast light on this sign which is so pure that even the slightest con-notation has been bleached out of it. The physical presence of the place, despite its 180 million years, is as spectral as the human consciousness which perceives it, the enigma of the latter being heightened not resolved in the presence of the former. Like Chateaubriand, Baudrillard is concerned with the geographical and the geological features of the site, but in a post-evolutionary age such features open out into a 'vision anthologique' that so far precedes human consciousness as to fade the latter out. The attitude of both writers to their respective scenes is one of religious awe; the differ-ence between them lies in the availability to the former of a still plausible hermeneutic theology while to the latter even the possibility of a semiology has become problematic:

Les déserts naturels m'affranchissent sur les déserts du signe. Ils m'apprennent à lire en même temps la surface et le mouvement, la géologie et l'immobilité. Ils créent une vision expurgée de tout le reste, les villes, les relations, les événements, les médias. Ils induisent une vision exaltante de la désertification des signes et des hommes. Ils constituent la frontière mentale ou viennent échouer les entreprises de la civilisation. Ils sont hors de la sphère de la circonférence des désirs. Il faut toujours en appeler aux déserts du trop de signification, du trop d'intention et de prétention de la culture. Ils sont notre opérateur mythique. (1986: 63)

[Natural deserts release me from the deserts of human signs. They teach me to read both surface and movement, both geology and immobility. They offer a vision expurgated of all the rest – towns, relations, events, media. They induce an exalted vision of the desertification of men and signs. They form the mental frontier against which the endeavours of civilisation come to grief. They lie beyond the sphere or circumference of desire. We should always appeal to the deserts against the excess of signification, of intention or of pretension of human culture. They are our mythic operators.]

In the light of the challenge of Death Valley, in what sense do the hermeneutic and the semiological both fail for Baudrillard? Once again comparison with Chateaubriand is illuminating. For both writers the desert is a screen, one that is at first blank but which in the case of Chateaubriand, as we saw, gradually fills with meaning. This is because the desert as a screen for the nineteenth century is that of the imagination, providing a screen on which can be projected some of the multiple references of the dynamic interpretant. Thus Chateaubriand loves deserts 'qui ouvrent à l'imagination les champs de l'immensité' ([1811] 1968: 384) ['which open up to the imagination immense fields of reverie']. For Baudrillard and the twentieth century, on the other hand, the screen provided by desert scenery is that of the cinema: 'Vous parcourez le désert comme un western' (1986: 57). This is because all of America is perceived by Baudrillard as cinemato-graphic: its hermeneutic is based not on a prior truth or belief but on the semiological dynamic inherent to modern media. The seductive, environ-mental influence of cinema and television is such that the interpretants even of the most sophisticated and educated (i.e. European) viewer are already programmed by the medium's framing strategies with the result that the viewing consciousness can only refer to the scene the interpretants already suggested by what one might call, to adapt Peirce's terminology, *co-televisual* experience. In other words, even in the wildest parts of the American West, the interpreting consciousness comes up against the hyperreal and simu-lacral images that it has already internalised through years of mediatised experience and which it is as impossible for it to delete as it was for earlier travellers to edit out of their vision of the desert images of the Bible. In this regard, Baudrillard's critique of the sign in *Amérique* is as validly applicable to the interpretative processes of Chateaubriand and Fromentin as to the televiewer of the late twentieth century. For, in the end, what signs can tell us about 'reality' has always been and always will be problematic. And in a sense, the more iconic signs are, the more simulacral they become, occlud-ing the object through their very representation of it. So the desert is an ideal site in which to experience the hyperreal. It has also always been the site of the sublime: in the Sinai Desert, Burton, nineteenth-century action hero that he was, exclaims 'What can be more exciting? What more Sublime' ([1855] 1893: I, 149), a perception enthusiastically seconded by Baudrillard in Death Valley 150 years later, as the passage above confirms. What signs in the desert thus teach us is that the sublime is, as Peirce might say, 'merely' hyperreal, the mysterious 'merely' simulacral, the ineffable 'merely' cine-matographic. The modern media thus clarify human semiological processes at the same time that they undermine any ground for belief in any ultimate hermeneutic vision accessible through them.

CHAPTER 6

Jungle books: (mis-)reading the jungle with Gide, Michaux and Leiris

Comme toujours dans ce pays démesuré, rien ne fait centre; les lignes
fuient éperdument dans tous les sens; tout est illimité.

(André Gide, 1927–8: 136)

Après Zaoro Yanga, savane, arbustes, paysage mal dessiné.

(Marc Allégret, 1987: 109)

Cette terre est rincée de son exotisme.

(Henri Michaux, [1929] 1968: 35)

Les Tropiques exactement tels qu'on les imagine. Paysage déconcertant
à force de ressembler à ce qu'on pouvait attendre.

(Michel Leiris, [1934] 1981: 174)

Although the semiotic problem presented by the jungle to twentieth-
century French writers remains as it was for the desert travellers of the
previous century, one of a tension between hermeneutics and semiology, it
is the problems associated with the latter that tend to loom largest.[1] Where
and what are the signs of the jungle? Can they be distinguished from the
amorphous phenomenological mass that is equatorial forest? If so, what
disciplinary tools – anthropological, botanical, geographical, zoological,
etc. – are best suited to a concerted analysis of them? What is the status
of the travel document in the light of these different possibilities? And
how can such hermeneutic preoccupations as do arise – whether anticipated (the search for the 'heart of darkness'; the anthropological project)
or unanticipated (the sociological or political considerations prompted by
European colonialism) – be reconciled with the primary semiological challenge of darkest Africa or Amazonia? Although these questions are not
necessarily explicitly posed at the outset of their journeys by any of the
writers on whom I shall focus in this chapter, they nevertheless emerge,
as I hope to show, as key issues underlining their travel journals, each of

which gives expression to the semiotic issues at stake with a varying dosage of hermeneutic preoccupation.

The first of the three writers in question, the one who sets out with the highest expectations on the hermeneutic level – Gide – is in the event the one who encounters the most persistent semiological problems, and the one whose text as it develops manifests the greatest change in thematic drift. Taking its cue from a *fictional* account of early twentieth-century colonial Africa – Conrad's *Heart of Darkness* (1902) – Gide's *Voyage au Congo* and *Retour du Tchad* (1927–8) nevertheless soon moves from a search for the heart of the Jungle and its black male inhabitants as objects – unavowed but nevertheless flagrant – of erotic/exotic fantasy, towards a more sociological and political analysis of the disastrous impact of colonialism on French Equatorial Africa and the Cameroons.[2] In facing the problem of how to square, on the one hand, primeval nature and commercial exploitation and, on the other, sexual fantasy with colonialist repression, Gide's approach fluctuates successively between aesthetics and anthropology, natural history and sociology. In doing so, it further complicates the quest for a coherent approach to an object – the Jungle – that, as I hope to show, presents itself to Gide as already highly problematic from a semiological point of view.

The second writer in this chapter's trio, Michaux, sets out to South America with much lower expectations on a hermeneutic level than Gide does two years before in Africa. Indeed the motivation governing *Ecuador* (1929) becomes very quickly apparent as a deconstruction of the travel journal genre, one that also calls into question, as one would expect from Michaux, the status and authenticity of the travel writer himself. Such a project involves a much higher degree of consciousness of what is at stake in travel writing than is apparent with Gide, whose apparent naïveté remains one of the unexpected charms of the African journal. In the event, Michaux's descent of the vast Amazon River by small boat and then paddle-steamer raises as many semiological issues as it dismisses hermeneutic ones, such questions as 'Et ce voyage, mais où est-il ce voyage?' ([1929] 1968: 16–17) setting the tone for the entire project. But Michaux is far too complex and subtle a writer for the message even of this, one of his earliest books, to be purely negative. On the contrary, the reader of *Ecuador* is obliged to negotiate issues fundamental to travel writing, whose confrontation at this stage liberated Michaux sufficiently to adopt the more complex approach visible, as we have seen, in subsequent works such as *Un barbare en Asie* (1933).

It is however in the travel journal of the third of the three writers, Michel Leiris, that the demands of semiology and hermeneutics are most clearly articulated and their complex interrelation most steadfastly pursued. For *L'Afrique fantôme* (1934b) constitutes a record of a personal quest and an ethnological expedition (Marcel Griaule's 'Mission Dakar–Djibouti', 1931–3)[3] in which the conflicting demands – methodological, scientific, social and emotional – of the two projects are confronted and analysed at the same that they are *lived* in all the reality of their indissoluble mixture by one subjective individual. A telling image of the extraordinary synthesis Leiris manages to achieve is that evoked towards the end of the book where, in Abyssinia, he participates in a possession ritual: sitting in the hut of the female magician, Malkam Ayyahou, mother of Emawayish, a native woman he loves, the carcasses of two disembowelled chickens bleeding on his head, he calmly records the details in his ethnographic diary ([1934b] 1981: 547).

Here the semiological – the status of the signs in the possession ritual (the sacrifice of chickens, their dismemberment, the distribution of their various parts among participants and in the immediate environment) – and the hermeneutic – the quest for an understanding of the mechanisms (social, psychological, religious) activated by such signs, are both consciously integrated into a recording process predicated on a subject whose personal feelings are, as related passages will show, susceptible to equally complex analysis. In other words, unlike Gide, for Leiris it is as important to turn the ethnographic gaze steadfastly on himself as on the exotic environment. In this way, as is also the case with Michaux (though perhaps to a lesser extent in *Ecuador*), Leiris penetrates to a 'heart of darkness' which, like that of Conrad, is to be found in an inner as well as an outer world. It may be of course that though this double ethnographic project is not explicitly stated in Gide the way it is in Leiris, it is nevertheless implicit in the *Voyage au Congo*. For the amorphous quality of the jungle as perceived by Gide may be an unconscious image of his unfathomability to himself, of his unwillingness to confront the ambiguities lying deep within.[4]

Whatever the case, for Gide, 'l'immense forêt vierge, la vraie' (1927–8: 18) rarely emerges as a static or fully indentifiable object. It is not a fixed phenomenon or event, but mobile and multiple; it is homogeneous and monotonous in both colour and form. Water merges with vegetation ('[M]ais toujours, arbre ou roseau, la végétation empiète sur le fleuve': 1927–8: 33); sky with water ('Vers l'ouest, ciel et lac sont d'une même couleur de perle': 1927–8: 36), vegetation with vegetation ('Pas une fleur; aucune note de couleur autre que la verte, un vert égal, très sombre et qui donne à ce paysage une tranquillité solennelle, semblable à celle des oasis monochromes': 1927–8: 38). The most satisfying jungle images that do emerge are those that as well as offering a sensuous presence also suggest future possibility or evoke the past, that is, transcend time, if not space. The perception of the jungle as a dynamic object is thus to a greater or lesser extent a function of pre-existing interpretants or of the application of a semiotic frame to its dynamic reality in an effort to fix or capture aspects of it. The semiotic process adopted by Gide is thus comparable to that analysed by Baudrillard, whereby the referent 'n'est que l'extrapolation au monde des choses (à l'univers phénoménologique de la perception) du découpage instauré par la logique du signe. C'est le monde tel qu'il est vu et interprété à travers le signe – c'est-à-dire *virtuellement découpé et découpable* à merci' (1972: 188) ['is only the extrapolation from the world of things (the phenomenological universe of perception) of the cutting-out process initiated by the logic of the sign. It is the world as it is seen and interpreted by the sign – that is, *virtually cut-out and cut-outable* at will'].

Gide's strategy thus entails a search for *découpages* that will cut the amorphous mass of jungle experience into comprehensible units, both on the level of the sign – clichés, *instantanés* and other images – and on that of the interpretant – mental images, memories, associated ideas, taxonomies, whether personal, scientific or cultural. The process is indeed partly automatic in that cultural tradition already provides the grids: 'Surtout je m'aperçois qu'on ne peut y prendre contact réel avec rien; non point que tout soit factice; mais l'écran de la civilisation s'interpose, et rien n'y entre que tamisé' (1927–8: 28) ['I realise in particular that one can't actually make real contact with anything there; it's not that everything is factitious, but that civilisation's screen interposes itself, and every perception is filtered']. Here Gide's awareness of the filtering process of human knowledge that interposes a 'screen' between consciousness and reality, what Peirce refers to as the 'dynamic object', is comparable to that applied as a fundamental framing device by French writers in the desert. The problem for Gide, however, is complicated by the fact that the jungle screen is constantly moving: the equatorial forest, like the desert for Baudrillard, is like a film. It is thus no accident that Gide's companion on the Congo trip, Marc Allégret (1987), should be a documentary film-maker, whose project is to capture both the static and dynamic aspect of the jungle and its native cultures. But the problem of movement encountered by Gide and Allégret is exacerbated by the fact that they are themselves constantly on the move – whether sailing up or down river, travelling by car or being carried in a litter by native blacks. Gide's text is thus as littered with poignant near-misses (e.g. 1927–8: 237) as it is with successful shots. The effect of this is to travel along an interface between two moving surfaces, whose momentary synchronisation is a function either of chance or of a culturally determined *découpage*.

These *découpages* can take many forms: there is the taxonomic programme based on scientific probability or imaginary expectation. It is often not fully realised, owing to either the desired species or imaginative qualities of the forest scene being lacking: 'Il faut bien avouer que cette forêt me déçoit. J'espère trouver mieux ailleurs. Celle-ci n'est pas très haute; je m'attendais à plus d'ombre, de mystère et d'étrangeté. Ni fleurs, ni fougères arborescentes; et lorsque je les réclame, comme un numéro du programme que la représentation escamote, on me répond que "ce n'est pas la région"' (1927–8: 43) ['I have to admit that I was disappointed by the forest. I hope to find better elsewhere. This one is not very high; I expected deeper shadows, more mystery and strangeness. Neither flowers nor tree ferns; and when I ask why they are not there, as though they were written into the programme, the reply is that "This is not the region for them"']. When a satisfactory 'take' on jungle scenery is made, it is often because it is framed in terms of an already known landscape model, usually French or northern, comparisons with 'la diversité nuancée de nos paysages du Nord' (1927–8: 38) being numerous, with Fontainebleau (174, 385) a privileged example: 'Chaque fois que le paysage se forme, se limite et tente de s'organiser un peu, il évoque en mon esprit quelque coin de la France; mais le paysage de France est toujours mieux construit, mieux dessiné et d'une plus particulière élégance' (174) ['Each time the landscape tries to take on shape, limit or order itself a bit, it makes me think of somewhere in France; but French landscapes are always better composed and more elegant in their lay-out']. The images most successfully captured are those that resemble what had been anticipated or recollect another scene, and thus participate in a system of semiotic tautology that characterises much Gidean travel experience:

Le spectacle se rapproche de ce que je croyais qu'il serait; il devient *ressemblant*. Abondance d'arbres extrêmement hauts, qui n'opposent plus au regard un trop impénétrable rideau; ils s'écartent un peu, laissent s'ouvrir des baies profondes de verdure, se creuser des alcôves mystérieuses et, si des lianes les enlacent, c'est avec des courbes si molles que leur étreinte semble voluptueuse et pour moins d'étouffement que d'amour. (1927–8: 40)

[The spectacle is beginning now to look more like I thought it would; it's resembling the pictures I've seen of it. Lots of very tall trees which far from presenting the gaze with an impenetrable curtain of vegetation, spread out a bit, open into deep, green glades, hollowing out mysterious alcoves; and if the lianas criss-cross each other it is with such soft curves that their embrace seems voluptuous, a loving hug rather than a strangulation.]

Gide's text collects such images as if they were inspired snapshots, successful in their evocation of the heart of the jungle, as in the perfect jungle image

(1927–8: 60) or as picture postcards, reproduced *faute de mieux* in their dreary banality, as in his evocation of Dakar by night (15). Sometimes these images come straight from magazines or journals, engravings or other mediatised representations, contemporary or historical:

Image de l'ancien 'Magasin pittoresque': la barre à Grand-Bassam. Paysage tout en longueur. Une mer couleur thé, où trainent de longs rubans jaunâtres de vieille écume. Et, bien que la mer soit à peu près calme, une houle puissante vient, sur la sable du bord, étaler largement sa mousse. Puis un décor d'arbres très découpés, très simples, et comme dessinés par un enfant. Ciel nuageux. (1927–8: 17)

[The sand bar of the Grand-Bassam looks like an image from the old illustrated journal, 'Le Magasin pittoresque'. A very wide landscape. A tea-coloured sea, streaked with yellowish bands of foam. And although the sea is more or less calm, a powerful swell approaches the sand-bank, spreading its foam. Then there is a screen of trees that stands out in the background, simply drawn, as if by a child. The sky is cloudy.]

Gide's terminology here ('décor', 'découpés', 'dessinés') once again reflects the semiological process clarified by Baudrillard as cited above.

The fact that Gide is neither geographer, botanist nor ethnographer, accounts for the at times shifting and unscientific approach he adopts to jungle phenomena.[5] Although soon after his arrival in central Africa he gives a long description of palm oil preparation, he adds 'Tout cela n'est pas bien intéressant à dire (encore que fort intéressant à observer); j'abandonne le reste aux manuels' (1927–8: 58), and the few anthropological insights he offers are either relegated to footnotes (1927–8: 223, 294–5), veer perilously near to racism (as in the natives' supposed inability to understand the concept of the word 'Pourquoi?': 1927–8: 112) or lapse into comic imagery: 'Ils [les enfants indigènes] restent à nous regarder manger, comme la foule, au Jardin d'Acclimatation, se presse pour assister au repas des otaries' (1927–8: 59) ['The children stay behind to watch us eat like a crowd at the zoo watching the feeding of the sea lions']. As an amateur lepidopterist, however, though not one in Nabokov's class, Gide shows some promise, though his interest in insects is neither primarily scientific nor merely a pleasure recollecting the innocence of childhood (see 1927–8: 24). The butterfly emerges rather as a metaphor for the beauty and vulnerability of the native, for aspects of jungle life and for the elusiveness of the jungle itself: a beguiling concept that can never fully be grasped. Most poignantly, the butterfly becomes an image of the fragility of native life beneath the onslaught of colonial exploitation, an idea allegorised in a passage in which Gide, attending the trial of a colonial administrator, manages, during the proceedings, to catch a butterfly that flies in through the courthouse window (1927–8: 27–8).

Indeed, the difficulty Gide encounters in adopting a consistent approach to his experience of Africa is undoubtedly exacerbated when the scale and horror of French colonial/commercial exploitation of native blacks becomes apparent to him. This leads him to supplement the more personal and less systematically conceptualised projects of his trip with a more concerted sociological perspective on the problem. As he says: 'Je ne pouvais prévoir que ces questions sociales angoissantes, que je ne faisais qu'entrevoir, de nos rapports avec les indigènes, m'occuperaient bientôt jusqu'à devenir le principal intérêt de mon voyage' (1927–8: 29, footnote) ['I couldn't have foreseen that these difficult social questions, that I was only beginning to make out, of our relations with the natives, would soon preoccupy me to the extent that they became the main interest of my trip']. Thus the machinations of the commercial exploiters of African labour and the politics of colonial administration become further lianas constricting the pathway of Gide's African journey, indeed an ideological jungle, the complete truth of which is as difficult to grasp as that of the equatorial forest: '[C]'est l'extraordinaire complication, l'enchevêtrement de tous les problèmes coloniaux [. . .] Je ne veux tenir pour certain que ce que j'aurai pu voir moi-même, ou pu suffisamment contrôler' (1927–8: 29) ['(I)t is the extraordinary complication, the tangling-up of all colonial problems (. . .) I will only hold as certain what I have seen for myself, or have been able to check properly'].

Genuine though Gide's concern for the well-being of natives may be, his prime interest in them is a function of sexual fantasy, a symptom of his unacknowledged but clearly evident homo-eroticism (as Daniel Durosay confirms in his introduction to Allégret, 1987: 13). So once again, from the amorphous mass of black Africans, the most satisfying images that emerge are those provided by attractive young black males, child or adult. Despite the presence of his young French friend Marc Allégret, Gide, in his 'Joie de se trouver parmi des nègres' (1927–8: 15) ['Joy at finding himself among black men'] launches into various homosexual romances with young blacks, for example the little bangle-seller with the beguiling smile and uninhibited affection (34, 36) whom he describes thus: 'Il ne comprend pas un mot de français mais sourit, lorsqu'on le regarde, d'une façon si exquise que je le regarde souvent' (1927–8: 34) ['He doesn't understand a word of French but smiles when one looks at him in such an exquisite way that one looks at him often']. Gide's erotic fantasies are sometimes unconsciously recreated in fragments of description, as for example that where the vigorous strokes of the black oarsman become an allegory of the male sexual act:

Lyrisme des pagayeurs, au dangereux franchissement de la barre. Les couplets et les refrains de leur chant rythmé se chevauchent. A chaque enfoncement dans le flot, la tige de la pagaie prend appui sur la cuisse nue. Beauté sauvage de ce chant semi-triste; allégresse musculaire; enthousiasme farouche. A trois reprises la chaloupe se cabre, à demi dressée hors du flot; et lorsqu'elle retombe un énorme paquet d'eau vous inonde, que vont sécher bientôt le soleil et le vent. (1927–8: 21)

[I remember the songs of the rowers at the dangerous crossing of the sand-bar. The couplets and refrains of their shanties are sung in an overlapping sequence. Each time the oar is thrust into the water, it is braced against the oarsman's naked thigh. What savage beauty in their melancholy songs, what muscular exhilaration, what wild enthusiasm. On the third oar-stroke, the boat rears up, its prow well out of the water; when it falls again great jets of spray soak us to the skin; we are soon dried out however by the wind and sun.]

Native masculinity also recalls Baudelaire's verse and thus answers to literary paradigms already engraved in Gide's memory, as in this evocation of 'Parfum exotique': 'Nous sautons dans un pousse, que tire un jeune noir "mince et vigoureux"' (1927–8: 16–17).

But literature as a framing device in Gide's *Voyage au Congo* acts as a *découpage* that cuts both ways. Either, as in the example just cited, it acts as a frame, heightening and detaching an image from an otherwise amorphous context; or, more frequently, it acts as a black-out, as an interlude between scene changes, or as a curtain to blot out the unfathomable monotony or impenetrability of the jungle scene. The role of reading can also be that of checking excessive identification with native life on a social or individual level. In this way, Gide's boxes of books create a safety barrier between him and the different symbolic systems of the native societies. Gide reverts to character or (cultural) type whenever the real or the other assert their presence too strongly. So when the noise of the tom-toms of the negro sailors aboard the *Ruby* becomes too deafening, he retreats to his cabin to read Bossuet's 'Oraison funèbre de Marie-Thérèse d'Autriche' (1927–8: 44). If tropical rainfall obliterates the view, Gide plunges back into the *Master of Ballantrae* (1927–8: 57), while on a boring stretch of the River Congo he reads the first three acts of *Le Misanthrope* (1927–8: 53). Gide's preferred reading is the French moralists (Bossuet, Molière, Racine) or the English classics (Milton, Browning, R. L. Stevenson), with Conrad the most prized of all: sweating it out in the tropical heat one night, Gide reads *Heart of Darkness* for the fourth time (1927–8: 356).

Marc Allégret's own travel journal of his African trip with Gide (published posthumously in 1987) provides a valuable foil to the older writer's perspective. In some ways Allégret's outlook is the more open and comprehensive of the two, though its interest lies not least in the insight it offers into Gide as jungle traveller. As his part-documentary, part-ethnographic, part-artistic film of the African trip confirms, Allégret shared Gide's initial approach to Africa as an aesthetic and fantasy adventure, the problems of colonial exploitation finding no echo in it. But as a young heterosexual male Marc's take on native life is very different from that of his older and homosexual mentor. So the fascination exerted by African women is recorded in his photographs and his film, as well as his journal, more openly than are the objects of Gide's more guarded desires (1987: 68). Similarly, in Allégret's journal, as in his photographs and film footage, the ethnographic and the erotic overlap, the unabashed and precocious sexuality of young native girls being evoked as artlessly as their physical beauty (1987: 85, 77). Allégret's response to Gide's homosexual practice is one of amused tolerance, his use of the nickname 'Bypeed' adding a humorously zoological touch to his observations – 'je prends le Bypeed dans une pirogue avec ses petits amis' (1987: 103). He records Gide's amorous advances to the native boys with the same detached amusement that he shows to any other aspect of animal or human behaviour: 'Bypeed fait des sourires et des caresses aux adolescents de Zaoro Dana qui ont suivi le *tipoye* et qui se laissent faire, un peu gênés' (1987: 119).

But Allégret's journal also, as one would expect of a budding artist and film-maker, interestingly nuances the conventional traveller's take on jungle scenery. Like Gide, Allégret is acutely aware of the European observer's tendency to capture the jungle within readymade frames. Picturesque native objects arrange themselves into 'Natures mortes', landscapes or sunsets into colour lithographs – 'C'est un peu chromo, un peu mauvais goût, car il y a tout: le fleuve magnifique, les collines à l'horizon, les arbres en silhouette' (1987: 62) – while even the heat recalls the glasshouses of Kew – 'Une chaleur suffocante (la serre pour les plantes exotiques, à Kew Gardens)' (1987: 62). However, an element of parody or caricature more than usually enters into Allégret's comparisons, a jungle storm providing a 'Spectacle [du théâtre de] Châtelet' (1987: 102) while the village of Abo Boya 'se prêterait admirablement à la photo "pittoresque"; une série de petits groupes de cases entourées d'immenses bananiers' (1987: 114). The ironic spotlight is also turned on human participants: in the village of Djemba, they meet 'Un vieux chef barbu, habillé à l'arabe, très pharisien des gravures des livres d'école du dimanche' (1987: 111), while in another village, accommodated in a hut whose roof is supported by sticks without walls, they feel themselves caged for the observation of the natives: 'Plus que jamais impression de zoo – et "défense d'agacer les animaux"' (1987: 106). Meanwhile, on arrival by river at the village of Dahi, 'Nous [. . .] mettons pied à terre [. . .] et sommes entourés d'une centaine d'hommes chantant à pleins poumons. Très anthropophages. La lune se lève au-dessus des collines, à l'horizon, comme un gros jaune d'œuf' (1987: 120–1). Although a refrain captured by Allégret is that of Gide's repeated attempts to slot jungle scenes into European categories – 'Rappelle un peu la forêt de Frascati, dit Bypeed' (1987: 93); 'Bypeed le compare aux sentiers de Cuverville' (1987: 95), etc. – he himself will avoid such comparisons. Similarly, although he may observe that some jungle landscapes are 'mal dessiné[s]' (1987: 109) and tire from time to time of the jungle's monotony, 'toujours la même végétation' (1987: 114), unlike Gide, he will usually refrain from blocking out the scenery by reading: 'Nous repartons vers les 4h15. Je suis plongé dans le *Master of Ballantrae*, ce qui me gêne un peu pour voir le paysage. Je m'arrache de mon livre' (1987: 120).

A couple of years after Gide and Allégret, Michel Leiris throws further light on this jungle reading habit, one that he himself shares with Gide – he admits to reading Dickens's *The Pickwick Papers* while travelling in Egypt ([1934b] 1981: 289), not to mention Conrad, in particular *Heart of Darkness* ([1934b] 1981: 243):[6] 'Autrefois je reprochais à Gide de parler fréquemment, dans le récit de son voyage en Afrique, de ses lectures, par exemple, Milton ou Bossuet. J'aperçois maintenant que c'est très naturel. Le voyage ne nous change que par moments. La plupart du temps vous restez tristement pareil à ce que vous aviez toujours été' ([1934b] 1981: 225) ['Before, I used to reproach Gide for talking so often in his African journal about the books he was reading, Milton or Bossuet. I see now that it's quite natural. Travel only changes you part of the time. The rest of the time you remain the sad little person you always were']. Reading, as Michaux points out a couple of years after Gide when he writes in *Ecuador*, 'Je ne suis plus à Quito, je suis dans la lecture' ([1929] 1968: 41), is a spatial as well as a temporal activity. It can transport the subject back to a culture thousands of miles away, detaching him or her from the exotic of the immediate environment. This point is further clarified by the passage from Leiris just cited, in which he underlines the necessarily intermittent character of contact with the real or the other of the exotic. The latter can be grasped only for a few privileged 'moments', images of which are only with difficulty separated from the amorphous flux of phenomena, jungle or other, before being adjusted to a given cultural frame and thus made susceptible to representation or expression. The way the critical reader approaches Gide's text (as also those of Michaux and Leiris) is not dissimilar: citation itself is a *découpage*, one necessary to analysis and comment, but one which inevitably also distorts precisely as it strives to highlight the authentic flavour and colour of the travel texts from which it is extracted. The critical process also thus participates in the ambivalence of the semiotic enterprise, in that it involves recognising signs (semiology) and offering a certain interpretation of them (hermeneutics), one that is open to a reading that is both subjective and communal. No travel writer is more conscious of this critical process than the Michaux of *Ecuador*.

For Michaux, it is names and words as signs rather than visual images that become the principal instrument of *découpage* in the jungle landscape. So, on arrival in Ecuador, his first response is a reflection on *names*:

Le nom. Je cherchais des noms et j'étais malheureux. Le nom: valeur d'après coup, et de longue expérience.

Il n'y en a que pour les peintres dans le premier contact avec l'étranger; le dessin, la couleur, quel tout et qui se présente d'emblée! Ce pâté d'on ne sait quoi, c'est ça la nature, mais d'objets, non, point du tout. C'est après de mûrs examens détaillés, et un point de vue décidé qu'on arrive au nom. Un nom est un objet à détacher. ([1929] 1968: 28–9)

[*Names.* I was looking for names but I was unlucky. Names are only worth something after the event, and in the light of long experience.

Only painters can really deal with the first encounter with the foreign; how quickly and completely painting and drawing capture it! Nature is first and foremost an unknown substance, it's not really made up of objects at all. It's only after detailed examination and from a fixed point of view that one can name anything. A name is a detachable object.]

The name is a symbolic sign: it has no real connection with its object and yet is a sign with access to multiple interpretations. Michaux chooses as the title of his book, *Ecuador*, a single proper noun, the name of a country, even though half the text in fact recounts a journey through Brazil. This may be because of the high degree of indexicality of proper names in general, and 'Ecuador' in particular, which elicits multiple interpretants. First, it refers to a major geographical feature, the Equator, the line dividing the globe *equally* into two hemispheres at the maximum circumference of the globe; second, a vast region stretching across three continents (Africa and part of Asia as well as South America); third, a South American country straddling in effect two hemispheres; fourth, an imaginative conception englobing multiple associations, personal and cultural. The signifier *Ecuador*, being Spanish for Equator, brings another layer of associations bound up with the history and culture of Latin America. In all, then, the name 'Ecuador', as an 'objet à détacher', constitutes a potent sign of the exotic.

But names as *découpages* tend to come, as Michaux says, 'après coup'. As the passage just cited suggests, the painter confronting the exotic or jungle landscape does not need to the same extent to cut it up to see it or to give it expression. The landscape presents itself immediately as a totality, the 'pâté' or plastic form of which can be more readily translated into the paint or modelling clay the artist might use to represent it. For the writer, on the other hand, there is always a gap between sign and object. This is because words are arbitrary signs, they bear little or no iconic relation to their object and are a function of a repertory of signs that is already culturally determined according to the various disciplines of European knowledge – botany, geography, geology, history, zoology, etc. As in the Garden of Eden, discrete objects only emerge when they are named. In an exotic context, as Michaux ruefully remarks, this process can necessitate detailed examination and a certain discretion. Thus Ecuador first appears to Michaux as just a mountain of mud ([1929] 1968: 50).

But although, like all other writers, Michaux is ineluctably dependent on words and names, he is deeply suspicious of them. For naming things is a specific kind of *découpage* that cuts across not only the unified or primeval chaos of the other or the exotic world but also the feelings of the perceiving consciousness. Words are like clichés in both the visual and linguistic sense of the word. As we saw with Fromentin in Chapter 5, when they are applied, they tend to cheapen or banalise both the object to which they refer and the emotional reverberation which attempts to express itself through them. They can strike a false note, as in the word *sucre*: '(le franc du pays). *Soucrès, soucrès*, comme on le prononce, le mot le plus goulu, le plus cupide qui soit' ([1929] 1968: 40). As a result of this, Michaux as a travel writer becomes acutely aware of the risks of parody attending evocations of the exotic. Local colour is thus looked upon with deep suspicion. So the Quito women's habit of wearing men's hats, which makes them appear like Amazons, is described by Michaux as 'chiqué' or 'revue de music-hall' ([1929] 1968: 38). Similarly, like that of Gautier at the Alcazar in Toledo, the experience of Michaux in Quito is sometimes inhibited by the presence of the desired exotic, in particular the way it solicits the knee-jerk reaction that Segalen had already decried in nineteenth-century pseudo-exotic writing. Occupying, as J.-P. Martin notes, 'une position avancée dans le front destructeur que la littérature commence à opposer à la notion d'exotisme' (1994: 314) ['an advanced position on the destructive front that literature is begining to set up against the notion of exoticism'], Michaux strives to avoid the 'travel impressions' style of writing that he refers to as 'Un insupportable bazar où l'on ne trouve pas de pain' ([1929] 1968: 16–17) ['An insupportable bazaar in which one finds nothing worth having'].

Michaux discovers two alternative routes out of the impressionist 'bazar'. The first is to reinsert the selected word or name back into a textual continuum which absorbs the banality of each. These mini-texts take the form of the loosely constructed fragments or poems that intersperse much of *Ecuador*. Their advantage is that they are able to express a greater degree of personal emotion, albeit at the expense of a certain bemusement on the part of the reader. This latter, Michaux argues, is in part a function of the nature of the phrases used by the writer, as he explains in the following passage:

La phrase est le passage d'un point de pensée à un autre point de pensée. Le passage est pris dans un manchon pensant.

Ce manchon de l'écrivain n'étant pas connu, celui-ci est jugé sur ses passages. Il est bientôt réputé beaucoup plus imbécile et incomplet que ses contemporains. On oublie que dans son manchon il avait de quoi dire tout autre chose, et le contraire même de ce qu'il dit. ([1929] 1968: 41)

[The phrase is the point of passage of one idea to another. This passage is enclosed in a mantle of thought.

Since the writer's mantle is not recognised, he is judged on his passages. He is soon reputed to be much sillier and more incomplete than his contemporaries. It is forgotten that in his mantle there was sufficient to express a quite different idea, even the opposite of what he said.]

Leaving aside this passage's extraordinary anticipation of the kind of play in language that Derrida will half a century later systematically analyse, one notes more particularly how it clarifies the nature of the tension between the necessarily conventional word used and the 'tout autre chose' that the writer had possibly intended. The advantage of this inevitable ambivalence may be that it enables Michaux, despairing of finding authentic regular formulae to express the exotic, to concentrate rather on reproducing the effect of *dépaysement* in the reader by disorienting him or her in the reading process by the unexpected insertion of poetic phrases or texts. In this way Michaux diverts attention from the exotic object to the latter's *effect* both on him and on his reader by setting up a play of interpretants that the form of the poem, in particular, is adept at mobilising.

The second exit from the tropical bazaar is that, already touched on, of parody and deconstruction. Michaux's aim here is not, however, merely to undermine travel-writing and travel-reading conventions for their own sake. Rather, as was already the case with Segalen in his *Essai sur l'exotisme* of twenty years before (1908), he sets out to reintroduce a sense of critical evaluation which would both problematise and intensify the travel writer's habits of perception and expression. This he does, in a manner anticipated by Segalen and that he will later perfect, as we saw in Chapter 2, in *Un barbare en Asie*, by turning the gaze of the other back onto the traveller at the very moment that the latter attempts to seize the former. The temptation of ethnography is thus both indulged and undermined as the western eye is itself observed by the look of the other, as here:

Le nègre a dans la tête une étrange expression. Comme les orangs-outangs. Et les orangs ont des yeux très humains. Le nègre: une eau dans la figure, c'est son œil.

Les blancs paraissent avoir dans les yeux un noyau plus au moins grand suivant les individus. Ce noyau jamais ne se dissout en regard. Il est la marque du secret, du phénomène cérébral, de la réflexion insoluble en physionomie. ([1929] 1968: 26)

[The negro has a strange expression on his face. Like orang-utans. And orang-utans have very human eyes. The negro has a spot of water in his face: it's his eye.

Whites seem to have in their eyes a nucleus that varies in size from individual to individual. This nucleus never dissolves into a gaze. It is the mark of secrecy, of mental activity, of a reflection that cannot be expressed in terms of physiognomy.]

In his comparison of Amerindians to orang-utans, Michaux seems to be making a racist interpretation but this misapprehension is soon corrected as the orang-utan eye is seen as similar to that of a human, the white man in the end coming off worst as his look is seen to hide as much as it shows of his feelings and humanity. 'L'Autre (l'indien)' is thus seen to be 'un homme comme tous les autres' (98) while the 'voyageur' as 'gobeur de l'intéressant' (120) turns out to be of a somewhat inferior species. The comic vignettes with which Michaux intersperses his text (and which appear only exceptionally in Gide's *Voyage au Congo*) thus become a necessary element of his strategy as a writer of the exotic where each 'take' is potentially a 'take-off', both of the viewed and the viewer: 'J'ai rarement entendu parler des Tropiques avec naturel. Ce ne serait guère possible. On avance ici comme des policiers. Et rien que pour s'asseoir, il faut prendre des précautions de laboratoire' (161–2) ['I've rarely heard anyone describe the Tropics at all naturally. That would scarcely be possible. You move through the jungle like a police officer. Just to sit down, you have to take clinical precautions'].

Moving from sign and interpretant to the object, to which, in the semi-otic process, the former refers the latter, Michaux, as writer of the exotic, experiences a comparable set of semiological difficulties. First of all, in encountering a relatively homogeneous object – person, country or town – the hurried traveller often has difficulty grasping it in its totality.[7] What should be felt as a full and complex experience either passes as in a dream or as a fragment in which somehow the essential is let slip, leaving the traveller with a sense of having missed the point ([1929] 1968: 37).

A more persistent problem, comparable to that encountered by Gide, is the difficulty Michaux has in separating the individual phenomenon from the encompassing totality. Like Gide in the Congo, Michaux travels by boat, descending much of the Amazon in a series of small canoes in one of which he spends much of the time lying on his back beneath a low and leafy roof:

L'auteur ayant parcouru 527 kilomètres en canoa imaginait à Rocafuerte trouver une chaloupe à vapeur, mais elle ne part que dans un mois; il continuera donc à descendre le Napo jusqu'à l'Amazone, parcourant quelque 1.400 kilomètres en canoa, calé sous un pamakari qui est un toit de feuilles arqué, qui descend jusqu'au bord, cercueil de 38° de chaleur, n'y ayant que des sacs de riz où l'on bute, et ni se peut lire ni rien, on est couché plutôt qu'assis et presque sans rien voir. ([1929] 1968: 147)

[The author having travelled 527 kilometres in a canoe hoped to find a steamer at Rocafuerte, but the next one wasn't departing for another month; he continued therefore to descend the Napo down to the Amazon making the 1,400 kilometre journey in a canoe, wedged beneath a pamakari, which is an arched shelter made of foliage descending to the edge of the boat, a coffin heated to 38 degrees centigrade, containing only bags of rice against which one was constantly thrown, in which it's impossible to read or do anything and in which one has to lie rather than sit, without being able to see out.]

The presence of water as simultaneously a containing flow, a means of transportation ('Pirogue trop petite et mobile. Plusieurs fois manque se coucher sur l'eau': [1929] 1968: 138), and as the essence of the jungle environment – clouds, water vapour, downpour, condensation, rapids, currents, waves – results in Michaux being swept along an interface between two humid surfaces at a faster rate even than that of Gide on the Logone. But it is the difficulty of isolating the signs as much as the expression or interpretation of them that is Michaux's prime concern on the Amazon, as the following passage shows: 'On entra dans le courant comme dans un engrenage. Sa brusquerie me renversa sur le dos comme je tendais à G. son kodak . . . Couché dans le fond de la pirogue, j'aurai juré qu'elle *ondulait*' ([1929] 1968: 132) ['We were wrenched into the current as if into a gearing system. The sudden jolt threw me onto my back as I was handing G. his camera . . . Recumbent in the bottom of the boat, I could have sworn that the keel was *undulating*']. Here, the snapshot approach to isolating and recording phenomena is comically abandoned as the exotic phenomenon itself, in the form of the surging Amazonian river current, literally bowls over the canoe's occupants as the swell's undulations make steady camera work impossible thereafter.

The few images that are salvaged from this drenched and mobile environment are thus stained or blurred by the enveloping humidity. Water vapour blots out aspects of the scenery as arbitrarily as clouds in Japanese prints – 'Le jeu du brouillard [qui] se joue au Japon' ([1929] 1968: 55–6) – while in some places the entire forest is obliterated by the downpour ([1929] 1968: 63). When the dynamic object is water, which creates, mobilises, obscures and disperses the essential reality of the scene, there is little the writer can do other than go with the flow, the odd observation appearing like flotsam in the drift. The water absorbs all qualities and qualisigns into itself, as in the 'rivières de chocolat' Michaux observes in Ecuador which transform themselves as they fall from improbable heights: 'Tombant, elle semble poussière; en bas fumée, fumée d'asphyxie, en haut cacao bouillant. Ce rio est le *Pastaza*. Sa chute la *chorrera del Aguayan*' ([1929] 1968: 57) ['Falling, it looked like dust; at the base it was smoke, an asphyxiating smoke, at the top it was boiling cocoa. This river is the *Pastaza*. Its falls the *chorrera del Aguayan*']. Here Michaux identifies, in a manner exactly analogous to Chateaubriand in Judea, the objects indicated by the signs only after the signs have themselves been observed in terms of qualisigns. In such a massive and amorphous environment violent *découpages* are necessary even to *see* the object. This is especially the case in the jungle landscape which has literally to be cut up (with a machete) to be seen and penetrated: trees, lianas, shrubs have to be massacred before the rare orchids and exotic trees can be accessed: 'C'est ainsi qu'il y a beaucoup de morts dans la forêt autant que de vivants et qu'on n'avance qu'avec la *machete*' ([1929] 1968:61). A similar problem arises with the fauna, often so abundant in their profusion as to preclude appreciation: so the spiders inhabiting the rest-house have similarly to be attacked with the machete while, to be observed, a monkey has to be shot ([1929] 1968: 143). Most often fauna are recorded as a cacophony of sounds, fragments of which are evoked in a kind of telegraphic style frequently used in *Ecuador* ([1929] 1968: 150). The phenomena of the exotic real only seem to separate and organise themselves into recognisable objects and species, flora and fauna (and tropical diseases) when experienced through a climate that organises itself vertically rather than horizontally:

Le plus haut, c'est neige et glace, la calotte de nombreux volcons. La région intermédiaire (les 3.000 m.) est encore froide et aride. Une demi-heure d'un train lent, voici une station, on vous offre des mandarines fraîches cueillies. On est piqué de quantité de mouches. On ne supporte plus le pardessus. (C'est qu'on est descendu à 2.300 mètres.) Encore quelques minutes de trajet: cannes à sucre, et quelques centaines de mètres plus bas, vers les 1.000 mètres, ce sont des ananas, bananiers, palmiers de toute espèce, singes, perroquets, typhoïde et paludisme. ([1929] 1968: 87–8)

[At the top, snow and ice cap the numerous volcanoes. At an intermediary altitude (3,000 metres) it is still cold and bare. Half an hour of slow train later and you find yourself in a station with freshly picked mandarins for sale. The flies begin to bite. The overcoat comes off. (This is because one is now at 2,300 metres.) After a few more minutes' descent, there is sugar cane, and a few hundred metres lower, at about 1,000 metres, pineapples, banana trees, all sorts of palm trees, monkeys, parrots, typhoid and malaria.]

Such a quasi-simultaneity of difference, reminiscent of that experienced by Fromentin in the Sahara ([1854] 1938: 8), is summed up by Michaux in a typically comic vignette: 'Il est difficile de déterminer le climat de l'Equateur. Dans les hauts plateaux, les gens ont coutume de dire, et c'est assez juste: les quatres saisons en un jour. [. . .]/Aussi l'habillement est-il une réelle difficulté pour peu que l'on soit dehors pendant plusieurs heures./L'on voit des désespérés sortir, avec chapeau de paille, veston de toile, pelisse et parapluie' ([1929] 1968: 89) ['It is difficult to determine the climate of Ecuador. In the high plateaux, people often say, and they are right: four seasons in a day. (. . .)/So what to wear becomes a real problem if you have to go out for several hours./You see some desperate individuals setting out wearing straw hats, linen jackets, pelisses and umbrellas'].

If, then, for Michaux, Amazonia 'est rincée de son exotisme' ([1929] 1968: 35), it is because of its nature as an object and of the difficulty of reading and representing it in terms of signs. As a phenomenon, equatorial America is 'rinsed' of its exoticism in that water is the dynamic object that both underlies and obliterates it in an unstoppable cycle of convection and precipitation. The only way of accessing or penetrating the vast aqueous system that is the jungle is through rivers and their tributaries, but these arteries are themselves a function of related hydraulic principles, this time applied in a horizontal vector in the form of a flow in which the traveller is inexorably swept along by eddies and currents that deny purchase on his surroundings. As a sign, Amazonia is rinsed of its exoticism in that, given its inherent dynamism and homogeneity, it is difficult to find words adequately to define its difference as a phenomenon, and the differences between the phenomena it englobes, and to express its unique vitality. Photographs and verbal impressions fall short in their representation of its dynamic reality, referring the interpretant less to the latter than to the clichés and commonplaces of a tradition already by Michaux's time a century old. As Meunier ruefully observes, 'l'Amazonie – son nom l'indique – est une terre de rêverie où se rencontrent [non seulement] les mythologies indiennes [mais aussi] la mythomanie blanche' (1987: 57) ['Amazonia, as its name suggests, is a land of reverie where not only Indian mythologies but also white mythomania meet up with each other']. Confronted with a similar situation in Africa, Gide, as we saw, tended to waver between different sign systems – literary, sociological, botanical – never completely abandoning, despite many disappointments, the fantasy of an ultimate centre and a correspondingly englobing sign. Michaux prefers, perversely but enrichingly, to explore the conditions that make any expression of the jungle's ultimate signification highly problematic. Leiris, on the other hand, as we shall now see, manages – by slowing down the flow of movement and by sustaining a range of scientific as well as subjective agendas, the interaction of which he succeeds to a remarkable degree in monitoring – to arrive at what is perhaps, from among these three writers, the most satisfying (mis-)reading of the tropics.

In changing, at the suggestion of his editor at Gallimard, André Malraux, the title of his African journal *De Dakar à Djibouti (1931–1933)* to *L'Afrique fantôme*, Michel Leiris draws implicit attention to the problematic that this chapter has been pursuing in relation to French jungle writers of the 1920s and 1930s, namely, that of the difficulty of grasping the real or the exotic other except as phantom or illusion. The specific connotation Leiris no doubt intended, as an ethnographic investigator of East African possession rituals, to attach to the word 'phantom' will be returned to later, but in the first instance it is the notion of Africa as a phantom, as an elusive principle as much as real object, that will be pursued. For if, like Michaux, Leiris believes that to write a travel book is 'une absurde gageure par quelque bout qu'on s'y prenne' ([1934b] 1981: 248) ['an absurd undertaking, whichever way one looks at it'], this is once again because of the challenge posed first by grasping the complexity of a totality as vast as a continent and second by expressing it in such a way as to represent as far as possible its dynamic reality. Leiris's comments on Gide's project in the *Voyage au Congo* clarify his position in this respect:

Depuis hier, discussions sur les carnets de route de Gide, que l'administrateur a jugé bon de nous prêter. Je les défends pour le principe, car ce livre a tout de même dénoncé pas mal de cochonneries. Mais toutes les descriptions, si brèves soient-elles, sont décidément bien vaines. On ne peut retracer un paysage, mais tout au plus le *recréer*; à condition, alors, de n'essayer aucunement de décrire. ([1934b] 1981: 248)

[Since yesterday we have been discussing Gide's travel notes, that the Administrator thought it a good idea to lend us. I spoke up for them as a general principle since they uncover a lot of shady goings-on. But all those descriptions, however brief, are really pointless. You can't redraw landscapes, you can at most *recreate* them, on condition that you don't, then, under any circumstances try to describe them.]

How does the writer then 'recreate' reality without describing it? Leiris, like Michaux, is as acutely aware of the dangerous seduction of the exotic and the picturesque as of the pitfalls that lie in the path of those who attempt to evoke them in new terms. So while in the earlier part of the trip in particular, Leiris will make comparisons or evoke scenes of Equatorial Africa that exactly recall those of Gide in the Congo a few years earlier – 'Parcours spécialement monotone. Vert ennuyeux' ([1934b] 1981: 63) or 'Joli pays boisé et rocheux – très Fontainebleau – mais quand même assez morne' ([1934b] 1981: 202) – he will increasingly give up any attempt to describe the picturesque, as for example the Chutes du Félou, which are viewed as 'trop pittoresques même pour [. . .] les décrire' ([1934b] 1981: 52).[8] Rather than focus on the object in aesthetic isolation, Leiris will, like Michaux, only with greater rigour, try to make contact with the *real* on a more visceral level: 'Grande joie d'être vautré, abîmé dans la réalité. Je suis gris de poussière. Je me mets sur le dos. Même plaisir que celui qui consiste à patauger en pleine boue, à faire l'amour sur un tas de fumier. Je ne me promène plus comme un corps sans âme, ni comme une âme sans corps. Je suis un homme. J'existe' ([1934b] 1981: 288) ['It's a great pleasure to wallow in reality, to be submerged in it. I am grey with dust. I am lying on my back. It gives the same pleasure as floundering in mud, or making love on a heap of manure. I'm no longer wandering about like a soul-less body, nor a bodiless soul. I'm a man. I'm alive'].

The real that Leiris evokes here then is that of what it means to be *human* and it is on this level that are based most of the observations and investigations, personal or ethnographic, that constitute *L'Afrique fantôme*.[9] This will lead him to focus on both himself and the other as human beings subject to conceptual frameworks, systems of sign, religious beliefs and mythologies that it is precisely the business of ethnography to explore. The problem raised by such an approach, however, is that of the incompatibility of ethnography as a supposedly objective science, and the subjectivity that inevitably enters into any project of investigation into personal experience. Like any other sign system within the European tradition, ethnography, in attempting to reach the real, nonetheless interposes between it and itself a conceptual screen that filters out or blocks any real or *human* contact between itself and its object: '*L'ethnographie ne pouvait que me décevoir: une science humaine reste une science et l'observation détachée ne saurait, à elle seule, amener* le contact; *peut-être, par définition, implique-t-elle même le contraire, l'attitude d'esprit propre à l'observateur étant une objectivité impartiale ennemi de toute effusion*' ([1934b] 1981: 13) ['*Ethnography was destined to disappoint me: a human science is after all a science and scientific observation cannot, of itself, guarantee real* contact; *it may even imply by definition the exact contrary, the mental attitude conducive to observation being an impartial objectivity that is incompatible with any expression of feeling*']. Leiris's grasp of the semiotic nature of this problem is clear, especially his awareness of the essential arbitrariness of sign systems, native as well as European. For all its greater closeness to the real, for all the sacredness that characterises the relation it establishes between sign and object, the native sign system is no less arbitrary a system of conventions than that of western knowledge, not least in that it can never marry itself seamlessly to the psyche of the numerous individuals who constitute the community. As Augé observes 'La question se pose aujourd'hui pour les anthropologues de savoir comment intégrer à leur analyse la subjectivité de ceux qu'ils observent' (1992: 54). Even the most delicate and sympathetic interrogation of the other thus involves a kind of violence[10] in that it aims to interrogate a supposed general system of representation that may not be fully applicable to the individuals participating in it, while the new relations established in the investigatory dialogue are not fully taken into account:

Pourquoi l'enquête ethnographique m'a-t-elle fait penser souvent à un interroga-toire de police? On ne s'approche pas tellement des hommes en s'approchant de leurs coutumes. Ils restent, après comme avant l'enquête, obstinément fermés. Puis-je me flatter, par exemple, de savoir ce que pensait Ambara, qui pourtant était mon ami? Je n'ai jamais couché avec une femme noire. Que je suis donc resté européen! (Leiris [1934b] 1981: 260)

[Why is it that ethnographic enquiry reminds me of a police investigation? You don't get that close to men by getting to know their customs. After your investiga-tions, they remain as closed to you as they did before. I can hardly flatter myself, for example, that I had any idea what Ambara was thinking; and yet he was my friend. I have never slept with a black woman. How European I've remained!]

The issue here is of course that each of the two projects at stake – the ethnographic and the personal – imply a different conceptual framework or *épistémè*. There are two ways for Leiris to understand the thinking of his African friend Ambara. First, the ethnographic route which, through observation and interrogation, will ideally lead him to grasp the deeper cul-tural and conceptual structures underlying Ambara's thinking as an African native. Second, the route of personal friendship[11] and companionship which will lead Leiris to understand Ambara's individual temperament. Good faith on both sides is a necessary condition of progress in both of these approaches. The following remark however shows Leiris's awareness of the mutual collusion that often vitiates the exchange of signs between European interpreter and native, an enterprise in which, as we shall see later, issues of power enter into the equation: 'Hypocrite Européen tout sucre et miel, hypocrite Dogon si plat parce que le plus faible – et d'ailleurs habitué aux touristes [. . .]. Le seul lien qu'il y ait entre nous, c'est une commune fausseté' ([1934b] 1981: 131) ['Hypocritical European, butter would not melt in your mouth; hypocritical Dogon, so bland because the weaker – and moreover used to humouring tourists (. . .). The only link between us is a shared bad faith'].

It is in exploring the element of individual sexual fantasy at the same time as investigating native mythology and religious practice that Leiris gets closest to the paradoxes at the heart of the personal and ethnographic project recorded in *L'Afrique fantôme*. To achieve this, it is necessary for Leiris to be explicit about his sexuality: he does not gloss over or fantasise it the way Gide did in *Voyage au Congo*. So, discussion of Leiris's sexual experiences, in terms of masturbation ([1934b] 1981: 303), auto-eroticism (235) and erotic dreams (148), as well as his later unfulfilled but complex desires in relation to the Abyssinian native woman Emawayish, become integral to a larger investigation of the construction of sexuality, in particular as compared between the different races. A major issue raised is that of the relation between sexual desire and *difference*, and what constitutes the latter. A problem the heterosexual western male confronts with the native woman is that, being both of a different colour and habitually fully or nearly naked, she is *too different* to constitute an object of desire. She is both more available and less distinctly demarcated from her surroundings, the difference of her colour cancelling out the potential appeal of her nudity. The deep fantasy investment of the western male in nudity becomes thus a source of reflection for Leiris, as indeed it does for Michaux, as the following two passages confirm:

Craie, argile, roc ou feuilles, couleurs de la nature.
    Mais le rose blanc du corps!
    Le blanc est nu parce qu'il est seul de son type. Il n'entre pas dans le système; et mis dans un tableau, il sort du tableau et fait la fortune du peintre.
    Au corps conviendrait un sol et une nature du type du ciel.
    On parle du nègre nu. Le blanc seul est nu. Le nègre n'est pas plus nu qu'un scarabée. Et quand on a couché avec une Indienne, on se demande si on l'a vue.
    Seulement, entre deux draps blancs, toutes les races sont nues. (Michaux, [1929] 1968: 40)

[Chalk, clay, crag or leaves, colours of nature.

But not the pinky whiteness of the body!

Whiteness is nudity because it is unique in its class. It doesn't enter into the system; and in a painting, it leaps out of the frame and makes the fortune of the artist.

The body requires a grounding in the natural world.

People speak of the naked negro, but only a white person can be nude. A negro is no more nude than a beetle. And when you have slept with an Indian woman, you wonder if you even saw her!

Only between two white sheets do all the races appear nude.]

[R]êve à peine érotique, qui se termine par une pollution involontaire. Brusque réapparution du sexe, au moment où je croyais le moins y penser.

Ce qui empêche, à mes yeux, les femmes noires d'être réellement excitantes, c'est qu'elles sont habituellement trop nues et que faire l'amour avec elles ne mettrait en jeu rien de social. Faire l'amour avec une femme blanche, c'est la dépouiller d'un grand nombre de conventions, la mettre nue aussi bien au point de vue matériel qu'au point de vue des institutions. Rien de tel n'est possible avec une femme dont les institutions sont si différentes des nôtres. A certains égards, ce n'est plus une 'femme' à proprement parler. (Leiris, [1934b] 1981: 148)

[A barely erotic dream that ends with an ejaculation. A sudden re-appearance of sex when I was least aware of thinking about it.

What, in my eyes, prevents black women from being really exciting, is that they usually appear nude and that therefore to make love with them would not put any social conventions at stake. To make love to a white woman is to strip her of a large number of social conventions, both literally to undress her and to divest her of institutional norms. No such thing is possible with a woman whose institutional norms are so different from our own. In some respects, she is not really a 'woman' at all.]

What both the above passages in their different ways affirm is that eroticism is in part a function of contrast, of which *nudity* is among the most powerful elements within the European tradition. Nudity must be an exception to maintain any erotic charge. Michaux, in a typically humorous manner, analyses this difference in terms of colour and aesthetics, raising issues that Gauguin, as we saw in Chapter 3, as a painter of the naked other, was also obliged to face. Leiris is equally attuned to the erotic charge of contrast, the following improbable vignette providing an African equivalent to conventional European pictorial representations of *Vénus surprise au bain*: 'Une fillette, surprise au bain, met sa main gauche sur sa vulve et de la droite décoche un salut militaire' ([1934b] 1981: 239) ['A girl, caught by surprise when bathing, places her left hand over her vagina, and, with her right, snaps into a military salute']. But, in the longer passage cited above, Leiris stresses a further dimension (one reflecting his involvement with the Surrealists and their notions of irrational desire), that of the link between eroticism and *transgression*. Sexual passion must challenge or appear to break the rules or conventions binding the social community. There is no doubt that, apart from the intense fascination that the Abyssinian woman Emawayish exerts on Leiris on a personal level, the erotic charge she emits is also a function of the transgression sexual contact with her would involve. First, she is already married and appears to have had several sexual relations with different native men. More importantly, she is ostensibly the object of Leiris's study as an ethnographer and thus, in theory at any rate, taboo as a sexual partner. Third, she, like her mother Malkam Ayyahou, is a kind of sorceress, presiding over and being actively involved in possession and exorcism rituals, activities which would clearly add an unimaginable, sacrilegious dimension to *sexual* possession in its more conventional sense. As Georges Bataille and other of Leiris's Surrealist artist and writer friends were also discovering, debauchery takes on its fullest intensity only when committed against the background of religion. While thus acutely aware of, and at times irritated by, the element of charlatanism inherent in the possession rituals enacted by Emawayish and Malkam Ayyahou, Leiris's African experience, even before the Abyssinian episode, has already alerted him to the 'Noblesse extrême de la débauche, de la magie et du charla-tanisme' and to the fund of deep religious feeling they activate in him: 'je suis décidément un homme religieux' ([1934b] 1981: 109). Like Bataille, who dedicated *L'Erotisme* (1957) to him, Leiris is aware that religious feelings are deeply bound up with blood and death, that 'la vraie religion ne commence qu'avec le sang' ([1934b] 1981: 548).

Much of the latter part of Leiris's African journal is correspondingly devoted to attempting to arrive at some sort of resolution of the tensions he experiences between ritual practice, ethnographic record and personal desire. Far from neutralising each other, the professional ethnographic and personal erotic projects of Leiris fuel each other's fire to an extreme of nervous excitement, particularly when they focus, as they mostly do, on the same object – that constituted by Emawayish, seductive daughter of the sorceress Malkam Ayyahou, together the principle practitioners of the possession rituals. Thus the profound desire to enter unreservedly into the visceral complexities of (for want of a better phrase) the African body causes Leiris momentarily to throw over the objective stance of the ethno-grapher, a lapse that is however immediately countered by the realisation that the ethnographic notebook constitutes a priceless document, not only of African ritual but also of the personal lyricism of Emawayish as one of its practitioners:

Songeant aux fulgurations incessantes de la vieille, au charme insolite qui émane de sa fille, mesurant l'immense prix que j'attache à fixer leurs paroles, je ne peux plus supporter l'enquête méthodique. J'ai besoin de tremper dans leur drame, de toucher leurs façons d'être, de baigner dans la chair vive. Au diable l'ethnographie! Le carnet d'Abba Jérôme – sur lequel je lui fais noter au vol ce que dit la vieille, ou bien sa fille, ou bien quelqu'un de l'entourage – m'est un monde de révélations dont la traduction, chaque fois, me plonge dans le délire . . . Je suis dans un état nerveux curieux; détaché, mais préoccupé fatalement de ces choses. [. . .] Sur plusieurs pages du carnet figurent des fragments de poèmes qu'elle [Emawayish] a chantés l'autre nuit, et je n'aurai de cesse qu'ils ne soient complétés. ([1934b] 1981: 436)

[Reflecting on the incessant raging of the old woman, and the strange charm exuded by her daughter, realising the huge price I attach to recording their words, I find myself unable to continue my work in a methodical manner. I need to become absorbed in their drama, to experience their way of being, to bathe in naked flesh. To the devil with ethnography! Abba Jérôme's notebook – on which I make him note down as they are spoken the words of the old woman, her daughter, or any other individual in her entourage – is for me a world of revelations, the translation of which, each time, plunges me into delirium . . . I am in a curious state of nervous excitement, detached and yet inevitably preoccupied personally by these things. (. . .) On several pages of the notebook appear fragments of poems that she (Emawayish) sang the other night, and I can't wait for them to be completed.]

The semiological issues raised by ethnographic observation and the hermeneutic questions that follow on from them are thus almost exactly paralleled in Leiris's experience by the difficulty of identifying the signs emitted by the complex personality of Amawayish, and then reading them in the light of the various 'zars' or demons by which she claims to be possessed.[12] Eventually Leiris came up with a triangular model that seems to express if not resolve the problematic interrelationship between ritual practice, ethnographic record and personal desire in which he is trapped:

Je ne parle pas. A qui parlerais-je? Je mange les grains qu'on me donne, bois le café qu'on me tend. Je regarde ces trois choses: le carnet d'Abba Jérôme, le diaphragme du mouton, le genou nu d'Emawayish, et sens plus que jamais mon irrémédiable isolement. C'est comme si ces trois points, formant un triangle dans ma tête (du fait que je suis le seul à connaître tous leurs liens), coupaient autour de moi l'univers au couteau comme pour m'en séparer et m'enfermer à jamais dans le

cercle – incompréhensible ou absurde pour quiconque – de mes propres enchante-
ments. ([1934b] 1981: 504)

[I don't speak. To whom would I talk? I eat the seeds that are given to me, drink
the coffee I am handed. I look at three things: Abba Jérôme's notebook, the sheep's
diaphragm, Emawayish's naked knee, and feel all the more strongly my irremediable
isolation. It's as if these three points formed a triangle in my head (since I am the
only one to understand their links), cut me off as with a knife from the rest of the
universe in order to separate me and shut me forever into the circle – absurd and
incomprehensible to anyone else – of my own enchantment.]

Leiris's triangle may be interpreted in more general terms as a statement
of the problematic nature of semiosis or meaning creation, in particular
as understood and theorised by Peirce. For the bizarre triad constituted
by the sheep's diaphragm, Emawayish's naked knee and the ethnographer's
notebook exactly reproduces that of the semiotic triangle, filling respectively
the roles of sign, object and interpretant. The sheep's diaphragm, as a key
component of the sacrifice central to the possession or exorcism rituals, is
a *sign* not only of the blood, sacrilege, violence, etc., involved, but also of
the Symbol which, as a semi-transparent membrane having an indexical
relation to its object, can also stand for or refer to a multiplicity of other
phenomena. The naked thigh is the *object*, the dynamic reality of which is
here unfathomable since it is an object *of desire* and thus again susceptible
to the conjuring up of a multiplicity of possible interpretants. Finally, the
ethnographic notebook is the *interpretant*, the instrument recording the
sign and referring it to its object, while also opening out in relation to
the latter a range of hermeneutic or interpretative possibilities. In addition,
for Leiris, these three signs are all also already *interpretants* – they are 'dans
[sa] tête' – signs therefore which interrelate with each other on a purely
semiotic level and which thus need have no real relation with the objective,
outside world. Like a demon or 'zar' in the mind of someone possessed, the
semiotic triangle can thus cut the individual off from reality, the violence
of such an excision being expressed here by Leiris in his use of the image
of the cutting knife, the language of castration.

The components of this triangle are variously and repeatedly thematised
in Leiris's African journal, but perhaps the most important angle of the
three is that of the interpretant, that represented by the 'carnet d'Abba
Jérôme'.[13] This notebook in which, using Leiris's pen, the native informant
transcribes and later translates the utterances of the natives observed, has
many symbolic overtones. First it is a sign of Ethnography, its instrument
and its record. Second it is a symbol of Power, and in particular the power
of the white man, perceived as such by African natives just as it was by the

South American tribesmen, whose appropriation of it was so memorably analysed, as we saw in Chapter 1, by Lévi-Strauss. In Leiris's journal, the misappropriation is effected by Teborah, Emawayish's good-for-nothing son:[14] '[qui] n'aide pas sa mère, répond – si on lui demande quelque chose – que "son travail, c'est d'écrire" (et ce disant il montre un nouveau carnet que je lui ai donné pour faire un manuscrit)' ([1934b] 1981: 536) ['who does not help his mother, and replies – if he is asked to do something – that "his work is to write" (and so saying shows a new notepad that I had given him to write on)']. Thirdly, the *carnet* is a symbol of the Book, the production of which is the ultimate goal of Leiris's equatorial adventure, and the object which in the end constitutes the ultimate *sign* of his African experience, englobing and transcending all the individual objects and encounters that it records. It is also of course the ultimate sign of Leiris himself as a human being, particularly given his commitment, as stated in the various drafts of prefaces he draws up within it ([1934b] 1981: 263–7), to arrive at objectivity through maximising exposure of the self in all its subjectivity.

Ultimately what emerges from Leiris's African journal is the parallel between the construction of subjectivity and the making sense of travel experience, the degree to which the other, the alien, the outside is admitted to the inner, the subjective, the familiar, and the reconfigurations that ensue. Using his findings as an ethnographer and relating them intimately to the observation and record of his personal feelings – for Séan Hand, *L'Afrique fantôme*'s originality lies not least in its establishment of a 'prototype ethnography of the ethnographer' (2002: 54) – Leiris clarifies and enriches our understanding of the semiotic process on which the travel/subjectivity relation is based, one in which that mysterious instrument that is the mind acts as the theatre for the sign's shifting yet pivotal role as intermediary or interface between object and interpretant:

Car, décidément, l'étranger, la brousse, l'extérieur nous envahissent de toutes parts. Nous sommes tous, soit des chasseurs qui renions tout, nous vouons volontairement au monde du dehors pour être pénétrés, faire notre nourriture et nous enorgueillir de certaines forces supérieures, grandes comme le sang qui bout au cœur des animaux, l'inspiration fatalement diabolique, le vert des feuilles et la folie; soit des possédés que cette même marée du dehors vient un jour déborder et qui, au prix de mille tourments qui parfois les font mourir, acquièrent le droit de signer définitivement le pact avec l'éternel démon imaginaire du dehors et du dedans qu'est notre esprit. ([1934b] 1981: 423)

[For certainly, the stranger, the jungle, the outer world invade us on every side. We are all hunters denying everything, devoting ourselves deliberately to the outside world so as to be penetrated by it, to make our food of it, to take pride in certain superior powers, as strong as the blood that courses through the hearts of animals, in certain forms of inevitably diabolical inspiration, the green of leaves and of folly; alternatively, we are all like people possessed, into whom this same tide from without one day overflows and who, at the price of many torments that sometimes bring death, gain the right finally to sign a pact with the eternal imaginary demon of outside and inside that is our minds.]

In *Nous et les autres* (1989), Tzvetan Todorov draws up a list of ten different categories into which modern French travel writers might plausibly be classified, the central four of which – *touriste, impressionniste, assimilé* and *exote* – are the ones that stand out as being particularly germane to the writers studied in this book. The *tourist* is a traveller in a hurry, more in search of monuments and sites than people (except to the extent that the latter may be reduced to 'local colour'), and whose symbol is the camera. The *impressionist* is a more leisurely and practised traveller who is as likely to write a journal or make sketches as to take photographs; the authors of most of the classic French travel texts of the nineteenth century were members of this group. The *assimilé*, as the name suggests, is someone who allows him/herself to be absorbed into the target culture, becoming versed in the deeper structure of the *épistémè* underlying it. Finally, the *exote*, above all as exemplified by Victor Segalen, is a writer who, while searching for and studying the other in its radical difference, stops short of becoming assimilated by it and thus losing his/her native identity. Travel writers such as Michaux and Leiris, who offer the deepest insight into the other, generally fall into the latter two categories and are careful to differentiate themselves from the former. Thus, like Segalen, Michaux mocks the *pseudo-exote*, preferring if necessary to sacrifice an individual response to the exotic if it risks dragging him into the pitfalls of impressionism. Gide in *Voyage au Congo* seems much less wary of such categories, revealing himself to be successively tourist and impressionist, with, as we saw, an occasional effort at a more scientific or at least sociological approach to the less picturesque aspects of his jungle quest. Leiris on the other hand, even more than Michaux, aware of the pitfalls of dilettante travelogue, succeeds best in sustaining the project of the *exote* as defined by Segalen, treading and maintaining a fine line between exoticism and assimilation. For no French writer delves deeper than he does into what is at stake in a concerted effort to understand the other, on both a personal and ethnographic level. At the same time, Leiris is aware of the ultimately utopian nature of any attempt to renounce his own culture to be absorbed into or possessed by the phantom of the other: 'Rester là [chez les Kirdi]. Ne plus rien faire. S'installer dans la montagne. Y prendre une femme et fonder un foyer. Désir utopique que me donnent ces gens, et leurs présents agrestes' ([1934b] 1981: 197) ['Why not stay there (among the Kirdi). Do nothing. Settle in the mountains. Take a woman and have a family. Utopian desire that these people inspire in me, with their rustic presents'].

The value of Leiris's project lies thus ultimately not only in its authentic and complex response to native life in the African tropics, but also in its grasp of the fundamental problems facing anthropology as a method, in particular in its relation to the subjectivity both of its practitioners and of the individuals who collectively constitute its object. Not surprisingly, therefore, *L'Afrique fantôme* is seen by contemporary anthropologists like Augé[15] and Clifford (1988) as a key text in its anticipation of the fundamental changes the human sciences would need to undergo in dealing with a post-modern, post-colonial world in which the boundaries between individualism and community are being redrawn.

CHAPTER 7

Grammars of gastronomy: the raw and the cooked – Lévi-Strauss, Barthes, Boman, Leiris

Mais le jaguar, rendu furieux par l'ingratitude de son fils adoptif qui lui a volé 'le feu [. . .]' restera plein de haine envers tous les êtres, et surtout le genre humain. Seul le reflet du feu brille encore dans ses prunelles. Il chassera avec ses crocs et mange sa viande crue, car il a solennellement renoncé à la viande grillée.

(Claude Lévi-Strauss, 1964: 75)

[C]'est toute une petite odyssée de la nourriture que vous vivez du regard: vous assistez au Crépuscule de la Crudité.

(Roland Barthes, [1970] 1980: 30)

Paradis gastronomique chauffé à blanc autant qu'une géhenne [. . .]. Odeur des carcasses de mouton accrochées aux gargotes voisines. Potage de rognons, avec artères coupées en rondelles et persil. Islamique à tout crin, en dépit du bol et des baguettes. A hurler. Fermons les yeux. Le bouillon est correct.

(Patrick Boman, 1989: 60)

Je suis ravi d'échapper pour un temps indéterminé à ce qui nous restait d'habitudes européennes, notamment les dîners consulaires.

(Michel Leiris, [1934b] 1981: 534)

Food, like any other vital aspect of human culture,[1] is in part a sign system and as Lévi-Strauss says (1965: 29), cooking is a language in which a society (unconsciously) translates aspects of its deeper structure. Or to put it another way, following Khiang-chih Chang, 'one of the best ways of getting to a culture's heart would be through its stomach' (1977: 4). Differences of underlying *épistémè* as between cultures correspondingly imply differences of structure or grammar. While certain fundamental oppositions seem to hold in most cultures, the elements or terms through which they are articulated can vary enormously. In most cases there is tension between syntagmatic or horizontal patterns of articulation on the one hand, and spatial and paradigmatic on the other. What may appear as natural opposites (sweet/sour) to one culture (e.g. European) might be perceived as complements to another (Chinese cooking of the Cantonese style). At the same time such an opposition may occur at a second level in a cooking or eating practice that would normally exclude it, as in the British proclivity to eat jam or other sweet conserves with meat dishes, an exception within European food culture. Food preparation and consumption, like cultures and societies, of course evolve with history and are susceptible to modification in relation to social distinctions and varying ritual practices (see Elias, 1939; Chang, 1977; Goody, 1982; Prakash, 1961). So a series of variables must always be taken into account when analysing and comparing different gastronomic systems.[2]

A glance at some of the earliest historically recorded cuisines is instructive in this respect. So, as Om Prakash comprehensively shows in his masterly compendium *Food and Drinks in Ancient India* (1961) the deep and early perceived links between food and mental make-up in India seem to have established a basis of cultural practice that, notwithstanding inevitable variations over the centuries, continues (at least until the mid twentieth century) to inform Indian cooking. Diet was from early on closely related to health and sexual well-being (the Kamasutra prescribes what should or should not be eaten) and the Indian obsession with spiritual purity extends to the related matter of cleanliness with respect to food and eating. If the cow is sacred in India it is in part so because of its multiple functions in Indian life (not just as flesh), not least in its supply of milk which, unlike in China, formed from early on a fundamental part of the Indian diet. Prakash records, for example, that in the Vedic period (2000–800 BC) some lived on milk alone (1961: 13). The rigid barriers of caste were reflected in Indian eating customs: meat and delicacies for the rich; milk products for the middle classes; food cooked in oil for the poor (1961: 130); while Brahmanas drank soma juice, Ksatriyas drank juice extracted from fruits and roots, Vaisyas drank curds, Sudras water. From the beginning of the early historic period (from AD 75) five elements of food corresponded to five elements of the body; four categories of food – beverages, non-chewed, chewed and licked – being characterised by six flavours – sweet, acid, salt, pungent, astringent, bitter (1961: 132–3). The Indian stomach was divided into four parts, two of which were filled with solid food, one for liquid and one for wind. Lighter, liquid diet was recommended in the summer and at all times a certain order of dishes was to be observed: first sweet, then acidic, then salty, then pungent, and the rest afterwards – an order markedly opposed to the standard modern European menu. Many foods that the modern

western world associates with India were late imports: the British established tea (originally from China) in the eighteenth century while the
Portuguese introduced chillies, tobacco and maize in the sixteenth. This
complex pattern of culinary and dietary checks and balances nevertheless constitutes what is for the most part a coherent system, one that
reflects the religious and cultural evolution of Indian life (Prakash, 1961:
240). Thus the Indo-European linear and syntagmatic linguistic model
is complicated – ramified or spatialised – to a marked extent by the
social and religious factors that also inform the structure of Indian
culture.

Chinese dietary and culinary traditions also seem, in comparison with the
European, more spatial and interwoven, but for reasons different from the
Indian model. One cannot of course generalise too simply about 'Chinese'
cooking since, in such a vast country, regional variations have a significant
part to play. Even though the main division of cooking in China is based
on the north/south divide, with more highly seasoned rice-based dishes
in the south and with wheat or other grain-based dishes (often noodles,
as we shall see with Boman) in the north, four or five different styles
of cuisine can be related to the regions of Honan, Shantung, Szechwan,
Fukien and Canton (see Goody, 1982: 106). However, the binary opposition
that is fundamental to Chinese philosophy, that of Yin (negative, dark,
feminine) and Yang (positive, bright and masculine), also provides the
deeper structure of Chinese eating habits. Since, as Chang points out, the
bodily functions observe the yin/yang principle, Chinese dietary practice
follows suit, seeking to achieve a harmony between well-being and health,
food being both nourishment and medicine. So, 'hot' food (oily, fried,
peppery, etc.) and 'cool' food (water plants, crabs, certain beans), liquid
(yang) and solid (yin), must be balanced, with the *fan* element (rice or
other grain staples) being complemented by the *ts'ai* element (vegetable
and meat dishes and soups). Although drinking is yang and eating is yin,
within eating itself some food is yang and some is yin, food and drink based
on grain being yin, and cooked meat dishes yang. Food thus becomes a code,
a ritual, a social language (Chang, 1977: 15) reflecting the deeper beliefs of
the culture, food semantics offering, as Chang says, 'a potentially fruitful
area of inquiry into the Chinese social system' (1977: 19). The following
food code or hierarchy as outlined by Chang (1977: 40) relates food to
the basic principles of Chinese cosmology (which includes as the five basic
elements: metal, wood, water, fire, earth) that date back as far as the Chou
dynasty (twelfth to third centuries BC):

Yin-shih
(drink and food)

Yin	*shih*	
(drink)	(food)	
	shih, fan	*shan, keng* etc.
	(grain)	(dishes)
[water]	[earth]	[fire]

Whereas the binary logics underlying Chinese food tend be ramified or complexified in its preparation, cooking and serving – as Chang points out (1977: 8), and as Barthes will, as we shall see, also remind us in Japan, all Chinese food is cut up by the cook rather than the eater so that there are no knives or forks on Chinese tables – in western eating practice such binary or other distinctions tend to be set out and observed in a more linear fashion. So in Europe the standard menu structure is one that has evolved, like European theatre, to become one of primarily successive courses or scenes appearing from the wings behind which the *entrées* have been consecutively – one might even say secretly – prepared and where each individual *plat* is a kind of event in itself. So in the standard sequence of soup, main course, salad, pudding or dessert, cheese, the main item is often signalled as the *pièce de résistance*.[3] Minor variations can of course be contained within the general system (the French take cheese before dessert, the English after, etc.). The binary tendencies of western thinking habits also tend to be more strongly observed by the separation of such oppositions as raw/cooked; sweet/savoury; hot/cold; liquid/solid; fresh/preserved. The more spatial orientation of eastern eating habits to be seen in China and Japan will thus be taken, by some of the writers studied in this section, as a reflection of a corresponding spatial approach to sign structures more generally: a language, for example, in which pictographic signs are disposed in vertical or horizontal disposition and in which there is a less pronounced development or more complex interaction of binary oppositions (see Granet, 1933). So for Patrick Boman (1989), the mixture of sweet *and* sour, raw *and* cooked in the same dish, and the ubiquity of the all-inclusive soup, reflect the totalising, organic nature of the Chinese ethos as compared to the more successive and analytical approach that has developed in the European tradition, while in *L'Empire des signes* (1970) Barthes sees, in such dishes as *sukiyaki*, the spatial or pictorial distribution of elements that characterises Japanese culture more generally.

As a fundamental part of human social structure, food and eating are heavily ritualised and invested with mythico-religious as well as psycho-social significance (see Elias, 1939). In so-called primitive societies, many myths of origin relate to fire, without whose transforming energies cooking (in temperate climates at any rate) would be impossible. In *Le Cru et le cuit*, Lévi-Strauss shows how a comparison of South-American Indian myths of origin (especially relating to fire) reveals the deeper structure of native thought, patterns that, like the underlying *épistémè*, are essentially unconscious. Myths, Lévi-Strauss argues, structure men's thinking, rather than the other way round: 'Nous ne prétendons donc pas montrer comment les hommes pensent dans les mythes, mais comment les mythes se pensent dans les hommes, et à leur insu' (1964: 20) ['We cannot then claim to show how men think in myths but rather how myths think through men, without their knowing']. The fundamental semiotic structure underlying myth is a kind of syntax in which varying paradigmatic substitutions operate but always within a certain fundamental logic. In this way, *Le Cru et le cuit* constitutes for Lévi-Strauss the outline of a 'syntaxe de la mythologie sud-américaine' (1964: 16).

It is mythological or religious significance which can also clarify the logic of what might otherwise seem a hopelessly heterogeneous inventory of culinary desiderata or prohibitions. So the following list of culinary taboos drawn up by Ch'en Ts'ang Ch'i (writing in the T'ang period, 618– 907), which reads like a further entry in Borgès's Chinese encyclopedia as cited by Foucault (1966), probably originated in ancient magical beliefs: 'the flesh of a black ox or goat with a white head, a single-horned goat, domestic animals that had died facing north, deer spotted like leopards, horse liver, and meat that a dog had refused to eat' (see Edward H. Schafer, in Chang, 1977: 131–2).

French travel writers' recurrent interest in food is symptomatic of a desire to come close to the other, to approach the epistemic structures buried beneath the surface of the exotic culture. Food is a way of tasting, exploring and ingesting the other in which the sensual and visceral can be experienced almost as powerfully as the sexual. Indeed the connection between food consumption and sexual consummation, as the words imply, is deep-rooted,[4] the link between incestuous sex and the origin of fire being, as Lévi-Strauss shows, a recurrent motif in South American myths. A sensitivity to the sexual connotations of food or words attached to it is also evident in Barthes:

Ce qui est honoré dans la crudité (terme que bizarrement nous employons au singulier pour dénoter la sexualité du langage, et au pluriel pour nommer la part extérieure, anormale et quelque peu tabou de nos menus), ce n'est pas, semble-t-il, comme chez nous, une essence intérieure de l'aliment, la pléthore sanguine (le sang étant symbole de la force et de la mort) dont nous recueillerons par transmigration l'énergie vitale. ([1970] 1980: 30–1)

[What is honoured in salads/crudities (a term which bizarrely we use in the singular to denote the sexuality of language, and in the plural to call the exterior, abnormal and somewhat taboo side of menus) is not, it seems, as it is in Europe, an essence intrinsic to the food, the full-blooded richness (blood being a symbol of both strength and death) whose vital energy we consume through a kind of transmigration.]

It appears again in Boman who describes as follows the taste of Chinese noodle soup: 'Comme si maintenant la bolée n'était sirotée que dans l'attente, à chaque instant plus insupportable, des quelques algues – subtil arrière-goût de sel d'un con aimé' (1989: 29) ['As if the dish were only sipped now in the expectation, at each moment more intense, of sea-weeds with the subtle salty aftertaste of a cherished cunt']. The gradual but progressive separation of food from ritual practice in the West is far less advanced in so-called primitive African and South American cultures. These latter thus offer the traveller valuable insights into the hidden symbolic significance of eating and food. So in certain rituals of Abyssinian tribes as observed and participated in by Leiris in *L'Afrique fantôme*, food (animal, vegetable and mineral – flesh, herbs, salt) and drink (fermented concoctions or brewed beverages like coffee) play a vital symbolic role.

A meal, then, is always to a greater or lesser extent a reconstruction of a model of the universe. Is the world a plate or a sphere? The world of China, as tasted by Boman, is aqueous, each bowl of soup more or less deliciously symbolising a hemisphere in miniature. That of Japan as *dégusté* by Barthes with its chopsticks and its low tables is a spectacular two-dimensional surface: raw and visual like a painting in progress. The world of Abyssinian ritual as partaken by Leiris is one of blood and flesh, both raw and cooked, in which the sacrificial knife cuts both ways. In this world of convivial butchery, there are no plates or table; ritual *découpages* are disposed across the room, the participants in it, and in the immediate outer environment.

A question raised in relation to the idea of food as ritual is that of manners. As is implied by the title of the third in the series of Lévi-Strauss's *Mythologiques* – *L'Origine des manières de table* – table manners are one of the symbolic systems separating men from animals. But, like all such systems, they vary from culture to culture. In the West, there is a strong taboo on emissions of human fluids or wind associated with the upper part of the alimentary tract in the dining room or restaurant. But these pushes the carcass a little further back on my head so that my forehead becomes visible. I don't know whether he does this so that the cross remains visible or because he thinks it looks more stylish.]

The use of the human body itself as a support for signs is, however, perhaps the most deeply ambivalent aspect of primitive ritual, for it implies that the recipient becomes a kind of text to be read by other participants in the ceremony while he tries to read the significance of what has been written on him. The use of a feather or *plume* plucked from one of the sacrificial cocks as the instrument of inscription, with blood for ink, heightens this ambivalence, especially in that the ink or blood will not only be marked on the participant's body but also consumed by him: the written signs are thus both exhibited and ingested, his body thus being totally invested in the signifying function. The relation between eating (or drinking) and signifying attains thus a kind of symbiosis: 'Je tiens le premier poulet par les pattes; Enqo Bahri, qui le tient par la tête, l'égorge au couteau. Malkam Ayyahou arrache vivement une plume blanche, l'humecte en la trompant dans la blessure. Puis elle me trace une grande croix sur le front et, par trois fois, me passe la plume entre les lèvres, pour me faire goûter le sang' ([1934b] 1981: 546) ['I hold the first cockerel by the claws; Enqo Bahri, who holds it by the head, cuts its throat with a knife. Malkam Ayyahou smartly pulls out a white feather, dampens it by dipping it in the wound. She then traces a large cross on my forehead and passes the feather three times between my lips so that I can taste the blood'].

The fact that throughout the ritual Leiris himself, in a further symbolic transformation, uses his own pen (*plume*) to record the event in his notebook is a further sign of the tension between native and western symbolic practice: 'La deuxième dépouille [de poulet sacrifié] est prête. Malkam Ayyahou essuie le sang que j'ai au front avec sa face interne: puis elle me coiffe de cette dépouille, par-dessus la première. Jusqu'à ce que le dépeçage soit terminé je reste ainsi, toujours assis, ne m'interrompant pas dans la prise de mes notes' ([1934b] 1981: 547) ['The second (chicken) carcass is ready. Malkam Ayyahou wipes the blood from my forehead with the inner part of the bird: then she puts it on my head, on top of the first. Until the carving up is finished I remain as before, seated, continuing to take notes'].

In this way Leiris gets as close as any other French travel writer to experiencing a cultural system in which the sign, as theorised by Baudrillard (1976) and others, is in a sacred relation to its object. For in the ceremonies conducted by his Abyssinian friends, he experiences the sign as a real and total object that is consumed both physically and in its human significance. In this way food literally becomes thought. Of course such a principle is also operative in Christian ceremony and indeed Leiris's participation in the African ritual makes him think of his first communion. However, the refined confections that are the wafer and the wine bring with them none of the visceral reality of sacrificial blood, for, as Leiris says, 'la vraie religion ne commence qu'avec le sang' ([1934b] 1981: 548). But, as we just saw, even as he experiences the visceral intensity of African symbolic practice, already he is transforming the object or the real it englobes into another symbolic form – that of writing as understood in the western tradition. The deeper implications of this transformation will be the subject of the next and final chapter.

Conclusion: writing difference – coming home to write

J'arrive aux Indes, j'ouvre les yeux, et j'écris un livre.
(Henri Michaux, [1933] 1967: 99)

J'écris rarement sur place. Je ne tiens pas de journal de voyage. Je parle d'un lieu dans un autre et pour un autre.
(Michel Butor, 1974: 29)

L'auteur n'a jamais, en aucun sens, photographié le Japon. Ce serait plutôt le contraire: le Japon l'a étoilé d'éclairs multiples; ou mieux encore: le Japon l'a mis en situation d'écriture.
(Roland Barthes, [1970] 1980: 10)

[L]'artifice du langage ne fait que souligner le côté dérangeant, décalé, d'une réalité qui ne s'y soumet pas.
(Marc Augé, 1994a: 189)

The aims of the travel writer are of course multiple, various and changing and even on the most basic or generic level never simple. But a denominator common to the writers studied in this book has been the aim, on the level of experience, to get as close as possible to the other, the exotic, the different as object; then to try to make sense of this object by grasping the deeper epistemic (mythological or semiotic) principles shaping the cultural and meaning structures of the other as a social or ethnic group; and finally to relay or communicate the message of both their experience and, where applicable, their grasp, in theoretical, individual or fictional terms, of the other to their own group. At the same time, many of the writers studied also reflect on the implications of this complex process for the status of the self as both recorder and writer of experience of the other. The first part of the process implies acute and, as far as possible, unmotivated observation, an openness to sensation and to feeling; the second implies a sensitivity to cultural resistances, a patient reflection on signs of difference and an alertness to mythological and ritual expression; the third implies a linguistic translation, one which operates on two levels: first the translation of experience of the object on an existential level into terms of linguistic or other signs; second, the translation of the signs of the other into symbolic configurations legible to the home culture.[1] Woven into this process is the anxiety writers feel in relation both to the status of their identity and to the text produced in the light of the shock, first of difference, and second of the return to the same.[2]

The first two stages both imply the accumulation of a substantial corpus of material or notes which will be processed to a greater or lesser extent in the third stage. In addition, although there is a logical dynamic that organises the three stages into a kind of sequential order, there is at the same time a necessary overlap between them: the taking of notes is as primary and fundamental an activity of the travel writer as making observations (see Leiris, [1934b] 1981: 547). This overlap is also reflected in the profound tensions between the component elements of the travel project. That between personal, individual experience and more objective, ethnographic study is a particularly rich one, one that we have seen operative in a range of texts studied. Indeed the institution of a kind of dialogue more or less consciously initiated between individual and human scientist is inaugural to the modern (that is, twentieth-century) travel text, finding expression already in the 1920s and 1930s among the early writers in the modern tradition such as Gide, Michaux, Leiris and Lévi-Strauss. The pole positions in this dialogue are established respectively by Leiris and Lévi-Strauss – the former in *L'Afrique fantôme* (1934b) affirming, as we saw, the importance of individual subjectivity; the latter, writing up his experiences of the later 1930s in *Tristes Tropiques*, authoritatively affirming the primacy of the objective stance: 'pour atteindre le réel il faut d'abord répudier le vécu, quitte à le réintégrer par la suite dans une synthèse objective dépouillée de toute sentimentalité' (1955: 61) ['to reach the real you must first repudiate the lived even if it means reintegrating it later into an objective synthesis stripped of any sentimentality'].

This tension between the personal and subjective and the scientific and objective is also visible in the *form* travel texts tend to take. If as a genre the journal tends to predominate, this is because as a form it is most susceptible to accommodating the multiple aspects of travel experience – personal impressions, scientific information, ethnographic observation, documents of various kinds. It implies a work in progress which, in retrospect, it might appear impossible to shape without some of the essential, though heterogeneous, elements of its content being eliminated. The degree of organisation or transformation to which such material is put might in theory be indicative of an individual writer's position in the individual/

the original French text) in formal and linguistic terms which reproduce as far as possible the glamorous, flickering, cinematographic mobility of the American *épistémè*:

J'ai cherché l'Amérique *sidérale*, celle de la liberté vaine et absolue des *freeways*, jamais celle du social et de la culture – celle de la vitesse désertique, des motels et des surfaces minérales, jamais l'Amérique profonde des mœurs et des mentalités. J'ai cherché dans la vitesse du scénario, dans le réflexe indifférent de la télévision, dans le film des jours et des nuits à travers un espace vide, dans la succession merveilleusement sans affect des signes, des images, des visages, des actes rituels de la route, ce qui est le plus proche de l'univers nucléaire et énucléé qui est virtuellement le nôtre jusque dans les chaumières européennes. (1986: 10)

[I sought *astral* America in the absolute and pointless freedom of the *freeways*; not in its social and cultural life; – I sought it speeding through the desert, in motels and mineral surfaces, not in the deep America of manners and mentalities. I sought it in the speed of the screenplay, in the indifferent reflexes of TV, in the film of days and nights projected across empty space, in the wonderfully unemotional succession of signs, images, faces, in the ritual patterns of driving behaviour – all that which is closest to the nuclear and enucleated universe that is virtually our own, right down to our European cottages.]

Faced with such a vision, the post-modern reader and writer of travel texts, more than ever before, is alerted to the necessity of acute semiotic awareness and of the need for a comparative semiotics of communications systems. In a world in which the semiotic, the ethnographic and the media are becoming increasingly difficult to distinguish from each other, the necessity for their close analysis, even as they are applied to their object – whether it be real, textual or mediatised in some other way – becomes correspondingly pressing.

Notes

INTRODUCTION: *NOSTALGIES DU SYMBOLE*

1. Derrida's critique of Lévi-Strauss (1967a and, in particular, in 1967b) is acute in its analysis of this nostalgia, focussing in particular on how Lévi-Strauss, notably in *Tristes Tropiques* (1955), attributed to writing (in the western general understanding of the word) the responsibility for the 'dégradation' (1967b: 194) of community which was hitherto 'présente à elle-même, sans différance' (1967b: 197). Derrida's aim in *De la grammatologie* of arguing for the fundamental homogeneity of 'parole' and 'écriture' naturally leads him to critique the position of Lévi-Strauss, and to identify the 'fatal accident' that introduces difference into primal society not as writing but as history: 'Fatal accident qui ne serait autre que l'histoire elle-même' (1967b: 195). If 'histoire' may be taken here as the violent irruption of a different sign system into a community, thereby bringing about irrevocable change, Derrida's contention would support the position argued for throughout this book.
2. The question of the meanings of exoticism in the colonial and post-colonial worlds were much discussed throughout the 1990s, the work in this domain of Chris Bongie (1991) and Charles Forsdick (2000a, 2000b) being particularly illuminating.
3. This development has in turn led to a burgeoning of post-colonial studies pursued in terms of ethnography (Augé, 1994a, 1994b; Balandier, 2002, etc.) and social anthropology (Goody, 1982), as well as literature (Forsdick, 2001; Khatibi, 1987).
4. The most outstanding recent contribution to the sociology of travel has been made by Jean-Didier Urbain in a remarkable series of studies (1991, 1994, 1998). For a useful recent appraisal of Urbain's contribution in this field, see Forsdick (2000b).
5. Fernand Braudel affirms Europe's role not only in the *making* of history but also in elaborating it as an intellectual discipline (1985: 33).
6. Bernard Mouralis supports this point when he writes 'c'est par le biais de l'exotisme qu'une culture commence à prendre conscience qu'elle n'est plus seule au monde [. . .]. Cette rencontre constitue un choc générateur de doutes' (1975: 66).

7. Frédéric Tellier, in an article which refers, in passing, to Tabatabai's thinking (p. 102), suggests that signs of a more self-critical approach are becoming evident in current Iranian reflection on Islam, on politics, and their interrelation; see Tellier (2002: 96–111).

8. For a further comparison of Peircian and Saussurian semiotics, see Gérard Deledalle (1979: 29–39).

9. Among the best recent general surveys in this area are Jean-Pierre Biondi and Gilles Morin (1993) and Raoul Girardet (1972).

10. This topic is fruitfully broached from an anthropological viewpoint by James Clifford in 'Spatial Practices: fieldwork, travel and the disciplining of anthropology', in *Routes* (1997), and in *The Predicament of Culture* (1988), and from a historical perspective by Joan Pau Rubiés in 'Travel Writing and Ethnography' (Hulme & Youngs, 2002: 242–60).

11. As Lévi-Strauss confirms in a 1994 interview with Frank Lestringant, 'vous n'êtes pas sans savoir le rôle joué au XXe siècle par Ferdinand de Saussure, ni l'influence considérable qu'il a exercé sur moi' (see Jean de Léry, [1578] 1994: 7).

12. Thomas More's *Utopia*, studied in Chapter 4, is an exception in that it is both not French and not based on a real journey; it will be discussed in some detail both insofar as it is a founding model of the Utopian ideal and insofar as it raises issues fundamental to later European travel writing and political reflection.

1 READING SIGNS: FOREGROUNDING THE SIGNIFIER – FROM GAUTIER TO BAUDRILLARD

1. Jonathan Culler was quick to make this point, noting that tourists are the 'accomplices of semiotics [. . .] reading cities, landscapes and cultures as sign systems' (1981: 128).

2. A classic example of this process is given by Bronislaw Malinowski in his study of magical practices among New Guinea Melanesian boatmen ([1922] 1966: 392–463).

3. This problem has been well explored by James Clifford (1988).

4. Derrida makes a similar point in his critical reading (1967b: 149–202) of Lévi-Strauss's 'La Leçon d'écriture' in *Tristes Tropiques* (to be discussed below). Where Lévi-Strauss argues that the introduction of writing leads to *asservissement* (1955: 347–60), Derrida argues in *De la grammatologie* that it also facilitates a certain *libération* (1967b: 191). It is the 'oscillation' (Derrida's term) between the two tendencies that the native group has to negotiate once it has apprehended or had imposed on it an alternative sign system, in this case that of (European) writing. Chris Bongie, in the light of Weber and Jameson, makes a similar point in Marxian terms when he writes 'In the passage from the traditional to the rationalised, value is at once lost (as reality) and gained (as abstraction)' (1991: 9).

5. The 'Leçon d'écriture' has antecedents in earlier French ethnographic writing, as Frank Lestringant reminds us in his 1999 edition of Jean de Léry ([1578] 1994: 381).

6. While valuing the nuances Chris Johnson – in the light of the reading of this passage from *Tristes Tropiques* by Derrida (1967b) and others – brings to Lévi-Strauss's 'La Leçon d'écriture' (Johnson, 1997), I would argue that it is precisely the introduction of writing *as a sign system* clearly problematising the link between sign and object that causes the concern of the Nambikwara community in relation to exchanges, both within and without the tribal group. Whereas the exotic objects the visiting ethnographer brings to the Nambikwara community in exchange for knowledge or native artefacts, despite their wondrous strangeness and power, bring about no major structural perturbations within the native signifying system, being integrated into existing patterns of exchange, the introduction of *new* signs which *stand* for objects, but whose object is not always clear, causes more of a problem. I agree with Johnson that responsibility for this upheaval falls as much to the ethnographer (in this case Lévi-Strauss) as to the colluding tribal chief, who is, we are told, abandoned by most of his tribe soon after the incident. Both, however, in my view, are victims of the fatality that accompanies a sudden or violent confrontation of different sign systems (see Derrida, 1967b: 194).

7. Segalen also, of course, explores the aesthetic potential of the unrecognised sign, and in poetic collections such as *Stèles* and *Peintures* strives to re-instate an element of the opacity and irreducibility of the exotic sign. This process has been suggestively analysed in semiotic terms by Christian Doumet in 'Corps-signe' in which he argues, for example, that *Stèles* 'met en œuvre *une poétique du signe poétique*' (2000: 46).

8. Jacques Meunier cites a comparable situation in his discussion of Carmen Bernand's study of an Indian community of Ecuador in *La Solitude des renaissants* (1985): 'Le malheur historique des habitants de Pindinlig se traduit par un décalage dramatique des mots et du réel. Perte de synchronie, perte de sens' (1987: 225).

9. A parallel to Barthes's conception of Japanese can be found in Segalen's of Chinese, see François Cheng (1979: 147–8).

10. Barthes also discusses Warhol's *Marilyn* in his essay 'Cette vieille chose, l'art . . .' in which he distinguishes precisely between object (or *personne*) and image (or *identité*), foreseeing a future in which, as in Baudrillard's world, images exist without objects, 'Un monde d'identités [. . .] mais non de personnes' (Barthes, 1964–84: III, 184).

11. Baudrillard's comment on the image of Marilyn in a later essay, 'L'Exotisme radical' (in 1990: 151–61), is illuminating in its equation of photographs of so-called primitive tribesmen with Hollywood stars. He writes: 'Il n'y a de photographique que ce qui est violé, surpris, dévoilé, révélé malgré soi, que ce qui n'aurait jamais dû être représenté parce qu'il n'a pas d'image ni de conscience de lui-même. Le sauvage, ou ce qu'il y a de sauvage en nous, ne se réfléchit pas. Il est sauvagement étranger à lui-même. Les femmes les plus

séduisantes sont celles qui sont les plus étrangères à elles-mêmes (Marylin) [*sic*]. La bonne photographie ne représente rien, elle capte cette non-représentativité, l'altérité de ce qui est étranger à soi-même (au désir et à la conscience de soi), l'exotisme radical de l'objet' (1990: 157).

12. Butor's *Mobile* (1962) of course preceded *L'Empire des signes* (first published in 1970), and in his 1963 review of it, Barthes underlines the importance of the semiotic rather than rhetorical strategies Butor employs in his innovative text (see 'Littérature et discontinu' in Barthes, 1964–84: I, 175–87).

2 THE OTHER AS INTERPRETANT: FROM SEGALEN AND MICHAUX TO THE *ETHNO-ROMAN*

1. Sometimes the other is encountered in the form of an animal, as in the memorable episode recounted by the sixteenth-century travel writer Jean de Léry during his Brazilian trip in which he writes of a giant lizard: 'fort estonnez que nous fusmes en nous regardans l'un l'autre, nous demeurasmes ainsi tous cois en une place. Ainsi apres que ce monstrueux et espouvantable lezard en ouvrant la gueule, et à cause de la grande chaleur qu'il faisoit [. . .], soufflant si fort que nous l'entendions bien aisément, nous eut contemplé pres d'un quart d'heure, se retournant tout à coup, et faisant plus grand bruit et fracassement de feuilles et de branches par où il passoit, que ne feroit un cerf courant dans une forest, il s'enfuit contre mont' ([1578] 1994: 269).

2. The complexity of Segalen's response to the 'exotic' and the various different ways in which his position has itself been interpreted by writers – both literary (Bongie, 1991) and ethnographic (Clifford, 1988; Gilsenan, 1986), in both a colonialist and post-colonialist age – has more recently been well elucidated, in particular by Charles Forsdick (2000a, 2000b), who writes in an essay in the latter work: 'For Segalen, exoticism is [. . .] not only an ideology, but can instead describe a process, dependent on openness, whose dynamics leave the *exote* vulnerable to the pitfalls of redefinition of self. Segalen's work is thus a shift from the polarisation of identity of self and exotic other' (see 'L'exote mangé par les hommes': 2000b: 24). Some of the 'pitfalls of redefinition of self' will be explored in the context of other French travel writers in my third chapter, 'Identity crises'.

3. This process is evoked by Edward J. Hughes, in 'Cultural stereotyping: Segalen against Loti', in terms of a 'vibrant alterity' (Forsdick and Marsan, 2000: 28).

4. An interesting parallel to Segalen's hallucinatory encounter with himself is to be found in the experience of a contemporary anthropologist, Bronislaw Malinowski (1884–1942), who recounts the following in his diary (1967), published several decades after his ethnographic research into the Polynesian islanders of New Guinea (see [1922] 1966): 'I had a strange dream; homosex., with my own double as a partner. Strangely auto-erotic feelings; the impression that I'd like to have a mouth just like mine to kiss, a neck that curves just like mine (seen from the side). I got tired and collected myself slowly' (1967: 13). This passage, placed in the context of the anxiety underlying the relationship

between self and other in the ethnographic exchange, is commented on by Vincent Crapanzano (1977: 70–1).

5. A useful account of this process is given by Marie-Annick Gervais-Zaninger in her article 'L'Insoutenable Résistance de l'autre' (in Ughetto, 1992: 45–50).

6. Jacques Perrin refers to this as 'la tentation du récit ethnologique' (Ughetto, 1992: 31).

7. See Ughetto (1992: 36–41).

8. See Michael Sheringham (1995: 210–20).

3 IDENTITY CRISES: '*JE* EST UN AUTRE' – GAUTIER, GAUGUIN, NERVAL, BOUVIER

1. For a fuller account of Gauguin's appreciation of Delacroix as colourist, see Gauguin ([1892–1903] 1974: 159–61).

2. For a different take on this passage, see Hughes (2001: 33–5). For confirmation of the general drift of Gaugin's experience, see Baudrillard when he writes: 'Il en est du voyage comme de la relation aux autres. Le voyage comme métamorphose, comme anamorphose de la Terre. Le féminin comme métamorphose, comme anamorphose du masculin. Le transfert comme délivrance de votre propre sexe et de votre culture. C'est cette forme-là, celle de l'expulsion et de la délivrance, qui l'emporte aujourd'hui sur le voyage classique, celui de la découverte' (1990: 155). For a brief but lucid account of the reaction of visiting Europeans, from the seventeenth century to the time of Gauguin, to the sexually ambivalent *mahu* figure within Tahitian society, see Rod Edmond, 'The Pacific/Tahiti: queen of the South Sea isles' in Hulme and Youngs (2002: 139–55, in particular the section on 'Alien practices', 144–9).

3. The downside to this process is the tendency to mythologise or even infantilise the other as encountered in the native environment. This problem has been well analysed by James Clifford (1988, Part 3, 'Collections': 186–215), Kirk Varnedoe (1984) and others, in particular in the context of the much-discussed exhibition '"Primitivism" in 20th-Century Art. Affinity of the Tribal and the Modern' held at the Museum of Modern Art, New York, in 1984.

4. See in particular Maillart's account of a pre-war drive from Istanbul to India in *La Voie cruelle* (published in English in 1947 and in French in 1952).

5. To facilitate his argument, Baudrillard here assimilates British pop icons such as David Bowie and Boy George to the American model.

4 UTOPIAS AND DYSTOPIAS: BACK IN THE US. BACK IN THE USSR – GIDE, BAUDRILLARD, DISNEYLAND

1. See, for example, Laurent Portes, 'Utopia in nineteenth-century French literature' in Schaer *et al.* (2000: 241–7).

2. The problem of the rights of the indigenous Indian population only really began to be addressed by Americans of European stock at the time of Tocqueville's visit.

3. Ella Maillart's *Parmi la jeunesse russe* (1932), written four years before Gide's *Retour de l'U.R.S.S.*, deliberately avoids the political issues at stake in rising Stalinism to concentrate on the warm and fruitful human relations she had with young Russian people.

4. This development is analysed in absorbing detail at exactly the same time by Boris Souvarine in *Cauchemar en URSS* ([1937] 2000).

5. Céline's experience of Russia as recounted in *Mea culpa* (1936) in some ways reads like a comic-book résumé of Gide's response to communist USSR, while his *Bagatelles pour un massacre* (1937) constitutes a kind of hysterical distillation, writ twentieth-century, of Custine's impressions of St Petersburg a century before.

5 SIGNS IN THE DESERT: FROM CHATEAUBRIAND TO BAUDRILLARD

1. For an illuminating insight into the way the desert is often perceived by the native inhabitant as rich in significance, see Rice (2002).

2. For a seminal account of Segalen's exoticism, see Forsdick (2000a).

3. For an insight into the complexity and modernity of aspects of Loti's approach to exoticist fiction and his problematisation of conventional narrative structures, see Barthes (1964–84: II); see also Bongie (1991) and Edward J. Hughes, in 'Cultural stereotyping: Segalen against Loti' (Forsdick and Marson, 2000: 28).

6 JUNGLE BOOKS: (MIS-)READING THE JUNGLE WITH GIDE, MICHAUX AND LEIRIS

1. Jacques Meunier remarks pertinently on the regressive character of jungle experience in which many basic processes – walking, identifying, orientation – have to be re-learned: 'tout voyage en forêt tropicale a un caractère régressif' (1987: 56).

2. Pierre Savorgnan de Brazza's travel journals of central Africa (1887–8) provide a direct antecedent and interesting point of contrast to those of Gide forty years later.

3. For a fuller account of this expedition, see Griaule (1934: 6–12), Leiris (1933; 1934a), Clifford (1988: 55–91) and Meunier who remarks, following some of Leiris's wry observations, that the Dakar–Djibouti team 'se comportera comme un gang d'antiquaires partis chiner dans des provinces lointaines et analphabètes' (1987: 186).

4. Gide's scepticism with regard to self-knowledge is of course well known. He writes for example of the classical dictum 'Connais-toi, toi-même', 'Maxime aussi pernicieuse que laide. Quiconque s'observe arrête son développement. La chenille qui chercherait à "bien se connaître" ne deviendrait jamais papillon' (Gide, 1947: 266).

5. A more coherent account of tropical jungle is given by British nineteenth-century *savanturiers* (Gilles Lapouge's term cited in Meunier, 1987: 248) such as Bates (1863) and Wallace (1869), no doubt as a function of the many years they

spent exploring it and the disciplinary frame that natural history provided and that consistently motivated their approach to the jungle. Bates spent eleven years in Amazonia (1848–59) while Wallace spent eight in Malaysia and Indonesia between 1854 and 1862, having already spent a couple of years on the 'Amazons' with Bates in 1848–50. Both writers, Wallace in particular, contributed decisive evidence in support of Darwin's theory of the origin of the species. These writers' scientific commitments did not of course prevent them from exploring many aspects of the cultural and religious practices of the natives they encountered on their travels, or from giving an engaging and candid account of their own experiences, with the result that their books are as comprehensively enthralling as any travel literature written over the past two centuries.

6. For the importance of Conrad, among others, as an intertext to *L'Afrique fantôme*, see Hand (1995: 178–83).

7. Susan Marsan makes an illuminating comparison between Michaux's problems in this respect and those of Segalen in his *Journal des îles* in '"De l'exotisme au quotidien": Segalen's *Journal des îles* and Michaux's *Ecuador*' (Forsdick and Marsan, 2000: 103–14).

8. Sean Hand (1995) contrasts Leiris's principally aesthetic reaction to the Falls at Felou with the more historically, politically and culturally informed response to the same site of his predecessor, Commandant Gallieni, whose *Voyage au Soudan français (Haut Niger et Pays de Ségou), 1879–1881* was published half a century earlier in 1881. Hand goes on to suggest that it is Gallieni himself, as much as any other figure, who is the 'real phantom of *L'Afrique fantôme*' (1995: 190), summing up in a brilliant concluding paragraph what appears essentially to be at stake in Leiris's project in this text: 'Leiris's exemplary work puts psychological, cultural, political and generic demarcation to the test. It dramatizes how self-identity is based on a determined Other; it shakes the epistemological foundation of certain scientific approaches, primarily anthropology, to the Other; it illustrates how a political revaluation, such as decolonization, must entail an anguished intellectual process of dispossession' and, most remarkable of all, offers a 'specific non-reading of the inchoate text of imperialism' (1995: 190).

9. Leiris, in anticipating the Dakar–Djibouti trip, had already written in 1930, admittedly a little tongue-in-cheek, 'je souhaite [. . .] que le plus possible de mes amis [. . .] fassent comme moi: qu'ils voyagent, non en touristes (ce qui est voyager sans cœur, sans yeux et sans oreilles), mais en ethnographes, de manière à devenir assez largement humains pour oublier leurs médiocres petites "manières blanches" (ainsi que disent certains nègres)' (1930: 413).

10. Marcel Griaule remarks that the art of the ethnographer is to be 'sage-femme et juge d'instruction', his native informer being both partner and adversary in the ethnographic process (1934: 11).

11. Leiris's experiences, as an ethnographer, both of personal friendship with native informants and of auto-eroticism (the latter is touched on below) find a striking parallel in that of Bronislaw Malinowski (see Stocking, [1996] 1999: 260, 263).

12. A useful résumé of what is at stake in the 'zar' rituals is given by Leiris in the article 'Le Taureau de Seyfou Tchenger' (1934a), illustrated with photographs of Malkam Ayyahou presiding. For a fuller account, see Leiris (1951).

13. Abba Jérôme was, in Leiris's words, a 'lettré abyssin [. . .] délégué par l'Empereur auprès de l'expédition pour l'aider dans ses recherches' (1934a: 77). For a tribute to his collaboration in analysing and documenting 'zar' rituals, see Leiris (1951: 11).

14. Jean Jamin recalls that a drawing by Teborah appeared on the cover of the 1951 edition of *L'Afrique fantôme*, see Jamin (1982: 201).

15. 'Il faudrait un jour rendre pleine justice à l'œuvre anthropologique de Michel Leiris et à ses vertus anticipatrices: *L'Afrique fantôme* est la première tentative anthropologique de coordonner, littéralement, l'observation de soi et celle des autres, la première expérience d'intimité anthropologique qui ne se résume pas à un naufrage dans la mythification d'autrui' (Augé, 1994b: 83).

7 GRAMMARS OF GASTRONOMY: THE RAW AND THE COOKED – LÉVI-STRAUSS, BARTHES, BOMAN, LEIRIS

1. In what follows I use the word 'culture' in the broadly classificatory, anthropological sense, implying the pattern or style of behaviour of a group of people who share it. In this way, as Chang argues, 'Food habits may be used as an important, even determining, criterion in this connection. People who have the same culture share the same [. . .] assemblage of food variables' (Chang, 1977: 3).

2. As Chang writes: 'An anthropological approach to the study of food would [. . .] isolate and identify food variables, arrange these variables systematically, and explain why some of these variables go together or do not go together' (1977: 3).

3. For a history of the European gastronomic tradition, see Roy Strong (2002).

4. The intimate connection between food and sex in human society is well stated by Farb and Armelagos (1980).

5. The table manners of the Tupinamba of Brazil, as encountered by Jean de Léry in his trip during the sixteenth century, are also taken by him as an illustration of cultural relativity. Avoiding the barbarous use of knife or fork, the polite way for the Tupinamba to pass food to the mouth is to throw it in with an infallible aim ([1578] 1994: 239–40); and although, like Europeans, they are hard drinkers, they do not mix food and drink, and remain silent while eating, mocking the uncouth European habit of mealtime chatter ([1578] 1994: 250–1).

6. Jean de Léry is as courageous in this respect as Lévi-Strauss, being put off neither by Tupinamba women's mastication of the manioc that goes into the native brew *Caou-in* (which he compares to French *vendangeurs* treading grapes) ([1578] 1994: 255–6), nor by the taste of lizard, which he describes as 'l'une des bonnes viandes que j'ay mangé en l'Amerique' ([1578] 1994: 267).

7. That the aesthetics of visual display in relation to food are imprinted early on the Japanese imagination is shown by Anne Allison (1991) in her ethnographic study of nursery school lunchboxes or *obentos*.

8. The noodle shops and soup stalls of northern China seem to have changed little since Sung times (960–1279), as Michael Freeman affirms: 'The noodle shops, a good deal humbler than the wine restaurants, fall into Meng Yuan-lao's category of "laborers' shops". They served up no wine but offered various kinds of noodle dishes, specializing in either noodles with meat or noodles with vegetables. Another kind of inexpensive restaurant which had mostly soups advertised their speciality by a calabash hung over the door. These shops did not really serve full meals but were convenient for a lunch or a snack for the customer in a hurry. Nor were they always physically permanent or substantial. Some evidently squatted on unoccupied city land and were often little more than latticework covered by thatch' (Chang, 1977: 161).

9. The question of the ethnographic/symbolic status of spit had already exercised Leiris and his colleague Marcel Griaule, leader of the 1931–3 Dakar–Djibouti expedition, in articles published in *Documents* (2 vols., 1929–30). On the basis of black African and Islamic evidence, Griaule had argued (vol. 1, 1929: 381), using the term *crachat-âme*, that spit was associated with the soul and so with both good and evil spirits: 'La salive est de l'âme déposée; le crachat est de l'âme en mouvement [. . .]. En résumé, de la maléficience à la bienfaisance, de l'insulte au miracle, le crachat se comporte comme l'âme: baume ou ordure.' Leiris, in the following entry, 'L'eau de la bouche', of the same volume, takes a more extreme view, equating spittle with a sullying of the noble mouth, in the West associated with language and intelligence: 'Juste au dessous des yeux, la bouche occupe une situation privilégiée, parce qu'elle est le lieu de la parole, l'orifice respiratoire, l'antre où se scelle le pacte du baiser bien plus, croit-on, que l'usine huileuse des mastications. Il faut d'une part l'amour pour restituer à la bouche toute sa fonction mythologique [. . .], d'autre part le *crachat*, pour, d'un seul coup, la faire tomber au dernier degré de l'échelle organique, en la douant d'une fonction d'éjection, plus répugnante encore que son rôle de porte où l'on enfourne les aliments' (Leiris, 1929: 381). For more on 'surrealist ethnography' and its ramifications in *Documents*, see Clifford (1988: 117–51), Hand (2002: 45–60) and Meunier (1987: 160–9). For an account of the diminishing tolerance to spitting within the European tradition since the Middle Ages, see Norbert Elias ([1939] 1978: 153–60).

CONCLUSION: WRITING DIFFERENCE – COMING HOME TO WRITE

1. An interesting insight into the translation aspect of travel writing is offered by Michael Cronin (2000).

2. This process has been illuminatingly investigated in the context of anthropology by Vincent Crapanzano (1977), who suggests that the 'shock of return' (1977: 71) is a function of both the writing-up process and the re-integration of the self into the home environment after a long period of confrontation with the other.

Bibliography

Affergan, Francis (1987a) *Exotisme et altérité. Essai sur les fondements d'une critique de l'anthropologie* Paris: Presses Universitaires de France.

(1987b) 'Calendaire d'exote', *Traverses*, 41–2, 125–8.

Allegret, Marc (1987) *Carnets du Congo: voyage avec Gide* (ed. D. Durosay and C. Rabel-Jullien) Paris: Centre National de Recherche Scientifique.

Allison, Anne (1991) 'Japanese mothers and *obentos*: the lunch-box as ideological state apparatus', *Anthropological Quarterly*, 64, 195–208.

Augé, Marc (1985) *La Traversée du Luxembourg. Ethno-roman d'une journée française considérée sous l'angle des mœurs, de la théorie et du bonheur* Paris: Hachette.

(1986) *Un ethnologue dans le métro* Paris: Hachette.

(1992) *Non-lieux. Introduction à une anthropologie de la surmodernité* Paris: Seuil.

(1994a) *Le Sens des autres. Actualité de l'anthropologie* Paris: Fayard.

(1994b) *Pour une anthropologie des mondes contemporains* Paris: Flammarion.

(1997) *L'Impossible Voyage. Le tourisme et ses images* Paris: Payot & Rivages.

Balandier, Georges (2002) 'De l'Afrique à la surmodernité: un parcours d'anthropologie. Entretien', *Le Débat*, 118, 3–15.

Barthes, Roland (1957) *Mythologies* Paris: Gallimard.

(1964–84) *Essais critiques* I, II, III & IV Paris: Editions du Seuil.

([1970] 1980) *L'Empire des signes* Paris: Flammarion.

Bataille, Georges ([1957] 1970) *L'Erotisme* Paris: Union générale d'édition.

Bates, Henry Walter ([1863] 1969) *The Naturalist on the River Amazons* London: Dent.

Baudrillard, Jean (1970) *La société de consommation, ses mythes, ses structures* Paris: Denoël.

(1972) *Pour une critique de l'économie politique du signe* Paris: Gallimard.

(1976) *L'Echange symbolique et la mort* Paris: Gallimard.

(1977) *L'Autre par lui-même* Paris: Galilée.

(1986) *Amérique* Paris: Grasset (Livre de Poche).

(1990) *La Transparence du mal: essai sur les phénomènes extrêmes* Paris: Galilée.

(1991) *La Guere du Golfe n'aura pas lieu* Paris: Galilée.

([1996]) 1997 'Disneyworld Company' in *Ecran total* Paris: Galilée.

(1997) *Le Paroxyste indifférent. Entretiens avec Philippe Petit* Paris: Grasset (Livre de Poche).

Bernabé, Jean, Chamoiseau, Patrick and Confiant, Raphaël (1989) *Eloge de la créolité* Paris: Gallimard.

Biondi, Jean-Pierre, and Morin, Gilles (1993) *Les Anticolonialistes (1881–1962)* Paris: Hachette (Coll. Pluriel).

Boman, Patrick (1989) *Le Palais des Saveurs-Accumulées* Paris: Editions Climats.

(1999) *Thé de bœuf, radis de cheval. (De Paris-Montparnasse à Paris-Est en évitant la ligne 4 du métropolitain)* Paris: Le Serpent à plumes.

Bongie, Chris (1991) *Exotic Memories. Literature, Colonialism, and the 'Fin de siècle'* Stanford University Press.

Borm, Jan (2000) *'In-Betweeners? –* On the travel book and ethnographies', *Studies in Travel Writing*, 4, 78–105.

Bouvier, Nicolas ([1963] 1992) *L'Usage du monde* Geneva: Droz (reprint Paris: Payot).

([1982] 1991) *Le Poisson-Scorpion* Paris: Gallimard (reprint Paris: Payot).

(1989) *Chronique japonaise* Paris: Payot.

(1990) *Journal d'Aran et d'autres lieux. Feuilles de route* Paris: Payot.

Bowie, Malcolm (1973) *Henri Michaux. A Study of his Literary Works* Oxford: Clarendon Press.

Braudel, Fernand ([1985] 2001) *La Dynamique du capitalisme* Paris: Flammarion.

Brillat-Savarin, Jean-Anthelme ([1826] 1975) *Physiologie du goût avec une lecture de Roland Barthes* Paris: Hermann.

Bruckner, Pascal and Finkelkraut, Alain (1979) *Au coin de la rue, l'aventure* Paris: Editions du Seuil.

Burton, Sir Richard ([1855] 1893) *Personal Narrative of a Pilgrimage to Al-Madinah and Meccah*, 2 vols. London: Tylston & Edwards.

Buruma, Ian and Margalit, Avishai (2002) 'L'Occidentalisme', *Le Débat*, 120, 152–62.

Butor, Michel (1958, 1971, 1978, 1992, 1996) *Le Génie du lieu*, 5 vols. Paris: Gallimard.

(1962) *Mobile. Etude pour une représentation des Etats-Unis* Paris: Gallimard.

(1974) 'Le Voyage et l'écriture' in *Répertoires IV* Paris: Editions de Minuit, 9–29.

Celestin, Roger (1996) *From Cannibals to Radicals: Figures and Limits of Exoticism* Minneapolis and London: University of Minnesota Press.

Céline, Louis-Ferdinand ([1932] 1952) *Voyage au bout de la nuit* Paris: Gallimard.

(1936) *Mea culpa* in *Cahiers Céline* VII (ed. J.-P. Dauphin and Pascal Fouché) Paris: Gallimard, 1986, 30–45.

(1937) *Bagatelles pour un massacre* Paris: Denoël.

Chang, Kwang-chih (ed.) (1977) *Food in Chinese Culture: Anthropological and Historical Perspectives* New Haven and London: Yale University Press.

Chateaubriand, François-René de ([1811] 1968) *Itinéraire de Paris à Jérusalem* (ed. J. Mourot) Paris: Garnier-Flammarion.

Cheddadi, Abdesselam (2002) 'Le Défi du savoir. Entretien', *Le Débat*, 119, 79–88.

Cheng, François (1979) 'Espace réel et espace mythique' in *Regards, espaces, signes. Victor Segalen* (ed. E. Formentelli) Paris: L'Asiathèque, 133–52.

Clifford, James (1988) *The Predicament of Culture: Twentieth-century Ethnography, Literature and Art* Cambridge, MA: Harvard University Press.

(1997) *Routes. Travel and Translation in the Late Twentieth Century* Cambridge, MA / London: Harvard University Press.

Conrad, Joseph ([1902] 1973) *Heart of Darkness* London: Penguin.

Cornelius, Paul (1965) *Languages in 17th- and 18th-Century Imaginary Voyages* Geneva: Droz.

Crapanzano, Vincent (1977) 'On the writing of ethnography', *Dialectical Anthropology*, 2 part 2, 69–73.

Cronin, Michael (2000) *Across the Lines: Travel, Language, Translation* Cork University Press.

Culler, Jonathan (1981) 'The semiotics of tourism', *American Journal of Semiotics*, 1, 127–40.

Custine, Astolphe de ([1843] 1990) *La Russie en 1839* Paris: Librairie d'Amyot (reprint Greg, 1971); also (ed. Hélène Carrère d'Encausse), 2 vols. Paris: Solin.

Deledalle, Gérard (1979) *Théorie et pratique du signe. Introduction à la sémiotique de Charles S. Peirce* Paris: Payot.

Derrida, Jacques (1967a) *L'Ecriture et la différence* Paris: Editions du Seuil.

(1967b) *De la grammatologie* Paris: Editions de Minuit.

(1992) *Moscou aller-retour* Paris: Editions de l'Aube.

(1996) *Le Monolinguisme de l'autre* Paris: Galilée.

Descartes, René ([1637] 1966) *Discours de la méthode* Paris: Garnier-Flammarion.

Diamond, Jared ([1997] 1998) *Guns, Germs and Steel. A Short History of Everybody for the last 13,000 Years* London: Vintage.

Doumet, Christian (2000) 'Corps-signe' in Forsdick and Marson (eds.): 39–49.

Elias, Norbert ([1939] 1978) *The Civilizing Process: The History of Manners* (trans. Edmund Jephcott) Oxford: Blackwell.

Etiemble (1964) *Connaissons-nous la Chine?* Paris: Gallimard.

Fabian, Johannes (1983) *Time and the Other. How Anthropology Makes its Object* New York: Columbia University Press.

Farb, Peter and Armelagos, George (1980) *Consuming Passions: The Anthropology of Eating* Boston: Houghton Mifflin.

Figes, Orlando (2001) 'Qu'est-ce que la Russie?', *Le Débat*, 116, 156–64.

Fischler, Claude (1988) 'Food, self and identity', *Social Sciences Information*, 27 no. 2, 275–92.

Forsdick, Charles (2000a) *Victor Segalen and the Aesthetics of Diversity: Journeys between Cultures* Oxford University Press.

(2000b) '*Viator in Fabula*: Jean-Didier Urbain and the cultures of travel in contemporary France', *Studies in Travel Writing*, 4, 126–40.

(2001) 'Travelling concepts: postcolonial approaches to exoticism', *Paragraph*, 24 no. 3, 12–29.

Forsdick, Charles and Marson, Susan (eds.) (2000) *Reading Diversity. Lectures du divers* University of Glasgow French and German Publications.

Foucault, Michel (1966) *Les Mots et les choses. Une archéologie des sciences humaines* Paris: Gallimard.

Fromentin, Eugène ([1854] 1938) *Un été dans le Sahara* (ed. M. Revon) Paris: Conard.

([1858] 1991) *Une année dans le Sahel* (ed. E. Cardonne) Paris: GF-Flammarion.

Gallieni, Joseph (1881) *Voyage au Soudan français (Haut Niger et Pays de Ségou), 1879–1881* Paris: Hachette.

Gauguin, Paul ([1892–1903] 1974) *Oviri. Ecrits d'un sauvage* (ed. D. Guérin) Paris: Gallimard.

Gautier, Théophile ([1840] 1981) *Voyage en Espagne* (ed. Jean-Claude Berchet) Paris: GF Flammarion.

([1860] 1877) 'A propos du *Voyage en Orient* de Nerval', *La Revue Nationale* (25 December 1860), cited in *L'Orient*, Paris: Charpentier, vol. I, 180–1.

Geertz, Clifford (1998) *Works and Lives. The Anthropologist as Author* Cambridge: Polity Press.

Geoghegan, Vincent (1987) *Utopianism and Marxism* London: Methuen.

Gide, André (1927–8) *Voyage au Congo suivi du Retour du Tchad. Carnets de route* Paris: Gallimard (Coll. Idées).

(1936–7) *Retour de l'URSS suivi de Retouches à mon Retour de l'URSS* Paris: Gallimard (Coll. Idées).

(1947) Les Nouvelles Nourritures Paris: Gallimard.

Gilsenan, Michael (1986) *Imagined Cities of the East: An Inaugural Lecture* Oxford: Clarendon Press.

Girardet, Raoul (1972) *L'Idée coloniale en France* Paris: La Table ronde.

Goody, Jack (1979) *La Raison graphique. La domestication de la pensée sauvage* Paris: Editions de Minuit (translation of *The Domestication of the Savage Mind* Cambridge University Press, 1977).

(1982) *Cooking, Cuisine and Class. A Study in Comparative Sociology* Cambridge University Press.

(1998) *Food and Love: A Cultural History of East and West* London: Verso.

Granet, Marcel ([1933] 1973) 'Right and left in China' (trans. R. Needham) in Needham, 43–73.

Griaule, Marcel (1929) 'Crachat', *Documents*, 1 no. 7, 381.

(1930) 'Un coup de fusil', *Documents* 2 no. 1, 46–7.

(1934) 'Mission Dakar–Djibouti', *Minotaure*, 2, 7–12.

(1943) *Les Saô légendaires* Paris: Gallimard.

Hand, Séan (1995) 'Phantom of the opus: colonialist traces in Michel Leiris's *L'Afrique fantôme*', *Paragraph. Mapping the Other: Anthropology and Literature's Limits*, 18 no. 2, 174–93.

(2002) *Michel Leiris. Writing the Self* Cambridge University Press.

Harbsmeier, Michael (1997) 'Spontaneous ethnographies: towards a social history of travellers' tales', *Studies in Travel Writing*, 1, 216–38.

Hartog, François (1971) *Le Miroir d'Hérodote: essai sur la représentation de l'autre* Paris: Gallimard.

Helbo, André (1975) *Michel Butor. Vers une littérature du signe, précédé d'un dialogue avec Michel Butor* Paris: Editions Complexe.

Hughes, Edward J. (2000) 'Cultural stereotyping: Segalen against Loti' in Forsdick and Marson (eds.), 25–38.

(2001) 'Without obligation: exotic appropriation in Loti and Gauguin' in *Writing Marginality in Modern French Literature from Loti to Genet* Cambridge University Press, 9–40.

Hulme, Peter and Youngs, Tim (2002) *The Cambridge Companion to Travel Writing* Cambridge University Press.

Jamin, Jean (1982) 'Les Métamorphoses de *l'Afrique fantôme*', *Critique*, 418, 200–12.

Johnson, Christopher (1997) 'Lévi-Strauss: the writing lesson revisited', *Modern Language Review*, 92 no. 3, 599–612.

Jullien, François (2001a) 'De la Grèce à la Chine, aller-retour. Propositions', *Le Débat*, 116 (2001), 134–43.

(2001b) 'Depayser la pensée: un détour par la Chine', *Le Magazine littéraire*, May, 99–103.

Khatibi, Abdelkebir (1987) *Figures de l'étranger dans la littérature française* Paris: Denoël.

Kristeva, Julia (1988) *Etrangers à nous-mêmes* Paris: Gallimard (Coll. Folio).

Lamartine, Alphonse de ([1835] 1887) *Voyage en Orient* Paris: Hachette.

Lane, Edward William (1836) *An Account of the Manners and Customs of the Modern Egyptians* London: Dent.

Leiris, Michel (1929) 'L'Eau de la bouche', *Documents*, 1 no. 7, 381–2.

(1930) 'L'Œil de l'ethnographe: à propos de la Mission Dakar–Djibouti', *Documents*, 2 no. 7, 405–14.

(1933) 'Danses funéraires Dogon. Carnet de route' (Premiers Documents de la Mission Dakar–Djibouti), *Minotaure*, 1, 73–6.

(1934a) 'Le Taureau de Seyfou Tchenger', *Minotaure*, 2, 75–82.

([1934b] 1981) *L'Afrique fantôme* Paris: Gallimard (Bibliothèque des Sciences Humaines).

(1951) *La Possession et ses aspects théâtraux chez les Ethiopiens de Gondar* Paris: Plon.

([1955] 1994) *Journal de Chine* (ed. Jean Jamin) Paris: Gallimard.

(1969) *Cinq Etudes d'ethnologie* Paris: Denoël/Gonthier (Collection Tel, Gallimard).

Léry, Jean de ([1578] 1994) *Histoire d'un voyage faict en la terre du Bresil* (ed. Frank Lestringant) Paris: Librairie générale française / Le Livre de Poche.

Lévi-Strauss, Claude (1955) *Tristes Tropiques* Paris: Plon.

([1958] 1974) *Anthropologie structurale I* Paris: Plon (reprint).

(1961) *La Pensée sauvage* Paris: Plon.

(1964) *Mythologiques I. Le Cru et le cuit* Paris: Plon.

(1965) 'Le triangle culinaire', *L'Arc*, 26, 19–29.

([1974] 1996) *Anthropologie structurale II* Paris: Plon (reprint).

Loti, Pierre ([1889] 1927) *Au Maroc* Paris: Calmann-Lévy.

McLuhan, Marshall (1962) *The Gutenburg Galaxy. The Making of Typographic Man* London: Routledge.

(1964) *Understanding the Media. The Extension of Man* London: Sphere Books.

Maillart, Ella ([1932] 1997) *Parmi la jeunesse russe* Paris: Payot & Rivages (Édition de poche).

([1947/1952] 1988) *La Voie cruelle* Paris: Payot.

Malinowski, Bronislaw ([1922] 1966) *Argonauts of the Western Pacific. An Account of Native Enterprise and Adventure in the Archipelagoes of Melanesian New Guinea* (preface James George Frazer), London: Routledge.

(1967) *A Diary in the Strict Sense of the Term* New York: Harcourt, Brace, & World.

Marin, Louis (1973) *Utopiques: jeux d'espace* Paris: Editions de Minuit.

Marson, Susan. ' "De l'exotisme au quotidien": Segalen's *Journal des Iles* and Michaux's *Ecuador'* in Forsdick and Marson (eds.), 103–114.

Martin, Jean-Pierre (1994) *Henri Michaux. Ecritures de soi, expatriations* Paris: Corti.

Maspéro, François (1990) *Les Passagers du Roissy-Express* Paris: Editions du Seuil.

Mauss, Marcel (1966) *Sociologie et anthropologie* (introduction by Claude Lévi-Strauss) Paris: Presses Universitaires de France.

Meunier, Jacques (1987) *Le Monocle de Joseph Conrad* Paris: Payot.

Michaux, Henri ([1929] 1968) *Ecuador* Paris: Gallimard (Coll. L'Imaginaire).

([1933] 1967) *Un barbare en Asie* Paris: Gallimard (Coll. L'Imaginaire).

(1974) *Par la voie des rythmes* Fontfroide-le-Haut: Fata Morgana.

Monod, Théodore ([1935] 1995) *Maxence au désert. Un Voyage en Mauritanie* Actes Sud / Hubert Nyssen.

Morand, Paul ([1930] 1988) *New York* (ed. Philippe Sollers) Paris: GF-Flammarion.

More, Thomas ([1516] 1965) *Utopia* (trans. Paul Turner) Harmondsworth: Penguin.

Moura, Jean-Marc (1992) *Lire l'exotisme* Paris: Dunod.

Mouralis, Bernard (1975) *Les Contre-littératures* Paris: Presses Universitaires de France.

Nash, Dennison (1981) 'Tourism and the anthropological subject', *Current Anthropology*, 22, 461–81.

Needham, Rodney (1973) *Right and Left. Essays on Dual Symbolic Classification* Chicago and London: The University of Chicago Press.

Nerval, Gérard de ([1851] 1980) *Voyage en Orient* (ed. Michel Jeanneret), 2 vols. Paris: Garnier-Flammarion.

Pascal, Blaise ([c. 1660] 1960) *Pensées* (ed. Z. Tourneur and D. Anzieu), 2 vols. Paris: Colin.

Peirce, Charles Sanders (1966) *Collected Papers* VII and VIII (ed. Arthur W. Burks) Cambridge, MA: Harvard University Press. See in particular Vol. VIII, Ch. 5 'On Signs', 210–13; Ch. 8 'To Lady Welby. On Signs and the Categories', 220–31; 'On the Classification of Signs', 231–45.

Pesquès, Nicolas (1997) *Madras, journal* Paris: André Dimanche.

Prakash, Om (1961) *Food and Drinks in Ancient India* Delhi: Munshi Ram Manohar Lal.

Ramburger, O. (1979) 'The deep grammar of haute cuisine', *Linguistics*, 17, 169–72.

Rice, Laura (2002), 'Critical appropriations: one desert, three narratives', *International Journal of Francophone Studies*, 4, 128–45.

Richard, Jean-Pierre ([1955] 1976) 'Géographie magique de Nerval' in *Poésie et profondeur* Paris: Seuil, 13–89.

Rifkin, Adrian (1994) 'Travel for men' in *Travellers' Tales. Narratives of Home and Displacement* (ed. G. Robertson *et al.*) London: Routledge.

Rolin, Jean ([1992] 1996) *Chemins d'eau* Paris: Payot & Rivages.

(1995) *Zones* Paris: Gallimard.

Sahlins, Marshall (2002) 'Les Cosmologies du capitalisme. Le "système-monde" vu du Pacifique', *Le Débat*, 118, 166–87.

Said, Edward W. (1978) *Orientalism* London: Routledge.

(1993) *Culture and Imperialism* London: Vintage Books.

Saussure, Ferdinand de ([1916] 1980) *Cours de linguistique générale* (ed. C. Bally and A. Sechehaye) Paris: Payot.

Savorgnan de Brazza, Pierre ([1887–8] 1994) *Au cœur de l'Afrique. Vers la source des grands fleuves* Paris: Payot & Rivages.

Schaer, Roland, Claeys, Gregory and Sargent, Lyman Tower (2000) *Utopia. The Search for the Ideal Society in the Western World* New York / Oxford: The New York Public Library / Oxford University Press.

Scott, David (2002) 'L'Image ethnographique: le timbre-poste colonial français africain de 1920 à 1950', *Sémiologie et herméneutique du timbre-poste. Protée*, 30 no. 2, 45–54.

(2003) 'The Smile of the Sign: semiotics and travel writing in Barthes, Baudrillard, Butor and Lévi-Strauss', *Studies in Travel Writing*, 7, 209–25.

Segalen, Victor ([1907] 1982) *Les Immémoriaux* Paris: Plon.

(1908a) *Essai sur l'exotisme, une esthétique du divers* Fontfroide: Bibliothèque.

([1908b] 1995) *Lettres de Chine* (ed. Jean-Louis Bédouin) Paris: Plon (10/18).

(1978) *Chine ou le pouvoir de l'étendue* (ed. Henry Bouiller) London: Taranman.

Sheringham, Michael (1995) 'Marc Augé and the ethno-analysis of contemporary life', *Paragraph*, 18 no. 2, 210–20.

Souvarine, Boris ([1937] 2000) *'Cauchemar en URSS' suivi de 'L'Ouvrier soviétique' et 'Le Paysan soviétique'* Marseille: Editions Agone.

Stocking, George W., Jr ([1996] 1999) *After Tylor. British Social Anthropology 1888–1951* London: Athlone.

Strong, Roy (2002) *Feast. A History of Grand Eating* London: Jonathan Cape.

Tabatabai, Javad (2002) 'L'Incompréhension des civilisations: le cas de la Perse', *Le Débat*, 119, 68–78.

Tellier, Frédéric (2002) 'L'Iran critique de l'islam politique', *Le Débat*, 121, 96–111.

Tocqueville, Charles Alexis de ([1835] 1951) *De la démocratie en Amérique*, 2 vols. Paris: Gallimard.

Todorov, Tzvetan (1989) *Nous et les autres. La réflexion française sur la diversité humaine* Paris, Seuil.

Tomaselli, Keyan G. (2001) 'The semiotics of anthropological authenticity: the film apparatus and cultural accommodation', *Visual Anthropology*, 14 no. 2, 173–83.

Tythacott, Louise (2003) *Surrealism and the Exotic* London: Routledge.

Ughetto, André (ed.) (1992) *Analyses et réflexions sur Henri Michaux. 'Un barbare en Asie', l'autre et l'ailleurs* Paris: Ellipses.

Urbain, Jean-Didier (1986) 'Sémiotiques comparées du touriste et du voyageur', *Semiotica*, 58, 269–86.

([1991] 1993) *L'Idiot du voyage. Histoires de touristes* Paris: Payot & Rivages.

(1994) *Sur la plage. Mœurs et coûtumes balnéaires* Paris: Payot.

(1998) *Secrets de voyage. Menteurs, imposteurs et autres voyageurs invisibles* Paris: Payot.

Vailland, Roger ([1951] 1996) *Boroboudour. Voyage à Bali, Java et autres îles* Paris: Editions Kailash.

Varnedoe, Kirk (1984) 'Gauguin' in *'Primitivism' in 20th-Century Art: Affinity of the Tribal and the Modern* (ed. William Rubin) New York: Museum of Modern Art, 179–209.

Wadley, Nicholas (ed.) (1985) *Noa Noa: Gauguin's Tahiti* Oxford: Phaidon.

Wallace, Alfred Russel ([1869] 1989) *The Malay Archipelago* London: Oxford University Press.

Young, Robert (1990) *White Mythologies: Writing History in the West* London: Routledge.

Index of writers and artists

Affergan, Francis 2, 57, 64, 75–6, 99
Allégret, Marc 161, 164, 167, 168–70
Allison, Anne 223 (n. 7)
Armelagos, George 223 (n. 4)
Audubon, John James 53, 55
Augé, Marc 1, 7, 14, 15, 17, 20, 48, 76–8, 80,
    82–3, 85, 107–9, 111, 115, 131–2, 133, 180, 188,
    209, 213, 214, 216 (n. 3), 223 (n. 15)

Balandier, Georges 216 (n. 3)
Barthes, Roland 12, 14, 15–16, 17, 18, 21, 23, 24,
    25, 31, 35–44, 45, 47, 53, 54, 55, 128, 189, 192,
    193, 194, 195, 199–201, 203, 204, 205, 209,
    211, 212, 214, 218 (n. 9), 218 (n. 10),
    219 (n. 12), 221 (n. 3)
Bashô 40
Bataille, Georges 183
Bates, Henry Walter 221 (n. 5)
Baudelaire, Charles 168
Baudrillard, Jean 1, 9, 11, 12, 14, 15, 16, 17, 18, 19,
    20, 23, 24, 25–6, 44–53, 54, 55, 80, 105–7,
    109, 110, 111, 112, 114, 115, 118, 120–5, 126,
    128, 130, 131, 132–3, 135, 136, 137, 138, 147,
    155–60, 164, 166, 207, 211, 212–13, 214–15,
    218 (n. 10), 218 (n. 11), 220 (n. 2), 220 (n. 5)
Bernand, Carmen 218 (n. 8)
Biondi, Jean-Pierre 217 (n. 9)
Boman, Patrick 15, 21, 108, 189, 192, 194, 195,
    201–4, 205, 212
Bongie, Chris 2, 216 (n. 2), 217 (n. 4), 219 (n. 2),
    221 (n. 3)
Borgès, Jorge Luis 4, 19, 21, 40, 69, 193
Bossuet, Jacques 168, 170, 212
Bougainville, Louis Antoine de 4
Bouvier, Nicolas 12, 15, 19, 58, 80, 82, 83, 100–5,
    108, 211, 212
Bowie, Malcolm 62
Braudel, Fernand 216 (n. 5)
Browning, Robert 168
Bruckner, Pascal 109
Burton, Sir Richard 137, 138, 140, 153, 160

Butor, Michel 15, 16, 18, 23, 50, 53–5, 98, 124,
    209, 219 (n. 12)

Céline, Louis-Ferdinand 221 (n. 5)
Cézanne, Paul 88
Chang, Khiang-Chih 189, 190, 191, 192, 193, 202,
    223 (n. 1), 223 (n. 2), 224 (n. 8)
Chateaubriand, François-René 14, 17, 18, 20, 98,
    136, 137–8, 142–6, 147, 148, 151, 153, 155, 158,
    159–60, 176, 211, 212
Cheng, François 23, 218 (n. 9)
Ch'en Ts'ang Ch'i 193
Clifford, James 188, 213, 217 (n. 10), 217 (n. 3),
    219 (n. 2), 220 (n. 3), 221 (n. 3), 224 (n. 9)
Conrad, Joseph 14, 162, 163, 168, 170, 212,
    222 (n. 6)
Cook, James 4
Cornelius, Paul 1, 2
Crapanzano, Vincent 213, 220 (n. 4),
    224 (n. 2)
Cronin, Michael 224 (n. 1)
Culler, Jonathan 217 (n. 1)
Custine, Astolphe de 14, 17, 19, 118, 123, 125–6,
    127, 128, 130, 131, 221 (n. 5)

Darwin, Charles 222 (n. 5)
Decamps, Alexandre 33, 35
Delacroix, Eugène 16, 33, 35, 88, 220 (n. 1)
Deledalle, Gérard 217 (n. 8)
Derrida, Jacques 14, 17, 20, 110, 111, 118, 126, 173,
    204, 216 (n. 1), 217 (n. 4), 218 (n. 6)
Descartes, René 8
Dickens, Charles 170
Doumet, Christian 218 (n. 7)
Durosay, Daniel 167

Elias, Norbert 190, 192, 201, 224 (n. 9)
Engels, Friedrich 114

Fabian, Johannes 24
Farb, Peter 223 (n. 4)